POLITICAL ECONOMY
AND CAPITALISM

POLITICAL ECONOMY AND CAPITALISM

Some Essays in Economic Tradition

By MAURICE DOBB, M.A.

LECTURER IN ECONOMICS IN THE UNIVERSITY OF CAMBRIDGE

GREENWOOD PRESS, PUBLISHERS
WESTPORT, CONNECTICUT

The Library of Congress has catalogued this publication as follows:

Library of Congress Cataloging in Publication Data

Dobb, Maurice Herbert, 1900–
    Political economy and capitalism.

    Includes bibliographical references.
    1. Economics.   2.   Capitalism.   I.   Title.
HB171.D7   1972   330.12'2   76–108389
ISBN 0-8371-3812-4

KEPT BECAUSE OF THE AUTHOR

CONTENTS

PREFACE

AN attempt to explore the whole territory of economics with so fragile a vehicle as eight slender essays might well be held sufficient evidence of a diffuseness doomed to be superficial. If these essays made any such pretension, there would, I think, be no answer to the charge. But while their apparent range is wide, they make no claim to do more than survey certain aspects of their field, and they advisedly ignore large areas which many may judge to be more deserving of study. The selection of themes has not, however, been a random one. It has been guided by the opinion that Political Economy and the controversies which beset it have meaning as answers to certain questions of an essentially practical kind—questions concerning the nature and behaviour of the economic system which we know as capitalism; and that this type of question is crucial both to any full understanding of the development of economic thought and to the relation between economic thought and practice. In the later career of a theory there is a common tendency for original questions of this kind to become submerged and forgotten, so that essential meaning is lost or obscured. It is the belief that economic thought, if it is to have realistic worth, must be freed of many notions to-day encumbering its roots which gives to these essays such unity as they can claim to have, and explains their preoccupation so largely with interpretation and criticism.

The book is necessarily addressed, in the main, to those who have some acquaintance with economic literature and with economic discussion. At the same time, care has been taken to avoid the technical preoccupations of professional economists, so far as the theme has allowed, and to make the discussion accessible to the wider circle of those who have a lively sense of the intimate relation between economic thought and practice in the world to-day and have little time for what is merely "light-bearing" without being "fruit-bearing". If some of what is written here may bear the character of thinking aloud rather than of finished thought, the thought has at least not been hasty but has extended over several years. In this process of groping I have incurred a debt to Mr. Dennis Robertson and Mr. Piero Sraffa, who have read some, and to Mr. W. E. Armstrong, Professor Erich Roll and Mr. H. D. Dickinson, who have read all or the greater part of these essays at various stages in their growth, and whose criticism has banished a number of confusions which might otherwise have remained. Mr. Clemens Dutt, Mr. A. G. D. Watson and Mr. George Barnard have also given me valuable advice and correction on a number of special points. But none of these must be blamed for errors which remain, or for any of the opinions which are expressed.

M. H. D.

CAMBRIDGE,
July 1937.

In the revised edition I have made some substantial alteration to the second half of Chapter IV, in order to elaborate certain aspects of Marx's theory of crises which in the earlier edition I had tended to ignore, and also some alterations, to meet the requirements of maturer thought, in the last dozen pages of Chapter VI. Elsewhere, although only too conscious of mistakes and deficiencies, I have confined myself to a few very minor changes.

May 1940. M. H. D.

Chapter I

THE REQUIREMENTS OF A THEORY OF VALUE

THERE are those whose attitude to classical Political Economy is contained in the statement that nothing is to be gained by examination of the elementary blunders of economists a century ago. In so extreme a form as this the attitude is probably rare. But there is a similar, if less impatient, opinion in general currency in academic circles which represents the classical economists as the crude, if brilliant, "primitives" of their art, from which our contemporary sophistication has no more than very minor lessons to learn. While classical Political Economy, it is said, may have posed many questions rightly and yielded certain brilliant guesses at the truth, its technique of analysis was inadequate to furnish logically satisfactory answers, and precision of thought as well as the solution of major problems were hindered by certain elementary confusions. Ricardo's genius was limited by his adherence to the crude and narrow labour theory of value, and by his "ignorance of the terse language of the differential calculus". Of Marx have we not been told that, taking as intellectual baggage a few hasty misreadings of Ricardo, he was led by commendable but unbalanced "sympathies with suffering" to positions which maturer reason must inevitably reject? The modern theory of value, product in the main of the final decades of the nineteenth century, divides the economics of to-day from that of a century ago much as Newton's principles divided the work of his successors from pre-Newtonian physics. Ricardo and Smith might be the Pythagoras and Aristotle of economic science; but they were little more than this. So much has this belief become part of the texture of economic thought that to dispute it is to render oneself suspect, either as an ignoramus or as a victim of perverse obsessions which should have no place in scientific judgment.

To-day there is a tendency to maintain that the early economists were not merely immature but were misled into false inquiries. Even the concept of utility, which originally was championed as providing a more adequate answer to the questions which the classics had propounded and as covering a greater generality of cases, is frequently discarded as untenable or otiose. It is a growing fashion to say, with Cassel, that a theory of value is unnecessary and that all the requisite propositions can be enunciated simply in terms of an empirical theory of price. We are told that a theory which represents exchange-relationships as functions of certain human preferences, expressed in human behaviour, is all that a true science of economics should have or needs to have, and that such a theory *ipso facto* constitutes the only theory of value which can exist when value is properly defined. To the study of economics, says Mises, the study of purposes or ends is as irrelevant as is a study of real costs; and the only theory of value necessary to economic study is an equational system which generalizes the relationships which must prevail between scarce means and given ends in all possible situations.[1] Professor Myrdal has recently

---

[1] *Die Gemeinwirtschaft*, Eng. trans. as *Socialism*, p. iii *et seq.*

declared that the search of previous economists for a theory of value, based on concepts either of real cost or of utility, represented an obsession with ethical and political questions; and that only the abandonment of this false search has led to the placing of modern economics on a scientific basis.[1] An American writer, addressing himself particularly to Socialists, has said that Marx failed to understand the requirements of a theory of value, and that the modern doctrine, because of its superior objectivity and greater generality, is more properly the economic theory of a socialist economy than the value-theory of Ricardo and Marx.[2]

Clearly, any decision on such a matter, even any understanding of what is involved, requires an answer to the question: What conditions must an adequate theory of value fulfil? Prior even to this question, it may be necessary to answer a further question: What relevance at all has a theory of value to the structure of propositions which constitutes Political Economy?

Croce has said that "a system of economics from which value is omitted is like logic without the *concept*, ethics without *duty*, aesthetics without *expression*".[3] But this analogy is unconvincing unless the purpose of economic inquiry is more precisely defined. Clearly there are a number of propositions about economic events which it seems possible to make without any prior postulation of a principle of value, still less of "adequate conditions" for a theory of value. Moreover, it seems quite possible to make a number of state-

[1] G. Myrdal, *Das politische Element in der Nationalökonomischen Doktrinbildung* (1932), Chapters 3 and 4.

[2] P. M. Sweezy in *Economic Forum*, Spring 1935.

[3] Benedetto Croce, *Historical Materialism and the Economics of Karl Marx*, p. 138.

3

ments about the behaviour of prices without any attention to *a priori* considerations concerning formal adequacy. Will not the sum of such statements, if consistent and true, itself constitute our theory of value? If a theory of value is conceived of as anything more than this, does it not define itself as something metaphysical, and something irrelevant to the positive inquiries which economists have in hand? Why not argue, not about formal adequacy, but simply about the sort of empirical statements to be made which are true to fact?

What is meant when one speaks of the formal adequacy of a theory in this context is the conditions which it must fulfil if it is to be capable of sustaining corollaries of a certain type of generality. One is referring to the relationship between propositions and the forecasts which can be built upon them. It is a question of the *level* of knowledge which one's set of statements constitutes—of how far one's knowledge is able to *reach*. It is a familiar fact that in the history of any branch of scientific knowledge inquiry has started with description and classification of events within a somewhat vague and undemarcated field. On the basis of such classification analysis is able at a later stage to construct certain limited generalizations. But such generalizations may for long remain applicable only to a limited type of situation or to a limited part of the field, and be incapable of sustaining forecasts of that more general type which relate simultaneously to the major events within the system and enable one to determine the configuration of the system as a whole. To achieve the latter requires that generalizations reach a certain degree, not only of comprehensiveness, but of refinement. A certain level of abstraction is required. Such a milestone in the path of knowledge seems to have been provided, for instance, in chemistry by the concept of atomic weight of chemical elements, and in physics by the Newtonian law of gravitation. In Political Economy it seems true to say that prior to the publication of *The Wealth of Nations* the study of economic questions had not passed beyond its descriptive and classificatory stage: the stage of primitive generalization and of particular inquiries. Only with the work of Adam Smith, and its more rigorous systematization by Ricardo, did Political Economy create that unifying quantitative principle which enabled it to make postulates in terms of the general equilibrium of the economic system—to make deterministic statements about the general relationships which held between the major elements of the system. In Political Economy this unifying principle, or system of general statements cast in quantitative form, consisted of a theory of value.

The question of the adequacy of a theory of value, therefore, means the conditions which such a set of statements must fulfil if it is to be competent to determine the equilibrium or movement of the system as a whole. The purely formal answer to this question is familiar enough. The set of statements must have the form (or be capable of expression in the form) of an equational system in which the number of equations, or known conditions, is equal to the number of unknown variables in the system to be determined—no less and no more. This, however, is purely the formal requirement. To sustain forecasts concerning the real world the theory must have not only form but also content. It must have not only elegance but also "earthiness"; and what is more concretely required when these conditions

5

are expressed in realistic terms is less familiar, and is, indeed, more frequently than not ignored.

An equational system means that certain relationships are defined which govern, or connect, all the variables within the system. These are the generalizations ' of which the theory is composed. A formal condition for this equational system to be capable of solution—for the "unknowns" to be "determined", or to have particular values assigned to them, when sufficient *data* about the situation are known—implies that somewhere in the system certain quantities which have the character of "constants" appear. The system as a whole is, of course, determined both by the relationships which the equations define and by these "constants". But in an important sense it is the "constants" which are the key which furnishes numerical values to the whole. They are the data which, when known in any particular case, enable one to calculate (by means of the equations) the position of all the rest. The significance of a "constant" is not that it is necessarily unchanging and unchangeable,[1] but that it is some quantity which in any particular case can be known *independently* of any of the other variables in the system. It must be something which can be postulated independently of the rest. It is some quantity brought in, as it were, from outside the system of events to which the set of equations refers; and in an important sense it is on this outside factor that the total situation is made to depend. When it is known, the "shape" and "posi-

---

[1] Prof. Ragnar Frisch has pointed out that when economic theory is expressed in a dynamic, and not in a static, form, dealing with movement as well as equilibrium, certain of these "influencing coefficients" will have the character of "given functions of time". (*Review of Economic Studies*, Vol. III, No. 2, p. 100.)

tion" of the situation can be fully calculated, for the reason that the unknowns are all ultimately expressed in terms of their relation to it, whereas it is not in turh expressed as a function of any of them. The quantity represented as a constant is, hence, determining, but not determined, so far as this particular context of events is concerned. For instance, the "gravitational constant" which figures in Newtonian physics expresses the acceleration of a body as (in part) a function of mass; and is valid in so far as one can treat mass as something independent of velocity. If, however (as more recent concepts are suggesting), the mass of a body in turn varies with its velocity, this constant is to that extent inadequate as a basis for calculating changes in velocity.

To take a slice of the real world and to analyse it in this way is equivalent to declaring this slice to be an "isolated system", in the sense that it is connected with the rest of world-happenings only through certain definable links, so that if we know what is happening at these links at any moment, we can calculate what will happen to the rest of this "isolated system". As Professor Whitehead has said, it means "that there are truths respecting this system which require reference only to the remainder of things by way of a uniform systematic scheme of relationships. Thus the conception of an isolated system is not the conception of substantial independence from the remainder of things, but of freedom from casual contingent dependence upon detailed items within the rest of the universe." [1]

In the abstract, of course, it is possible to create any number of "isolated systems". One can construct equational systems about events, and make them coherent

[1] *Science and the Modern World*, pp. 58-9.

and solvable, merely by observing the formal rules and inventing the necessary constants which are required to determine the whole—by assuming certain things to be independent, whether they are in fact so or not. In this way quite a number of theories of value can be devised, with no means of choice between them except their formal elegance. This is an easy, much too easy, game. On the other hand, it is true that in the real world there are no completely "isolated systems". A law of value, therefore, while it must be subjected to realistic, and not merely formal, criticism, can be expected to be no more than an *approximation* to reality, capable of sustaining a certain type, but not every type, of forecast, and achieving the highest degree of generality that is consistent with the complexity of the phenomena which one seeks to handle. The ultimate criterion must be the requirements of practice: the type of practical question which one requires to answer, the purpose of the inquiry in hand.

The smaller the degree of generality that one's questions require, the easier it often is to find a principle which will fit the case. The more particular, and less general, the problem to hand, the greater the number of surrounding conditions which one is justified in assuming to be constant. The problem of determining the result then becomes relatively simple provided one can know enough of the surrounding conditions (indeed, at the extreme of particularity one generally in practice knows too few of the relevant conditions to forecast the result, so that what one may gain in apparent simplicity one more than loses in insufficient knowledge). For instance, if one wishes to determine the price at which fish will sell in a particular market on one particular day, the result is given if only one knows the supply of fish on the spot, the ephemeral desires of housewives and the amount of cash which the latter at the moment have to spend. All of these things can be reasonably treated as independent both of one another and of the price at which the fish is sold. Again (to take a mcre long-period example) if one is dealing with a particular commodity in isolation from the rest, one is entitled to take the level of wages, of profit and of rent as independent factors, as part of the given *data* of the problem; and a simple "cost of production" explanation suffices (given conditions of "constant returns") to determine the result. When, however, one is dealing with the generality of commodities, or even with large groups of commodities, or with a long instead of a short period of time, these simple assumptions break down: what in the isolated particular case one treated as independent factors cannot now be so treated. In this case one is no longer justified in using the level of wages, of profit and rent as determining constants, for the reason that these will be influenced by the values of commodities as well as influencing them. It follows, therefore, that an essential condition of a theory of value is that it must solve the problem of distribution (*i.e.* determine the price of labour-power, of capital and of land) as well as the problem of commodity-values; and it must do so not only because the former is an essential, indeed major, part of the practical inquiry with which Political Economy is concerned, but because the one cannot be determined without the other. In other words, neither Distribution nor Commodity-Exchange can be properly treated as "isolated systems". To express it more generally, a principle of value is not adequate which merely expresses value in terms of some one or other particular value: *the determining constants must express a relationship with some quantity which is not itself a value.* This was the reason for which Ricardo rejected mere "supply and demand" explanations, and Marx scorned the "cost of production" theory of J. S. Mill: because such theories sought an explanation of value in terms of quantities which could only be treated as independent in circumstances which precluded the principle from having the requisite generality; in Mill's case in terms of a given level of wages and rate of profit for which he adduced no independent principle of determination.[1] This was the reason too why Ricardo was so concerned to demonstrate the unsuitability of Malthus' attempt to represent the value of commodities in terms of the value of labour-power,[2] and why Marx so brusquely set aside the relativism of Bailey.[3]

There is a further requirement which deserves explicit mention if only for the reason that it so frequently passes unobserved. It seems clear, from the nature of its subject-matter and the type of statement which it is required to make, that an economic theory must be

[1] Cf. below, pp. 16 and 137.
[2] Cf. below, p. 89 f.
[3] A writer recently commenting favourably on Bailey has referred to "irrational disquisitions which depend upon a qualitative or monist conception of the nature of exchange-value" and regrets that value-theory "has not been more influenced by the proposition that the objective exchange-values of a commodity are to be found in the other commodities for which it can be exchanged (and not in some different inherent quality)". (Karl Bode, in *Economica*, Aug. 1935.) This comment would seem to miss the essential issue in the criticism of Bailey. It may be perfectly proper to *define* exchange-value as "the other commodities for which (a given thing) can be exchanged"; and it was so defined by Ricardo and Marx. But it does not follow that a determinate theory of value can be cast purely in such terms.

quantitative in form. If this is so, it is necessary that the determining relation or relations which figure in the equational system should be capable of expression in terms of quantitative entities in the real world. They must be translatable into actual dimensions which can be factually apprehended and known. This is elementary; but it is not always observed by those who construct principles on purely formal lines. This does not necessarily mean that a theory of value needs to relate the exchange-value of commodities to some single dimension or real entity; although in practice it may work out that this has to be done. But to permit any full quantitative statements to be made, such governing dimensions or entities to which the price-variables are connected must themselves be related in a way that enables them to be reduced to a common term. For instance, if one's equations were to express the price of a commodity as some particular function of two quantities, u and v, one would need to know how u and v were themselves related for one's statements to have any precise meaning. (If we were to know that commodity a, for example, was equal to $5u$ and $1v$, while commodity b was equal to $1u$ and $5v$, it would be impossible, in the absence of further knowledge of the relationship between u and v, to state whether a was greater than b or b was greater than a.) This is simply to say that u and v must be actually capable of numerical expression. For this reason it would not be sufficient for a cost-theory of value to express value as a function, say, both of labour and abstinence, or of quantity of man-power and quantity of nature used in production, unless the theory was able to embrace some further condition or *datum* which afforded a common term to the two elements of cost. And for this purpose it would not be legitimate to assimilate labour and abstinence or man-power and nature in terms of their market *values*, since this would be to make the determining constants, or the knowns of the problem, dependent on the unknowns which were to be determined. Similarly, a principle which made value a function of "desire" and "obstacles" would need to include some such condition as the postulate that in equilibrium the differential coefficients of "desire" and "obstacles" (subjectively estimated) were equal. This is evidently the meaning of Marx's emphasis, in the much misconstrued opening chapter of *Das Kapital*, on the necessity of finding some uniform quantity, not itself a value, in terms of which the exchange-value of commodities could be expressed; as it is clearly also the explanation of Marx's statement in a letter to Engels that, in his opinion, the major contribution of his first volume was the separation of labour-power and labour [1]—the former a commodity represented in its value and the latter an objective representation of human activity and an entity capable of independent quantitative expression. This seems to provide the reason why the two major value-theories which have contested the economic field have sought to rest their structure on a quantity which lay outside the system of price-variables, and independent of them: in the one case an objective element in productive activity, in the other case a subjective factor underlying consumption and demand.

This crucial "value-constant" classical Political Economy found in a relationship of *cost*. The exchange-value of a commodity was defined in the purely relative

[1] *Marx-Engels Correspondence*, pp. 226 and 232.

sense of the amount of other commodities for which it was customarily exchanged. But a determinate solution for this system of exchange-ratios was sought in the principle that these ratios were governed ultimately by the quantity of labour required (in a given state of society and of technique) to produce the commodities in question. It was this solution which constituted the famous labour-theory of value. Prior to Ricardo this principle was not enunciated in any complete or clear-cut form. Frequently, indeed, it was formulated obscurely, and even ambiguously; Adam Smith having referred both to the *amount* of labour and also to the *value* of labour used in production.[1] As used by Ricardo and Marx the conception of labour was an objective one; labour being conceived as the expenditure of a given quantum of human energy; even though it was later to be translated into subjective terms as a mental "sacrifice" or psychic "pain" involved in work. Viewed objectively in this way, the determining relation was a technical one, and not a value-relation. In any given technical situation it would be a given factor, synonymous with the degree of labour-productivity, and independent of the *value* of labour-power (*i.e.* the wage-level). Moreover, it was a

[1] For instance: value "is equal to the quantity of labour which it enables him to *purchase or command*"; and "the real price of everything, what everything costs to the man who wants to acquire it, is the *toil and trouble of acquiring it*". (*Wealth of Nations* (Ed. 1826), pp. 34-5.) Ricardo commenting on this says that Adam Smith sometimes speaks "not (of) the quantity of labour bestowed on the production of any object, but the quantity which it can command in the market: as if these were two equivalent expressions, and as if because a man's labour had become doubly efficient he would necessarily receive twice the former quantity in exchange for it". (*Principles*, p. 6.) In *Letters to Malthus* (Ed. Bonar, p. 233) we find Ricardo writing: "You say a commodity is dear because it will command a great quantity of labour; I say it is only dear when a great quantity has been bestowed on its production."

13

relation capable of being expressed in terms of "greater" or "less". Given conditions of "constant returns" it was independent also of demand: the productivity of labour in terms of commodity *a* and commodity *b* would remain unaffected whether much of *a* was demanded and little of *b*, or much of *b* and little of *a*.

This principle of the identity of value-ratios with labour-ratios rested on conditions which defined the nature of the dominant tendencies in an exchange-society. In an exchange-society characterized by the division of labour, by competition and the mobility of resources, competition would ensure that labour was distributed between the various lines of production in such a way that these ratios were equal. It depended, therefore, on a particular conception of the equilibrium of such a society; and it depended on the conception of the level of wages as being *uniform* for labour of uniform quality, though not on that level being *constant*. But the statement was subject to two important qualifications. First, with respect to land, it held true only under *marginal* conditions of production, or for production under the least favourable natural conditions being utilized at the time. This indeed must be so in the case of any form of cost-theory. Secondly, it implied the important simplifying assumption that the ratio of labour to capital employed in different lines of production was everywhere equal: what Marx termed equality in the "organic composition of capital" or what later economists would have called uniformity of the "technical co-efficients". This assumption meant that value was only an abstract approximation to concrete exchange-values. That it should be so has generally been held to be fatal to the theory; and was the *onus* of Böhm-Bawerk's criticism of Marx. But all abstractions remain only approximations to reality: this is their essential nature; and it is no criticism of a theory of value merely to say that this is so. Whether such assumptions are permissible or no is a matter of the type of question, the nature of the problem, with which the principle is designed to deal. The criticism only becomes valid if it shows that the implied assumptions preclude the generalization from sustaining those corollaries which it is employed to sustain. It is frequently said that Ricardo, at least in the first edition of his *Principles*, did not appreciate the importance of his implied assumption. It has even been suggested in the case of Marx that he did not notice the crucial qualification, and that he then wrote his third volume to evade a difficulty which he had not previously observed; with the result that he produced a substitute theory which was indistinguishable from the "cost of production" theory of Mill.[1] But these are rash and ill-founded presumptions. It is altogether more reasonable to suppose that Ricardo gave cursory mention to the qualifying assumption in his first edition, not because he did not appreciate it, but because he considered it unimportant for the purpose of the main inquiry he had in hand. It is too seldom remembered to-day that the concern of classical Political Economy was with what one may term the "macroscopic" problems of economic society, and only very secondarily with

---

[1] That this view is incorrect is sufficiently shown by the fact that in his *Misère de la Philosophie*, published many years before the first volume of *Kapital*, Marx pointed out that a rise of wages would have a different effect on different industries, causing the price of goods to rise in some and actually to fall in others owing to the fact that "the relation of manual labour to fixed capital is not the same in different industries". Cf. below, p. 73.

15

"microscopic" problems, in the shape of the movements of particular commodity prices. Ricardo, at any rate, did not pretend that his principle was adequate to determine the latter. But Ricardo, more than others, was first and foremost concerned with problems of distribution—with the movement of the three great revenues of society, rent, profit and wages—and with commodity-values in relation to this.[1] Hence he was concerned not with particular commodity-values, but with broad classes of commodities, such as agricultural produce and manufactures, or with commodities on the one side and money on the other. To this type of problem he considered his approximation an adequate one, and affording the degree of generality which the scale of his problem required. So it was with Marx in the scope of the problem so far as it was covered in his volume I. When he approached the problem of particular commodity-prices in his volume III by means of a further approximation in the shape of his theory of the "price of production", it had this essential difference from the cost of production theory of Mill. Marx had criticized the latter because it had left "cost of production" itself unexplained: it had described cost of production as consisting in the wages paid for the labour used *plus* an average rate of profit, without affording any explanation of the determination of the rate of profit itself.[2] In Marx's theory of the "price of production" profit figured as a quantity determined in terms

---

[1] Ricardo wrote to Malthus: "Political Economy you think is an inquiry into the nature and causes of wealth; I think it should rather be called an inquiry into the laws which determine the division of the produce of industry among the classes which concur in its formation." (*Letters to Malthus*, p. 175.) In the Preface to his *Principles* he wrote: "To determine the laws which regulate this distribution, is the principal problem in Political Economy."

[2] Cf. below, p. 137.

of the law of the first approximation, as presented in volume I, profit depending on the surplus or difference between the value of labour-power and the value of finished commodities. In this crucial respect the second approximation depended on the first (as, for example, do the successive approximations of the law of projectiles in physics), and was not a contradiction of it in its essentials. The solution of the "microscopic" problem was conceived as dependent on the solution of the "macroscopic" problem; microscopic phenomena as ruled (with appropriate modifications) by the macroscopic law. The theory of gravitation is not rendered absurd and useless merely because it requires substantial modification to explain why airships and aeroplanes can rise in the air.

The essential importance of this labour-principle was that it could be employed to determine the value of labour-power itself (under certain given conditions). The key question as both Ricardo and Marx saw it was: What determined the difference between this and the value of commodities in general? For instance, if wages rose, would this difference be narrowed, or would the price of commodities rise *pari passu*? On this difference profit and in turn the rate of profit depended. If this could be determined, then, not only was a key afforded to the problem of distribution—to the variation of class revenues—but the constituent elements of Mill's "cost of production" and Marx's "price of production" were also determined.

This, it may be said, is still to approach the matter in a formal way. Any principle may be made formally consistent at a sufficient level of abstraction; but that is not to say that it has realistic worth. Why should a cost-theory of value based on labour, which is admittedly only one of the factors in wealth-production, have a superior claim to any alternative cost-theory that one might devise: for instance, a principle which took capital or land as the determining quantity? To concentrate on labour alone is, surely, arbitrary dogmatism: it is to imply the sequel in this initial assumption, without affording any independent ground for believing the sequel to be true? This, it is true, is ultimately a practical and not a formal question. The truth of an economic principle must lie in whether, in making abstraction of certain aspects of the problem, it does so in order to focus upon features which are in fact crucial and fundamental features of that slice of the real world to which the theory is intended to apply.

In the case of land or capital clearly there were serious practical objections to taking them as a basis: difficulties which would have exceeded any of those which are charged against the labour-theory. Classical Political Economy was already focussing attention on the non-homogeneous character of land, and was using the differences in the quality of land, along with its scarcity, as basis of the classical theory of rent. Acres are more dissimilar than man-hours of labour. In the case of capital there was the more crucial objection that it is itself a value, depending upon other values, in particular on the profit to be earned. How, then, could this quantity be used as basis for a determinate explanation of profit? If, on the other hand, the term were to be taken as designating, not a value, but the concrete things—machines and structures, etc.—which capital-values represent, then these could only have quantitative significance in this context as "stored-up labour". As for a combination of these factors to form a composite cost-principle: there is the additional objection that there is no discoverable common term by which these diverse quantities could have been related; and such a principle would have remained vitiated by an essential dualism. How, for instance, even if acres could be taken as homogeneous, could one relate man-hours and acres and capital-units?

But there is a practical reason which is more decisive than this. That labour constitutes a cost in a unique sense was, of course, an assumption. But it was an assumption born of a particular view of what was the essence of the economic problem. As such it was not an arbitrary definition, but an attempt to depict the essential shape of real events; and by its adequacy in doing this it must ultimately be judged. Any theory of value necessarily constitutes an implicit definition of the general shape and character of the terrain which it has decided to call "economic". The crux of the economic problem, as this theory represented it, and as it had been traditionally viewed, lay in the struggle of man with nature to wrest a livelihood for himself under various forms of production at various stages of history. As Petty had said, labour is the father, nature the mother of wealth. To this relationship the contrast between human activity and the processes of nature was fundamental; human activity being endowed with primary significance as the initiator and begetter of change and increase. If when we speak of the economic problem we refer, not to its formal character, but to its real content, and intend to indicate some element common to the various forms which the economic struggle has taken at different stages of history, it is hard to see what statement is possible which does not include this ever-changing relationship be-

tween labour and nature, and the fundamental contrast between these two factors, as a crucial element. And if we
seek to give any quantitative expression to this relationship
—to man's mastery over nature—it is hard to see what
simple notion one can use other than the expenditure
of human energies requisite (in a given state of society)
to produce a certain result. Among the earliest distinctions in Political Economy was that between "riches"
and "value"; the crux of this contrast being that, while
nature as well as human activity was productive of wealth
or riches, value, being a social relationship, was an
attribute of human activity and not of nature. The
essence of value, in other words, by contrast with riches,
was conceived to be cost, and the essence of cost to lie
in labour, by contrast with nature. Labour, conceived
objectively as the output of human energy, was the
measure and the essence of Ricardo's "difficulty or
facility of production". This contrast between labour
and nature, conceived as parallel to the contrast between
value and riches, was clearly a primary notion, to which
the consideration that man is a tool-using animal and
manufactures instruments to increase his power over
natural forces (whence follows the distinction between
labour devoted to the creation of instruments and labour
devoted to their use) was secondary. All this is elementary enough. At the same time, it would seem to be
sufficiently fundamental for any value-concept which
ignores these simple notions to have very limited power
to sustain pronouncements about essential processes in
the real world.

Whether human labour is a cost in a unique sense is,
therefore, a practical question, for judgment, not for
logic, to decide. True, human activity is itself differenti-

ated as labour which embodies itself in tools and instruments and labour which is devoted to the use of these instruments in the direct and current production of commodities. But while the making of such instruments and their subsequent maintenance and repair represents a cost in this crucial sense, there is no comparable cost in the mere *use* (as distinct from using-up) of these instruments, or in the mere postponement of their use in time.[1] As Böhm-Bawerk himself has said (in criticizing the use-theory of Interest): "it is by the passing of available energy into work that the 'use' of goods is obtained by man"; there is no other sense of "use" than the "putting forth of physical powers", or energy; and "for any 'use of goods' other than their natural material services there is no room either in the world of fact or in the world of logical ideas".[2] Hence, in basing itself on this simple but fundamental characterization of economic activity, the labour-principle was not merely providing a formal concept: it was making an important qualitative statement about the nature of the economic problem (a qualitative statement often confused with an ethical one), and imparting the implications of this statement to its corollaries. So also, indeed, was the utility-theory; although the qualitative statement it made was of a quite different order, being concerned, not with relations of production, but with the relation of commodities to the psychology of consumers. In expressing value as some function of utility, it was characterizing the equilibrium which it defined as an

[1] The question of "real cost" viewed subjectively as something psychological, and hence of so-called "abstinence", is a different matter, and is considered separately below.

[2] *Capital and Interest* (Ed. 1890), pp. 220 and 231.

equilibrium of a specific kind, related in a certain way to a "maximum" of utility (a statement which has independent meaning quite apart from any moral or ethical postulate). The statement which the labour-theory implied was that exchange-values bore a certain relation to the output and using-up of human energies, and in doing so provided a term which gave some meaning to the distinction between a gross and a net product and to the concept of surplus, and provided a criterion for differentiating one type of income from another. Thus it is possible in these terms to distinguish exchange-relationships which represent a passing of value-equivalents from those which do not: for instance, the sale of labour-power representing the exchange of income against human energies expended in production, contrasted with the sale of a property-right over the use of scarce resources, representing no such passing of equivalents and constituting an income by no means "necessary" in the fundamental sense in which a subsistence-income to labour is necessary or the return to a machine of a value equal to what the operation of that machine has used up (in a physical sense). And if so radical a distinction as this exists, it must surely be of crucial importance in determining the behaviour of different income-classes and the reaction of economic changes on them? Without some such value-conception, fundamental distinctions of this kind can have no place in economic theory. With a different value-principle they disappear; and (as will later be seen) in the modern subjective theory of value the very concept of surplus, contrasted with cost, loses any essential meaning, and a criterion for any fundamental distinction between different class incomes is lacking.

Ricardo, it may be, only dimly sensed the requirements of a value-theory. At least, there is no evidence that he based it on any developed methodology. Yet it seems clear that in essentials the instinct of his robustly analytical mind was right. There is little doubt, however, that Marx was more fully alive to the methodological problem than his contemporaries and most of his successors. His analysis of capitalist society was approached from the standpoint of a general philosophy of history, by which it can be said that the descriptive and classificatory emphasis of the historical school and the analytical and quantitative emphasis of abstract Political Economy were combined. More essentially even than with Ricardo his concern was with the movements of the main class revenues of society, as key to "the laws of motion of capitalist society" which his analysis was primarily designed to reveal. To this inquiry he considered his value-principle fully adequate as well as necessary. That both he and Engels were well aware of the limitations as well as the requirements of the abstractions he used is suggested by the following passages, in which their mutual theory of the rôle of abstraction in thought and practice is revealed. "The formulation in thought of an exact picture of the world system in which we live is impossible for us and will always remain impossible. . . . Mankind therefore finds itself faced with a contradiction; on the one hand, it has to gain an exhaustive knowledge of the world system in all its inter-relations; and on the other hand, because of the nature both of man and of the world system, this task can never be completely fulfilled. . . . Each mental image is and remains in actual fact limited, objectively through the historical stage and subjectively

23

through the physical and mental constitution of its maker. . . . Pure mathematics deals with the space forms and quantity relations of the real world—that is, with material which is very real indeed. In order to make it possible to investigate these forms and relations in their pure state, it is necessary to abstract them entirely from their content, to put the content aside as irrelevant."[1] In a letter to Conrad Schmidt discussing specifically Marx's theory of value, Engels wrote:—"The conception of a thing and its reality run side by side like two asymptotes, always approaching each other yet never meeting. This difference between the two is the very difference which prevents the concept from being directly and immediately reality and reality from being immediately its own concept. Still . . . it (the concept) is something more than a fiction, unless you are going to declare all the results of thought fictions."[2]

But it was not many years after the publication of *Das Kapital* before a rival value-theory was to rise and with remarkably little resistance to conquer the field. This was the utility-theory, which seems to have germinated simultaneously in several minds, being enunciated alike by Jevons in this country and by Menger and Wieser and Böhm-Bawerk of the Austrian School. The new theory had the attraction of ingenuity and elegance as well as of novelty (although, like most ideas, it was not unforeshadowed); and owed its invention in part to the use of conceptions of the differential calculus, with its emphasis on increments of a quantity and rates of increment. It seems clear that Böhm-Bawerk at any rate appreciated the problem which the classical theory had

---

[1] Engels, *Anti-Dühring*, pp. 46-7.
[2] *Marx-Engels Correspondence*, p. 527.

sought to solve. While he is sparing, almost niggardly, in paying tribute to Marx even for formulating the question accurately, there is every indication that he framed his theory directly to provide a substitute answer to the questions which Marx had posed. It is, at least, a remarkable fact that within ten years of the appearance of the first volume of *Kapital*, not only had the rival utility-principle been enunciated independently by a number of writers, but the new principle was finding a receptivity to its acceptance such as very few ideas of similar novelty can ever have met. If only by the effect of negation, the influence of Marx on the economic theory of the nineteenth century would appear to have been much more profound than it is fashionable to admit.

Utility, as something individual and subjective, was the quantity to which value was anchored by this new theory. Value was expressed as a function, not of utility treated as an aggregate, but of the increment of utility at the margin of consumption. In place of an objective cost-relation, lying behind production, a subjective relation between commodities and individual states of consciousness was taken as the determining constant in the equational system. As Professor Pigou has said, the "economic constants" are conceived as "depending upon human consciousness".[1] By this means, it was claimed, a greater degree of generality was attained than had been possible for classical Political Economy. It was applicable whatever the technical combinations of factors of production might be; and so was unrestricted by assumptions about the "organic composition of capital". For this reason it sufficed to determine simultaneously and completely both the "macroscopic"

---

[1] *Economics of Welfare*, p. 9.

and the "microscopic" configuration of economic society. Many proceeded to claim that, since the fundamental instincts of human consciousness remained the same, the principle would hold for any type of economic society. To academic economists it came, as Wicksell has described it, as something of a revelation. At the same time it implied certain limiting assumptions of its own, quite different in character and significance from those surrounding the classical principle. In particular, since states of human consciousness could only find expression in value-terms, usually in terms of money, abstraction had to be made of the different income-positions of different individuals. Consumers had to be treated in abstraction from their character as producers, and *vice versa*. The problem of value had to be treated as though it could be solved independently of the effects on demand of the distribution of income: otherwise a demand-schedule could not be regarded solely as a function of utility and as independent of the value of commodities and of productive-agents. This has led some writers to maintain that the principle is only fully applicable to a society of equal incomes—in other words, to a society where there is no problem of distribution left to explain. And it led Wieser to define "natural value" as the exchange-ratios which would rule in a communist society. Further, by taking as its foundation a fact of individual consciousness, it not only separated his attributes *qua* consumer from his attributes *qua* producer and income-receiver, but made abstraction of all *social* influences upon individual character—all reactions of the society of which he was part and the economic relations into which he entered on his desires and aversions, his pleasures and pains. The significance of this abstraction will be more fully discussed later; but it was clearly inevitable that the corollaries of such a principle should have an individualist bias, since an individualist description of human society was contained in its assumptions. Whether such a description is justified or not is not a formal or logical question but a question of fact.

There has been some dispute as to whether utility, so defined, can properly be treated as a quantity at all. Into this dispute we need hardly enter, since it seems to have little importance for the issue in hand. The truth may well be that utility, though a mental fact, can be defined in such a way as to give it what Kant termed "intensive magnitude"—of enabling it to be conceived in terms of "greater or less".[1] Whether, when so defined, it is something which exists is another matter. But for the present the question of its existence as an entity need not concern us. If existent it can only have economic significance when objectively expressed through an individual's behaviour on a market—in a concrete act of purchase or sale. The immediate mental activity behind such an act of purchase is sometimes referred to as a "desire" (behaviourists would term it, presumably, a behaviour-reaction) to distinguish it from the more fundamental fact of consciousness to which the term satisfaction or utility is applied. Here for long the subjective theory of value has continued to rest on a very slender pediment: so slender that Marshall hid it in a footnote. That it does so rest seems to have remained surprisingly unnoticed by many. This premise consists in the identification of "desire" with "satisfaction". As Marshall said: "We fall back on the

[1] Cf. an article by O. Lange in *Review of Econ. Studies*, June 1934, also a reply to it, *ibid.*, October 1934, and W. E. Armstrong in *The Economic Journal*, September 1939.

measurement which economics supplies of the motive, or moving force to action, and we make it serve with all its faults, *both* for the desires which prompt activity and for the satisfactions that result from them."[1] Professor Pigou has defended this identification as a sufficient approximation and as true of "most commodities, especially those of wide consumption that are required as articles of food and clothing".[2] Without this simple assumption there is no ground for expressing demand as a function of utility; and hence no ground for connecting value-phenomena with such a quantity at all. How far they can be regarded as connected even at a low level of approximation will be part of the criticism of a later chapter.

As has been said, it is increasingly fashionable to-day to discard utility as either a shadowy or a superfluous entity. "Satisfaction" and other such deeper mental states are thrown to psychology or to ethics, and foundation-material sought in the sterner stuff of desires, empirical preference-scales and behaviour-reactions. Prices are the resultant of certain schedules of demand-prices—of certain empirically observed market-offers; and economics as a science of "catallactics" is presented as the last word of amoral purity and scientific objectivity. But is this escape a legitimate mode of escape? Is it an escape consistent with the requirements of a theory of value? On the purely formal plane, of course, the equations can be made adequate enough: the necessary "constants" can be defined as "constants"; and there is the logical end of the matter. But whether such equations, when given realistic interpretation, can con-

---

[1] *Principles*, pp. 92-3.
[2] *Economics of Welfare*, First Ed., p. 25.

28

sistently sustain the corollaries they are required to do is a different question. What quantity, independent of value-movements, have we left on which to rest our system? If demand is not to be a function of utility, by what is it determined? By empirically observed preference-scales; which have a suspicious appearance of being the same entity under a different title! These preference-scales are not necessarily grounded in either any instinct or any basic rationality. What warrant have we to assume them to be creators rather than the creatures of market-price? Is not much of the objection to mere "supply and demand" explanations appropriate also here? Is it not perilously similar to an attempt to frame the "gravitational constant" without the concept of mass, substituting, let us say, some such entity as the "attractional propensity" of an object in its stead? If this criticism is valid, then we are left with a formal technique, which can be used to explore the implications of certain definitions and to furnish a descriptive account and a classification of certain types of value-relationships; which can postulate realistic tendencies and make realistic prognoses in the case of certain particular problems treated separately and in isolation, but with respect to the "macroscopic" phenomena of economic society is impotent to pronounce judgment. An economic law is not merely a conditional sentence stating that if a situation be defined in this or that way it will necessarily have this or that attribute. Such is no more than tautology. As Cannan has said (in discussing the "law of diminishing returns")[1] an economic law or tendency must state the probability of some actual course of events occurring. And it is to permit statements of this kind to be made that a law of

---

[1] *Theories of Production and Distribution*, p. 168 *et seq.*

value must be adequate. Otherwise, whatever its formal elegance, it is not worthy of the name.

We have mentioned that there is a crucial respect in which any type of demand-theory, whether it be well or ill-grounded, seems necessarily to be inferior to a cost-principle as a basis of interpretation of economic events. It is that only in terms of the latter can the concept of surplus acquire a meaning; while without it (or something akin to it) no criterion of differentiation between class-incomes seems able to exist. The reason for this is that a cost-principle essentially makes some statement concerning the nature of productive activities—of the relation between men in the activity of production—whereas a demand-theory is a generalization about consumption and exchange—about the relation between men *qua* consumers and the commodities which result from production. Any question of a type which includes the concept of surplus is a question about the connection between a given income and productive activity, and hence *ipso facto* involves a concept of cost; cost and surplus here figuring as correlative terms. A principle which interprets value purely in terms of demand can define the productive "contribution" of a person or a class only according to the value of what *eventuates*: it cannot define this contribution according to the activity or process in which the contribution *originates*, since it includes no statement about any productive relationship of this kind. Hence any participant in production which acquires a price—any agent which figures on the market at all—must *ipso facto* have made a "contribution", this being synonymous with the value which consumers have directly or indirectly placed upon his services. Not merely the labour of weavers, the wool fed to the looms, the wear and tear of machines, but also the loan of scarce resources represents value contributed to the productive process. Even such things as "goodwill" and time and risk-bearing may represent value-contributions; since the latter consist in the sum total of conditions which are both essential to production and are scarce. If a thing acquires a price, it *ipso facto* performs a service; the sum total of values contributed must (at least, under competitive conditions) equal the value of the result; and the whole inquiry concerning "surplus-value" becomes meaningless.

But the inquiry becomes meaningless because of the form in which the problem is stated, and not because it does not refer to something actual in the real world. Indeed the concepts of cost and of surplus are not merely abstract categories, product of a certain mode of thought, but are among the most fundamental as well as the earliest in economic inquiry, which we meet with even when Political Economy was at its purely descriptive stage. So long as cost and gross product could both be represented in terms of the same thing, the concept was easily expressed without the intervention of a value-theory. On a farm a certain amount of corn is fed each year to the sustenance of men and of animals, and a certain amount of seed corn is placed in the ground. At the end of the season the harvest of corn exceeds what has been used up to produce it. The difference figures as the surplus, or net produce, on which the Physiocrats placed such emphasis as the life-blood of society and the determinant of the level of civilization which a given society could attain. But when it is wool that is fed to the looms and flour to the weavers, and cloth which is the result, the difference between the original and the final quantities can only be expressed in terms of value. The question immediately arises as to why such a value-difference should exist at all and, if it persists, what causes it to do so. Why should not competition either raise the original values to equal the final values, or lower the final value to equal the original value of the constituent elements?[1] This problem of the creation and of the disposal of this surplus-value was a central one for classical Political Economy, as indeed it must be for any theory of distribution. The significance of the labour-principle of value was that it gave a quantitative meaning to the original value-contribution made to the productive process in a sense which enabled it to be different from the final value of the product. As a cost-principle it evaluates a productive contribution in terms of the physical using-up of something which has to be replaced by human activity. If the labour or activity required to replace what is used up is less than the labour embodied in the total product, a surplus emerges. The crucial question is then this: Is this surplus distributed in proportion to the productive contribution of the participants in production (in proportion to the share of each in the cost involved), or is some class which has made little or no productive contribution successful in annexing it, and if so, how and why? This is no ethical inquiry alien to the realm of rigorous scientific definition. Yet it is an inquiry which modern economics has successfully eliminated. It will

---

[1] Böhm-Bawerk, for example, posed the question in this way in discussing the reason for a "surplus-value" on capital: "Why should the pressure of competition on the capitalist's share never be so strong as to press down its value to the value of the capital itself? . . . If this were to happen, the surplus-value, and with it the interest, would . . . disappear." (*Op. cit.*, p. 171.)

be part of the argument of subsequent chapters that this inquiry has been eliminated, not by accident, but for a crucial reason: namely, that subjective economics, in its obsession with demand and exchange, postulates little or nothing about the activity of production except that certain agents of production exist which are necessary and are scarce.

CHAPTER II

CLASSICAL POLITICAL ECONOMY

It is not surprising that classical Political Economy should have stirred its age, and exerted an influence which was revolutionary both to traditional notions and to traditional practice. In the history of thought in the social sciences its arrival was epoch-making because it created the concept of economic society as a deterministic system: a system in the sense that it was ruled by laws of its own, on the basis of which calculation and forecast of events could be made. For the first time a determinism of law in the affairs of men was demonstrated to exist, comparable to the determination of law in nature. In thus stressing the essential unity of economic events, Political Economy at the same time stressed the interdependence between the various elements of which the system was composed. To introduce a change at any one point was to set in motion a chain of related changes over the rest of the system; and these movements could be defined as having a certain form and also a certain order of magnitude in relation to the size of the initial impulse. The form and magnitude of such related movements were given by the series of functional relations stated by the equations of which (as we have seen) the classical theory of value in effect consisted; so that its theory of value was an essential, and not merely an incidental, feature of classical Political Economy.

34

In postulating, not only the fact of interdependence, but also interdependence of a certain form, the theory held implications which were of crucial importance for practice. Negatively, it implied that certain types of explanation were inappropriate to interpret a situation, and certain types of action by Governments were impotent to achieve their desired ends. Positively, it implied that the true explanation of phenomena was restricted to certain specific causes to which alone these phenomena could be directly related.

To-day, at the distance of a century and a half, there is a not uncommon tendency to overlook both the startling effect of this conception of an economic determinism on the thought of its age and the crucial position which it occupied in the development of economic doctrine. There is an inclination to forget the fundamental truths embodied in the classical structure and their significance as a basis for simple corollaries which to-day have become traditional: perhaps as a basis even of any deterministic thought and forecast in the economic realm. Recent years have seen a renewal of criticism of traditional Political Economy, even in some quarters an iconoclastic impatience to raze the classical structure to the ground. In this reaction against notions which have hardened into dogmatism and become props of an apologetic system of thought, there is much that is vigorous and healthy. Without criticism, thought stagnates and ideas shrivel to scholasticism; and it is true that in the heritage of economic thought there is much to be uprooted. Yet with certain brands of this modern criticism impatience seems to have banished discrimination; and there appears to lurk the danger, in rejecting all classical notions as product of unreal assumption, of

striking a blow at economic truths which may be fundamental, not merely to a given set of conclusions, but to
any forecast in the economic realm. In particular, there
is the danger of confusing too readily certain enduring
truths which were the essential contribution of classical
Political Economy, properly so-called, with the shapes
into which these notions were subsequently fashioned
in more scholastic or apologetic hands. When in place
of these classical corner-stones nothing of equivalent
calibre is provided, and when (as too frequently seems
to happen) the gap even passes unnoticed, there is ground
for apprehension lest the room is merely being cleared
for a species of economic mysticism to reign in a realm
of chance where any miracle may happen provided some
conjuror of the requisite moods and expectations can be
made to appear. This, of course, is not to say that any
criticism of classical doctrine is to be deplored because
it has a tendency to substitute doubt for dogmatic
certainty. This must be the first effect of any criticism.
But it is to say that two types of criticism are to be
distinguished which are frequently represented as similar.
There is the criticism of Political Economy which retains
certain essential limbs of the classical structure, as representing important constituents of truth, at the same time
as it emphasizes additional relationships which have the
effect of remodelling the structure and revolutionizing
the practical significance alike of the whole and of its
several elements. Of this type, as we shall see, was
Marx's critique of Political Economy—Marx who cited
classical Political Economy to refute the sophisms of
Proudhon. On the other hand, a criticism which takes
as its text the rejection of the classical structure *in toto*,
and is blind to the necessity of creating new structural

principles adequate to fill the room of those which it rejects, seems destined, in the main, to be nihilistic in its tendency.

To contemporaries the reign of law that Political Economy postulated was hard to credit. What could be believed of inanimate bodies was more difficult to envisage in the social realm, where events were the product of human action and of the unbound human will. To suggest that a system of commodity production and exchange could operate of itself, without collective regulation or single design, seemed at first incredible. To postulate that a system of apparent economic anarchy was ruled by law seemed a miracle too strange to trust. How could order emerge from the conflict of a myriad of independent and autonomous wills? The answer which the economists provided depended on the fact of competition. When a seller is one among many operating on a market, his own actions can exert no more than a negligible influence on the total market situation. He will, therefore, be forced to take existing market-values as given, and mould his own action to the values which confront him. Each, separately viewed, will be ruled by, and will not be rulers of, market-values. Hence, if they are driven by the motive of maximizing their gains relative to the situation in which each finds himself, all will tend to respond to value-movements in a *uniform* way. What results in the market at large will, of course, be product of the totality of separate actions; but of actions originating with individuals in a situation where the individual will is irrelevant, both because separately it is impotent and because, with respect to the total situation, it is blind. It was for this reason that the market could be ruled as though by an "invisible

37

hand" which exacted that the hand of each served a purpose and achieved a result quite other than the individual will had conceived and intended. This was the alchemy by which private vices might compound to yield public benefits.

But the theory implied something more than this. It implied the assumption not only that the individuals in each market were numerous and competed with one another, but also that individuals and resources were *mobile* and prices flexible (at least within the boundaries of a single country and given a sufficient period of time). Consequently exchange-values themselves could be said to behave in a certain way: to observe certain uniformities, and to conform to certain essential relationships.[1] These controlling relationships were relationships between men as producers. The fact that men and the productive resources which men handled would move between different lines of production in search of maxi-

---

[1] True, all elements in the situation can be said "mutually to determine" one another (as Marshall emphasized in criticizing Böhm-Bawerk). But so can this be said of everything in the universe at a moment of time. This does not prevent its being true that (as was said in the previous chapter) in relation to our knowledge of the situation and to practice, there are certain factors in the situation which are "key" to all the other variables, and hence are to be singled out as essential and determining factors. Otherwise all causal statements would be impossible. It is of interest to note that Engels remarked that "cause and effect . . . are conceptions which only have validity in their application to a particular case as such; but when we consider the particular case in its general connection with the world as a whole they dissolve in the conception of universal action and interaction". (*Anti-Dühring*, p. 29.) This did not prevent him from referring to the "primacy" of (for instance) the economic factor in history as a basis of interpretation and forecast in a particular historical context. The recognition of interaction does not imply the impossibility of any causal statement: merely the recognition that any such statement necessarily isolates certain determining influences as the most important in a given context.

mum advantage ensured not only that wages and profits tended to uniformity over the whole range of industry, but also that the ratios at which commodities exchanged on the market tended to correspond to the ratios of their real costs. This latter represented their "normal" or "natural" values. Relations of exchange, therefore, reflected relations of production and were controlled by them. Political Economy became primarily a theory of production. As Marx later expressed it: "In principle there is not exchange of products, but exchange of labours which compete in production. It is on the mode of exchange of productive forces that the mode of exchange of products depends."[1]

Several crucial principles were implied in this view; principles which both held a central place in classical discussion and have been the particular target of recent criticism. First, it implied that the quantity of money, viewed both as a standard of value and a medium of exchange, was irrelevant to the determination of any of these essential relationships. Since money represented merely a convenient technique of exchange, either for calculation or as an exchange-intermediary, it could make no difference to the essential productive relationships, and hence could not (in the last analysis) affect the system of exchange-ratios. An increase or decrease in the quantity of money, since it would ultimately tend to affect all prices equally, would leave the relation between them unaffected: it would simply raise or lower the prices of all things (including land, labour-power and capital-instruments) uniformly, while leaving the ratios at which they exchanged against one another the same as before. This was used in particular by Ricardo

---

[1] *Misère de la Philosophie* (1847 Ed.), p. 61.

to combat the former notion (to-day again put in currency) that the rate of interest depended on the abundance or scarcity of money; as, again, it was used by Say to dispute the view that "capital is multiplied by the operation of credit", on the ground that "capital consists of positive value vested in material substance, and not of immaterial products, which are utterly incapable of being accumulated".[1] In stating the central propositions of Political Economy, abstraction could be made of money and of the money-measure of demand. Indeed, if this had not been possible, the classical economists would have been unable to postulate any such thing as an equilibrium of exchange-ratios without, at least, introducing as datum some additional and sufficient condition concerning the behaviour of money.[2]

Secondly, there was the principle which was embodied in Say's famous Law of Markets. While history has endowed it with the name of Say, the enunciation of

---

[1] Say, *Treatise on Pol. Econ.* (1821), Vol. II, p. 145. Already in the first edition (1803) of his *Traité* he had taken Locke to task for saying that the rate of interest depended on the supply of money.

[2] Mr. Keynes's denial of this doctrine in his *General Theory of Employment, Interest and Money*, Chapter 13, applies, of course, to a situation where there are unemployed resources, and hence the possibility of a change of output if demand increases. In his Appendix to Chapter 14 he states (p. 191) that it would apply to long-period equilibrium, given "flexible money-wages". It is to be noted that in his proposition (on p. 168) that $M = L(r)$ (where $M =$ "total quantity of money", $L =$ liquidity-preference, and r the rate of interest) M is defined as money measured in wage-units (*i.e.* relative to the price of labour-power), so that the equation embraces the case where wages and prices rise proportionately to M. What the equation is designed to stress is that, where factors of production are in elastic supply, an increase in M is capable of altering output, and not prices, by influencing investment *via r*. But the Ricardian school may have been justified in ignoring this possibility in an age when factory industry was still in its infancy and a chronic reserve of equipment did not exist on the scale it does to-day.

the principle probably owes as much, or even more, to James Mill; it was sponsored by Ricardo and runs throughout the writings of the Ricardian School.[1] Essentially it is to say that since exchange, which is a two-sided process, is ultimately to be viewed as a series of transactions between two sets of producers, each of them bartering its products against the other's, there could never be a problem of general or all-round excess of products. There might, it is true, be an excess of certain types of product, into the production of which relatively too much of the labour-force of society had been drawn. This would show itself in a fall in the price of these particular commodities below their "normal value", and the migration of producers into other industries. But if the increased production were general to all industries, there could be no excess (provided the increase were in the "proper" proportions), since both sides of all of the two-sided transactions between producers, in which exchange consisted, would be increased *pari passu*, and the increased desire of each party to barter his products would be balanced by the increased desire of the other. James Mill put the matter clearly and dogmatically: "The

---

[1] In the first edition (1803) of Say's *Traité d'Économie Politique*, the chapter on "Des Debouchés" (Chap. 22 of Tome I) occupied no more than three pages, and is concerned solely to combat the Mercantilist view that markets consist in abundance of money and that increase of wealth is dependent on increase of exports. The germ of the future doctrine is contained in the words: "It is not abundance of money which makes sales easy, but the abundance of other products in general" (p. 153). His second edition, when he rewrote the chapter and enlarged it to sixteen pages (Chap. 15 of Tome I), did not appear till 1814. Meanwhile, Mill's *Commerce Defended* had appeared in two editions in 1808, in which the doctrine was elaborated and its significance for the question of over-production was stressed. Ricardo, however, always attributed the doctrine to Say.

production of commodities creates, and is the one and universal cause which creates a market for the commodities produced. . . . A nation's power of purchasing is exactly measured by its annual produce. The more you increase the annual produce, the more by that very act you extend the national market. . . . The demand of a nation is always equal to the produce of a nation." [1] J. B. Say asserted that: "It is production which opens a demand for products. . . . To say that sales are dull, owing to the scarcity of money, is to mistake the means for the cause. . . . Sales cannot be said to be dull because money is scarce, but because other products are so. . . . A product is no sooner created than it, from that instant, affords a market for other products to the full extent of its own value. Thus the mere circumstance of the creation of one product immediately opens a vent for other products." [2]

At first sight such an argument seems quite arbitrary dogmatism, with little relation to real events. Supply and demand can never be unequal because they are defined in such a way as to make them equal! Yet the principle was something more than a tautology in so far as it implied a description of economic society as characterized by this particular type of inter-relationship; and as such it was flesh of the flesh of the Ricardian system. As money could be neglected in the determination of exchange-values, so for the same reason could

[1] *Commerce Defended* (1808), pp. 81 and 83.

[2] Say, *Treatise on Political Economy*, Tr. Prinsep, 1821, Vol. I, pp. 165, 167. Say even went so far as to state (which was quite a different matter) that "one kind of production would seldom outstrip the rest, and its products be disproportionately cheapened, were production left entirely to itself"; while his translator added that "there is no possibility of production outrunning consumption, so long as that consumption is free". (*Ibid.*, pp. 169, 178.)

the "amount of demand" (viewed as an absolute figure) be neglected as a factor determining the processes of production and exchange. The "market", as an independent factor in the problem, disappeared as soon as one viewed the economic process as a unified whole. Demand then became a dependent, not an independent variable. In each transaction, separately regarded, there were always, of course, two terms: supply and demand, goods and money, producer and market. But to conclude from this that the same two terms must appear as independent factors in the situation viewed as a whole was to commit the fallacy of composition: it was to neglect the fact that this single transaction was but one-half of a pair of transactions, in which "demand" or "the market" expressed in money appeared as a common term. As Marx later put it:[1] exchange was essentially a series of transactions of the type $C - M - C$, with money as a simple intermediary between transactions which were essentially one.

Thirdly, there was J. S. Mill's dictum that "demand for commodities is not demand for labour", the "complete apprehension" of which Leslie Stephen declared to be "perhaps the best test of an economist", and which Mill himself described as "a paradox (which) hardly any even among political economists of reputation, except Mr. Ricardo and M. Say, have kept constantly

[1] Marx stated this to be true of a "simple exchange society" (*i.e.* of small independent producers). As we shall see later, he also stated that a crucial modification was introduced in a capitalist economy, *i.e.* an economy characterized by the existence of a class whose sole concern was with investment of capital in a series of transactions of the type $M - C - M'$ (where M' was $> M$ by an amount equal to the rate of profit). This introduced an opposition into the apparent unity of the exchange process, and created the possibility of a rupture and a breaking of the process into its two parts.

and steadily in view". "The demand for commodities determines in what particular branch of production the labour and capital shall be employed; it determines the *direction* of the labour; but not the more or less of the labour itself, or of the maintenance or payment of the labour. These depend on the amount of the capital, or other funds directly devoted to the sustenance and remuneration of labour." [1] By "demand for labour" Mill, of course, meant not demand in terms of money, but demand in terms of commodities: in other words, he was thinking of the determination of real wages, not of money wages. To have said that "demand for commodities" conceived as a total of *money*-expenditure by consumers could not permanently influence the ratio of exchange-values, including the exchange-value of labour-power, would have been to repeat, with a particular reference, the former of the two principles which have just been described. It is clear that Mill intended his proposition to imply something additional to this; and that when he spoke of "demand for commodities" he intended it in a purely relative sense—the only alternative meaning it could have had in this context. Using it in this relative sense, he apparently intended to imply *both* that a demand for some particular commodity as compared with another exerted no appreciable influence on the level of wages and *also* that an increase in the amount which consumers spent on commodities in

---

[1] *Principles*, Ed. Ashley, pp. 79-80. Jevons, who attacked this doctrine (*Principles of Economics*, pp. 126-33), declared that it originated with Ricardo in the third edition of his *Principles*. But what Ricardo here asserts is that the demand for labour depends on the *mode* of expenditure by consumers (due to the different ratios of labour to capital in different employments)—a qualification of Mill's statement, rather than an anticipation of it. (Ricardo, *Principles*, Third Ed., p. 476.)

general relatively to what they invested would not increase the share of the product which accrued to labour, but rather the reverse. The former of these two propositions was a repetition of the familiar classical doctrine that the configuration of demand was irrelevant to the distribution of the product between profit and wages (except in so far as it might accelerate the tendency to diminishing returns on land, and hence raise the cost of subsistence). Like so much of Ricardian reasoning, it rested on a particular assumption: namely, that the proportions between capital and labour were equal in all industries. Without this assumption, the statement would no longer be valid. Nevertheless, it can be held to embody this important truth: that, unless the shift in demand had any substantial bias in the direction of more or of less labour-using lines of production (*i.e.* towards industries of either higher or lower "compositions of capital" as Marx termed it), the change could be treated as irrelevant to the determination of the exchange-value of labour-power.

The second proposition (referring to the proportion of income spent compared to the proportion of income saved) depended, however, on a particular view of the nature of capital and of the relation between capital and labour in the production-process. This raises issues which will be separately discussed in a later chapter. But since the classical economists were wont to regard capital as consisting essentially in "advances to labour", the proposition had a simple and (within its limits) an important meaning: namely, that it was on the quantity of capital, viewed as a wages-fund, relative to the supply of labourers, that the level of wages depended. Since an increase in the proportion of income which was spent would involve a diminished accumulation of capital, it followed that the demand for labour, as properly viewed, would be reduced thereby rather than increased.[1]

Finally, we have the principle which was treated by Ricardo as the outstanding corollary of his theory of value. It is summed up in the statement which, treated in isolation, has often been derided as no more than a tautology: "when wages rise, profits fall". The truth which the statement was intended to imply is more fully represented in another statement of Ricardo that "profits depend on high or low wages, and on nothing else".[2] In other words, profit is uniquely determined by the ratio of the value of labour-power to the value of commodities in general, and these two quantities can move independently of each other. This relation is approximately, although not precisely (owing to the fact of rent) equivalent to the proportion of the labour-force of society which requires to be devoted to the production of the labourers' subsistence.[3] This proposition was

[1] Of course, there was the possibility that the change in spending might result in an equivalent and opposite change in "hoarding" of money. In this case no change in capital accumulation would result. But such hoarding the classical economists apparently (it was rarely mentioned by them) treated as simply a withdrawal of money from circulation, with an effect equivalent to any change in the quantity of money: namely, an effect on all prices equally.

[2] Ricardo used "high wages" as synonymous with a high "*proportion of the whole produce necessary to support the labourer*". (*Notes on Malthus*, Ed. Hollander and Gregory, pp. 134-5.) James Mill said that if profit be used "to denote the ratio of values [*i.e.* the *rate* of profit] it may be shown that profits in that sense depend wholly upon wages". (*Pol. Econ.*, pp. 58-9.) It was this latter statement, as we shall see below, referring to the *rate* of profit as distinct from total profit, that Marx amended with his concept of the "organic composition of capital".

[3] When Professor Pigou in his *Theory of Unemployment* took the quantity of labour in what he termed wage-goods industry and in non-wage-goods industry as a fundamental and determining relation, he was, of course, using a conception closely similar to Ricardo's.

clearly fundamental, not only to the practical conclusions which Ricardo derived from his economic doctrine, but also to certain subsidiary propositions which are to-day treated as virtually axiomatic, and without which the economist would find himself in an Alice-through-the-Looking-Glass sort of world. It implied that the rate of profit (treated as "a ratio of values") could be increased neither by an increase in the quantity of money (except temporarily) nor by an increase of consumption, as Malthus was asserting. Ricardo used it to demonstrate that, contrary to the assertion of Adam Smith, an expansion of foreign trade could only raise the rate of profit in so far as it was able to lower wages by cheapening the workers' subsistence.[1] Marx used it to refute the contention of Proudhon that a rise in wages would result in an equivalent rise in commodity prices so that trade unionism could do no more than chase its own tail. How central it is to much else in economic reasoning can be judged from the fact that, were it not true, there would be no reason to conclude that a rise in the wage-level tends to encourage, and a fall to discourage, the use of machinery.[2] For if the price of labour can rise without producing any fall in the rate of profit (viewed as the return on capital), the cost of machines will be raised (due to the increased price of the labour-power used to make them) proportionately with the cost of hiring labour; and the cost of mechanized processes will increase *pari passu* with the cost of processes which depend solely upon direct labour. But such a result requires that prices and wages all increase simultaneously. Classical doctrine, however, was assuming a situation

[1] Cf. below, pp. 225–6.
[2] Cf. Wicksell, *Lectures*, Vol. I, pp. 100, 167.

where a rise of wages can take place without any equivalent rise of prices, with the result that profits fall. Indeed, it was assuming that some prices will actually fall as a result of a rise of wages, even though other prices rise. Those commodities will have most tendency to fall which embody little direct labour and require a relatively large amount of capital to finance them; and since this is the essential characteristic of labour-saving machinery, a particular encouragement will be given to its purchase and use.[1]

But these principles were mainly incidental to the central corollary of Political Economy—the grand precept of *laissez-faire*. Here the imposing unity of Political Economy as a theoretical system was translated into a consistent system of practical doctrine. Here abstract principles were clothed in the flesh of actual policies, and schematic interpretation of the world of events was fused with precept and action. Political Economy had created the concept of economic society as an autonomous system, ruled by laws of its own. These laws operated,

---

[1] Mr. Keynes has stated (*The General Theory of Employment*, p. 191) that many of these classical propositions rest on the assumption of "full employment" as a necessary condition, and hence can have no application to conditions of changing output or departures from equilibrium. It is certainly true and important that some of these propositions require substantial modification in a situation of unemployed resources: for example, a change of money-demand can alter total output instead of exhausting its influence in an alteration of prices. But it does not seem to follow that these classical propositions have *no* application to the real world; unless it is assumed that in the real world all resources are permanently in infinitely elastic supply. What it seems clear that the classical economists intended to assume was the existence of tendencies *towards* a position of full employment. Hence they regarded their propositions as establishing the limiting factors on economic development in the long period. Certain of these classical propositions also depended on other assumptions—assumptions affecting the stability of the system—which will be referred to in Chapter VI.

the system "went of itself", independently of the care of government and the whim of sovereign and statesman. Regulation by the State, previously held to be essential if order was to emerge from chaos, was seen to be unnecessary. The presumption was afforded that such regulation would be positively harmful, in that it would obstruct the working of economic forces, produce disequilibria where harmony would otherwise rule, without any evidence that it could achieve results more consistent with the general interest, but rather the contrary. A description of how the system worked *ipso facto* became a presumption as to how it should be allowed to work. True, classical Political Economy contained no final demonstration that *laissez-faire* produced the *optimum* result in human welfare. This was left for the utility principle to do (quite fallaciously) half a century later in hedonistic terms. The economists were content with the claim that *laissez-faire* was superior as a condition for the production and increase of wealth: a claim which they were particularly concerned to demonstrate by contrast with State-aided monopolies or with State restrictions on foreign trade. There was every temptation to believe that a system which achieved an equilibrium by an internal coherence of its elements operated better left alone than when ignorantly interfered with. At any rate, it was a belief which inevitably found favour in an age when whatever exhibited the reign of "natural law" was implicitly held to be half divine.

Closely related with this practical doctrine was another sharp edge of criticism which Political Economy turned against contemporary policies. As essentially a theory of production, it carried the implication that a consuming class which had no active relation to the production of material commodities—which drew revenue but yielded no productive contribution, in the sense of incurring some "real cost" as an equivalent—played no positive rôle in economic society. Its existence was a drain upon wealth rather than an assistance to wealth-creation; and in so far as its interest dominated the counsels of the State, it was likely to be a fetter and an obstruction. This was the light in which Political Economy, at least in its Ricardian tradition, viewed the landed interest, which dominated the unreformed Parliament, restricted the mobility of labour by parish settlement and the Speenhamland system, and maintained the Corn Laws for the protection of corn prices and land-rents. In addition to labour, the only active element in production was capital, which financed the progress of technique and of the division of labour.[1] While wages fed the labourer and his increase, profit was the source of and incentive to capital accumulation by the industrious class, intimately related to industry and finding in industry the focus of its interest and ambitions. Rent, by contrast, was the price of a property-right in scarce natural resources: it was an extraction of a part of the fruits of production to maintain a passive and unproductive class. "Rent," said Ricardo, "is in all cases a portion of the profits previously obtained on the land. It is never a new creation of revenue, but always part of a revenue already created."[2] In so far as this class

---

[1] James Mill in his *Elements of Pol. Econ.* (Third Ed.) spoke of "two instruments of production: one primary, the other secondary": namely, labour and capital (p. 84). Rent, however, was "something altogether extraneous to what may be considered as the return to the productive operations of capital and labour" (p. 68).

[2] *Essay on the Influence of a Low Price of Corn on the Profits of Stock* (1815), p. 15.

was thrifty and accumulated its rents as capital for industry, the payment, while it might be otiose, did no harm: it was returned to production as new capital to finance a new productive cycle. But this from nature and tradition such a class was less inclined to do than was the industrial bourgeoisie. If they invested they might well have more inclination towards government bonds or monopolist trading companies than towards industry. (Had not a writer like Lord Lauderdale defended the existence of the National Debt on the grounds that it served as a solid investment for such funds?) And in so far as rents were spent in maintaining this class in idleness, in the upkeep of establishments and staffs of menial servants, it represented a tax on the productive system for the maintenance of unproductive consumption.

How preoccupied the classical economists were with practical interpretation such as this, even in their more abstract analyses, is too seldom, I think, appreciated. William Spence (against whom James Mill had written his *Commerce Defended*) had made it a principal defence of the landed interest that consumption was a prior condition of production and that expenditure therefore was conducive to national wealth. In 1808 he had written: "It is clear, then, that expenditure, not parsimony, is the province of the class of land proprietors, and that it is on the due performance of this duty, by the class in question, that the production of the national wealth depends. . . . For the constantly progressive maintenance of the prosperity of the community, it is absolutely requisite that this class should go on progressively increasing its expenditure." [1] Malthus inclined towards this opinion; and his doctrine of

---

[1] *Britain Independent of Commerce*, pp. 36-7.

"effective demand" was clearly directed to the conclusion that landlords were not to be condemned as a class of unproductive consumers, but rather to be praised as an element in the necessary balance of a healthy society: a balance between the accumulating instincts of the industrialist and the market for their products provided by a consuming class. Against this view the principle that demand was irrelevant to the determination of values (and hence of profits), that the productive process created its own demand, and that parsimony, not consumption, was a creative act provided directly a polemical weapon. And throughout the nineteenth century the classic heresy whose refutation was taught by every economic teacher was that the spending of the rich was beneficial to industry. Similarly, many other points of controversy between Ricardo and Malthus were related directly to this central issue. Malthus wrote his *Inquiry into the Nature and Progress of Rent* (1815) primarily to disprove the view of "some modern writers" who "consider rent as too nearly resembling in its nature, and the laws by which it is governed, the excess of price above the cost of production, which is the characteristic of monopoly", and to show that high rents (or the circumstances producing them) were an aid to improvements in the land.[1] In their discussion of the effect of agricultural improvements on the rent of land, Ricardo argued that these would cause rents to *fall* (and hence be opposed to the interests of landlords as a class), while Malthus on the other hand asserted that they would cause rents to *rise*.[2]

[1] Pp. 2 and 27-30. Marx termed this essay "a pamphlet for the landlords against industrial capital". (*Theorien über den Mehrwert* (Ed. 1923), Vol. III, p. 61.)

[2] Cf. *Letters of Ricardo to Malthus* (Ed. Bonar), 94 *et seq.*, and Malthus, *Principles*, 205 *et seq.*

As a critique levelled simultaneously against the authoritarianism of an autocratic state and against the privileges and influence of the landed aristocracy Political Economy at its inception played a revolutionary rôle. As a systematizer of thought in a sphere previously void of consistent principles it came as a revelation; while, as a vindicator of freedom in the economic realm, its influence in the bourgeois revolutions of the nineteenth century was scarcely surpassed by those philosophies of political rights which lit the torch of liberalism on the Continent. Only later, in its post-Ricardian phase, did it pass over from assault on privilege and restriction to apology for property. Among its concepts the notion of the determination of value-relations by the relations of men as producers, and the distinction between what was necessary to production and what was unnecessary as turning upon concrete human activities, were fundamental. These governing relations of production were the concrete forms which the social division of labour assumed in a given state of demand and of technique. Whether these relations were rightly to be treated as fundamental is, of course, ultimately a practical question. But the fact that the economic theory of the rising industrial bourgeoisie should have had this emphasis finds an evident historical explanation as an expression of the rôle in society which this class filled: the perspective from which this class viewed the process of social change enabling it to reach this essential and realistic conception. But this historical reason at the same time implied a limitation. Included among the productive relations between men in society is the class relation between capitalist and labourer. This Political Economy took for granted, but did not penetrate; was content to de-

53

scribe and to include among its conditions, but did not analyse; treating this division into classes either as part of the order of nature or as simply one form which the division of labour spontaneously assumed in a free society, and not as an historical product of a special type. That the characteristics of this unique relationship might affect the manner in which their economic laws operated, and might radically transform the interpretations and the forecasts based upon these laws, the economists did not consider, because they had not recognized the essence of this relationship. Their successors, as we shall see, drifted away from and not towards this recognition, with their tendency increasingly to drop these relations between men as producers from the picture, or at best to retain them as insubstantial ghosts of their former selves.

CHAPTER III

CLASSICAL POLITICAL ECONOMY AND MARX

FOR Marx the analysis which the classical economists had conducted disclosed only half of the problem. As Engels put it in an important passage in his *Anti-Dühring*, they had shown the positive side of capitalism, in contrast to what had preceded it. In demonstrating the laws of *laissez-faire* they had provided a critique of previous orders of society; but they had not provided an historical critique of capitalism itself. This latter remained to be done, unless capitalism was to be regarded as a stable and permanent order of nature or an unchanging final term of social development. It remained to be done in order to give capitalism its proper place in historical evolution and to provide a key to the forecast of its future. Economic science to date, said Engels, "begins with the critique of the survivals of feudal forms of production and exchange, shows the necessity of their replacement by capitalist forms, and develops the laws of the capitalist mode of production and its corresponding forms of exchange in their positive aspects; that is, the aspects in which they further the general aims of society". Equally necessary was the dialectical completion of Political Economy by "a socialist critique of the capitalist mode of production; that is, with the statement of its laws in their negative aspects, with the demonstration that this mode of production, through its own development, drives towards the point at which it makes itself impossible ".[1]

The crux of the matter was a precise interpretation of Profit as a category of income. The economists had postulated conditions which regulated the exchange-values of commodities. These they had explained in terms of a cost-theory; and they had also provided what was virtually a cost-theory of the value of labour-power itself. Profit was then regarded as a residual quantity, the size of which was determined by these other given factors—the value of the product and the value of labour-power. So far the explanation might appear to be satisfactory enough. But, as it stood, it was seriously incomplete; since profit had been left as a mere residual element without being itself explained. The nature of profit, the why and wherefore of its existence as a category of income at all, remained a secret; and until this secret was revealed, not only were important practical questions left unanswered, but there could be no certainty that the terms of the relation which was said to determine profit (namely, wages and the value of the product) could properly be treated as independent. In the theory of rent, the limited supply and consequent scarcity of available land was adduced as the reason for the emergence of rent and its acquisition by the landowner. Classical theory had adduced no parallel reason for the emergence of profit and its acquisition by the capitalist. Its necessity had simply been assumed. There remained the question: Why, even though there might exist a difference between the expenses of production and the value of the product, should this difference accrue to the capitalist and his partners rather than to anyone else? Why in a regime

[1] *Anti-Dühring*, Eng. trans., p. 171.

of economic freedom and competition did not such a surplus tend to disappear either into rent or into wages? If its persistence was to be explained in terms of a cost-theory, how was this consistent with the labour-theory of value? Or was it to be interpreted in terms analogous to the theory of rent? That this was no superfluous inquiry can be seen from the importance of the type of practical question which depended on it: for instance, what would be the effect if profit were taxed or otherwise appropriated, or if wages rose and encroached upon profit, or if the rate of profit for any reason tended to fall? Was the maintenance of a capitalist class as much the fostering of an unproductive burden on industry as the Ricardians had alleged the existence of a landed class to be? Would the interest of this class in protecting profit become as much a fetter on the productive forces as was the interest of landlords in the protection of rents?

Sensing this *lacuna* in their argument, the economists, particularly the successors of Ricardo, sought to develop an explanation of profit along two lines—on the one hand, by inventing a new category of "real cost", for which profit was the exchange-equivalent; on the other hand, in terms of an alleged special "productivity" of capital (and hence, by imputation, of its creator the capitalist). It is these shallow and inconsistent theories which afford the principal evidence of that decline of Political Economy after Ricardo which so many commentators have refused to recognize, and which elicited from Marx the title of "vulgar economics". It was against these concepts that Marx directed his fiercest polemics—in particular what Böhm-Bawerk termed [1] his "weighty attacks" against the productivity theory of

---

[1] *Capital and Interest,* p. 173.

capital. To Marx the explanation of Profit lay, not in any inherent property of capital as such, not in any real cost or productive activity contributed by the capitalist (no more than land-rent was to be explained in terms of the properties of nature or any activity of the land-owner), but in the class structure of existing society—that class division into propertyless and dispossessed which lay behind the appearance of equality and free contract and "natural values" in terms of which the laws of Political Economy had been framed.

According to Marx's view of history, progress had seen the march of various class systems, each generating and in turn conditioned by the technical conditions and their associated modes of production at the time. Class antagonisms, rooted in the relationships of different sections of society to the prevailing means of production, had been the basic motive-force of the process—of the passage from one form to the next. As became clear from an examination of its origins, capitalism was also a class system: different in significant respects from preceding ones, yet nevertheless a system rooted in a dichotomy between possessing masters and subject dispossessed. It was natural that Marx should look to the peculiarities of this class relation to find a key to the essential rhythm of capitalist society—to find the dis-equilibria, the tendencies to movement, and to movement *in* its base and not merely *on* its base, behind the veil of economic harmonies which an analysis merely of exchange relations in a free market seemed to reveal. As contrasted with equality of rights, here was revealed inequality of economic status; as contrasted with contractual freedom, economic dependence and compulsion.

Clearly, the essence of this relation between capitalist

58

and labourer, on which the emergence of profit hinged, must bear a major analogy to the relation between owner and labourer in earlier forms of class society— for instance, between master and slave or between lord and serf. In these earlier forms of society there was no doubt about the character of the relationship as one of force and exploitation, or about the nature and origin of the income of the owning class. The latter annexed the surplus product, over and above the subsistence of their labourers, by virtue of law or custom. The relationship was openly written as what it was. But in capitalist society this was not so. Relations assumed exclusively a value-form. There was no surplus product, but only a surplus-value, which was presumably controlled by the law of value oper- ating in a competitive market where normal exchange was a transfer of equivalent against equivalent. How under such circumstances could one explain the emerg- ence of a surplus-value at all? How was it to be made consistent with the theory of value, which was itself an abstract expression of the operation of a free competitive market? The formula of exchange on a free market was $C-M-C$. No one, it seemed, could acquire a money- income without first offering C, some equivalent com- modity-value, in exchange. The possibility of buyers and sellers moving freely from one side of a market to another and between markets ensured that in neither half of this exchange-cycle, neither $C-M$ nor $M-C$, did any surplus-value emerge. How then could one class start with M, a sum of money-capital, and by introducing it into the cycle of exchange draw out a larger value than the value originally put in: $M-C-M'$? "To explain the general nature of profit," said Marx, "you

must start from the theorem that on an average commodities are sold at their real values, and that profits
are derived from selling them at their real values. If
you cannot explain profit upon this supposition, you
cannot explain it at all." [1]   Tudor monopolies or feudal
liens on the labour of others could no longer be used
to explain how a class drew income without contributing
any productive activity.   Gains of chance or of individual
"sharp practice" could exert no permanent influence in
a regime of "normal values".   Universal and persistent
cheating of the productive by the unproductive seemed
impossible in an order of free contract.   At most this
could explain individual gains and losses among the class
of capitalists—what one gained another losing: it could
not account for the income of a whole class.   Therefore,
to explain Profit as had Sismondi simply as "spoliation
of the worker", acquired by the entrepreneur "not because
the enterprise produces more than it cost him, but because he does not pay all that it costs him, because he
does not give to the worker a sufficient compensation for
his work",[2] or, in Bray's description of it, as product of
"a system of unequal exchanges",[3] was not a sufficient
explanation: it afforded no answer to the central difficulty
and still left the contradiction unresolved.

James Mill had actually drawn attention to the analogy
between a wage-system and slave-labour.   "What is the

---

[1] *In Value Price and Profit.*   Here he also said of the comparison
between slavery and a wage-system: " On the basis of the wages system
even the *unpaid* labour seems to be *paid* labour.   With the slave, on the
contrary, even that part of his labour which is paid appears to be unpaid."
In the former " the nature of the whole transaction is completely masked
by the intervention of the contract and the pay received at the end of
the week".

[2] *Nouveaux Principes*, Vol. I, p. 92.

[3] *Labour's Wrongs and Labour's Remedy*, p. 50.

difference," he asked, "in the case of the man who operates by means of labourers receiving wages (instead of owning slaves)? . . . He is equally the owner of the labour with the manufacturer who operates with slaves. The only difference is the mode of purchasing. The owner of the slave purchases at once the whole of the labour which the man can ever perform: he who pays wages purchases only so much of a man's labour as he can perform in a day, or any other stipulated time. Being equally, however, the owner of the labour so purchased, as the owner of the slave is of that of the slave, the product which is the result of this labour, combined with his capital, is all equally his own." [1] But here Mill left the matter. For Marx it was the beginning of what was essential. The solution which he reached for this central problem turned on that distinction which he regarded as so crucial between labour and labour-power. Capitalist production had its historical root precisely in the transformation of human productive activity itself into a commodity. Labour-power became alienated as something to be bought and sold, and as itself acquiring a value. Since the proletarian was devoid of land or instruments of production, no alternative livelihood existed for him; and while the legal coercion to work for another was gone, the coercion of class circum-

---

[1] *Elements of Pol. Econ.*, pp. 21-2. Cf. also Richard Jones, *Introductory Lectures on Pol. Econ.* (1833), pp. 58-9. This "only difference" may, however, make the position of the wage-earner economically inferior to that of the slave, as well as enabling it to be better, since if the labourer is not the property of the master, the latter has no long-period interest in the former's upkeep (the wear and tear of labour and its depreciation through destitution is not a cost to the employer as is the wear and tear of his machinery). Hence it may well be in the employer's interest to treat a free labourer less well than he would a horse or a slave.

stance remained. Since the individual labourer (at least in the absence of organization and association) was devoid alike of alternative or of a "reserve price", the commodity he sold, like other commodities, acquired a value equal to the labour which its creation cost; and this consisted in the labour required to produce the subsistence of the human labourer. Hence the emergence of profit was to be attributed, not to any procreative quality of capital *per se*, but to the historically conditioned fact that labour in action was able to realize a product of greater value (depending on the quantum of labour involved) than the labour-power itself as a commodity was valued at. Hence the transaction between labourer and capitalist both was and was not an exchange of equivalents. Given the social basis which constituted labour-power as a commodity, an exchange of equivalents took place which satisfied the requirements of the law of value—the capitalist advanced subsistence to the labourer and acquired labour-power of equivalent market-value in return. The capitalist acquired the labour-power of the worker; the worker obtained in exchange sufficient to replace in his own person the physical wear and tear that working for the capitalist involved. Economic justice was satisfied. But without the historical circumstance that a class existed which had the sale of its labour-power as a commodity for its only livelihood to confront the capitalist with the possibility of this remunerative transaction, the capitalist would not have been in a position to annex this surplus-value to himself.

The rival interpretation which Lauderdale and Malthus had advanced in terms of the productivity of capital involved a relapse either into mysticism or into the superficialities of mere "supply and demand" explanations, which Marx in common with Ricardo condemned.[1] Marx never wished to deny that capital, or rather the concrete instruments in which stored-up labour was embodied, were creative of wealth or "riches": to have done so would have been patently absurd. In fact, he explicitly states that "it is wrong to speak of labour as the only source of wealth".[2] No more did Ricardo deny that land even uncultivated might yield utilities. But this was not to say that land or capital were productive of *value*. In fact, the more lavish was nature with the fruits of the earth, the *less* value were the latter likely to have and the *less* chance was there that land would yield a rent. Value, Marx emphasized, was not a mysterious intrinsic attribute of *things*: it was merely an expression of a social relation between *men*. It was an attribute with which objects were endowed by virtue of the form and manner in which the disposition of human labour took place between various lines of production in the course of the division of labour throughout society; and this disposition of the social labour-force was not arbitrary, but followed a determinate law of cost by virtue of Adam Smith's "unseen hand" of competitive forces. To explain surplus-value, therefore, in terms of some property of an object (capital) was to relapse into what Marx termed the Fetishism of Commodities—a species of animism in which post-Ricardian "vulgar economy" became increasingly enmeshed. This consisted in attributing animistically to things *in abstracto* the cause of exchange-relationships, when actually the latter were merely the resultant of the social relationships between *men*. It

---

[1] Cf. above, pp. 9-10.
[2] *Critique of Political Economy*, p. 33.

was to explain the course of a puppet-show exclusively in terms of the qualities and behaviour of the puppets. "A definite social relation between men assumes in their eyes the fantastic form of a relation between things."[1] "The existence of the revenue, as it appears on the surface, is separated from its inner relations and from all connections. Thus land becomes the source of rent, capital the source of profit, and labour the source of wages."[2] A Political Economy which spoke in these terms, which used as its constants properties of objects abstracted both from individuals and the class circumstances of these individuals, could deal only with surface appearance, could afford only a partial analysis of phenomena, and hence postulate laws and tendencies which were not merely incomplete, but also contradictory and false. At such a level of abstraction there could be no *differentia* because none of the essential differentiating qualities were included in the assumptions. Factors of production were treated solely in their technical aspect as indispensable each to the whole and hence each to the other: an abstraction which yielded an *ex hypothesi* demonstration of an essential harmony between them. It was not surprising that on this plane of reasoning no concept of rent or surplus could appear, and that equivalents should always exchange against equivalents because the situation was so defined that this must be so.

A more recent example may perhaps be cited of the lack of meaning attaching to certain fundamental concepts when exchange relations are treated in abstraction from men as producers and from their relation to a

[1] Marx, *Capital*, Vol. I, p. 43.
[2] Marx, *Theorien über den Mehrwert* (Ed. 1923), Vol. III, pp. 521-2.

background of social institutions. Pareto has pointed to the significant distinction between "activities of men directed to the production or transformation of economic goods", and "to the appropriation of goods produced by others". Clearly, if one views the economic problem simply as a pattern of exchange relations, separated from the social relations of the individuals concerned—treating the individuals who enter into exchange simply as so many x's and y's, performing certain "services", but abstracted from their concrete relation to the means of production (*e.g.* whether propertied or unpropertied, whether passive *rentiers* or active labourers)—then Pareto's distinction can have no meaning in a free competitive market. "Appropriation of goods produced by others" can only result from the incursion of monopoly or of extra-economic fraud or force. From the regime of "normal" exchange-values it is excluded by the very definition of a free market. This is, in fact, the answer which is given by Professor Pigou. Citing Pareto's distinction, he proceeds to suggest that "acts of mere appropriation" can be excluded by the assumption that "when one man obtains goods from another man, he is conceived to obtain them by the process, not of seizure, but of exchange in an open market, where the bargainers are reasonably competent and reasonably cognizant of the conditions".[1] It may be said that this conclusion is perfectly consistent with the scope of the inquiry. But does not the very answer which this scope demands suggest the unreality of such limits and the barrenness, at least on matters fundamental to problems of *Political* Economy, of so limited an analysis? Yet the whole tendency of economics since the days of the post-

[1] *Economics of Welfare*, p. 130.

Ricardians has been to narrow the scope of economic inquiry in this way: moreover, while doing so, at the same time to persist in rendering pronouncements on fundamental issues similar to those with which the classical economists were concerned.

Suppose that toll-gates were a general institution, rooted in custom or ancient legal right. Could it reasonably be denied that there would be an important sense in which the income of the toll-owning class represented "an appropriation of goods produced by others" and not payment for an "activity directed to the production or transformation of economic goods?" Yet toll-charges would be fixed in competition with alternative roadways, and hence would, presumably, represent prices fixed "in an open market, where the bargainers on both sides are reasonably competent and cognizant of the conditions" Would not the opening and shutting of toll-gates become an essential factor of production, according to most current definitions of a factor of production, with as much reason at any rate as many of the functions of the capitalist entrepreneur are so classed to-day? This factor, like others, could then be said to have a "marginal productivity" and its price be regarded as the measure and equivalent of the service it rendered. At any rate, where is a logical line to be drawn between toll-gates and property-rights over scarce resources in general? Perhaps it will be said that the distinction depends on whether the toll-gate owner himself constructed the road. If so, it is precisely to break through the restricted circle of abstract exchange-relations to seek a definition in terms of the productive activity of the person in question, as separate from and more fundamental than the opening and shutting of toll-gates. But notions which confine themselves to the circle of pure exchange-relations are clearly unfitted to rise above the wisdom of a contemporary critic of Ricardo, who, in attacking Quesnay and Smith, roundly declared that, since none could charge a price who did no service, all classes which drew an income must *ipso facto* be "productive", and their income the measure of their value to society.[1] Perhaps it will be said that such distinctions are not the province of economics. But this injunction, if it were obeyed, would both render economics barren of most of its practical fruit and make it something radically different from what the founders of the subject designed and intended.

It must not be thought that, in criticizing this type of abstraction, Marx was tilting at all abstractions from the standpoint of a crude empiricism. He was criticizing a particular method of abstraction on the ground that it ignored the essential and mistook shadow for substance and appearance for reality. Any generalization, from its very nature, must, of course, make abstraction of certain elements in a situation; and to this extent "theory" and "fact" must necessarily be at variance. Indeed, the method of Marx, as we have seen, was an abstract method as much as that of the classical economists: The theory of value which Marx took over from classical Political Economy, and developed in important particulars, was an abstraction which based itself not simply on certain features general to any exchange economy, but on essential characteristics of capitalism

---

[1] George Purves, *All Classes Productive of National Wealth* (1817). This gentleman had commenced by declaring that "the grand fundamental question, on which the whole science of statistics must more or less depend" is "whether all classes are productive of wealth or whether some are unproductive".

as a system of commodity-production. It seems to be generally forgotten, when Marx is criticized for giving no adequate "proof" of his theory of value in *Das Kapital*, that he was not propounding a novel and unfamiliar doctrine, but was adopting a principle which was part of the settled tradition of classical Political Economy and without which he considered any determinate statement to be impossible. Clearly in these circumstances he had no intention of prefacing his analysis of capitalist production with more than a definition and contrast of certain basic concepts such as value, exchange-value and use-value. These and kindred concepts were admittedly abstractions which had only a more or less imperfect representation in the real world. But here his method was no more and no less abstract than that of his predecessors. Competition itself was an abstraction, and so was the "perfect market" in which "normal values" emerged. "Normal values", like Euclidean points and straight lines, were to be found in the real world only as "limiting cases".

The two abstractions which have caused most clamour among Marx's critics—the concept of homogeneous "simple labour" and the assumption in volume I of *Capital* of equal "organic compositions of capital" in all lines of production—were also common to preceding and contemporary economists, and the ground of many of their most signal corollaries. The latter assumption figured prominently, as we have seen, with Ricardo. In the theory of international trade, for instance, it was the basis of the proposition that a high or low wage-level in a country did not affect the terms of trade, but only caused an equivalent and opposite change in the level of profits.[1] As we have also seen, it underlay John Stuart Mill's dictum that "demand for commodities does not constitute demand for labour". The assumption of homogeneity of units of a factor of production is common to economic method up to the present day. Without it the conception of a "normal" return has no meaning: tacit or explicit, it is part of any discussion of the "general level of wages" or of a theory of "normal profit". When Marx in the third volume of *Capital* admitted that the assumption of equal "compositions of capital", which formed the basis of his value-principle in the first volume, was only a first approximation, Böhm-Bawerk made great play with the "great contradiction" between the first approximation of the first volume and the later approximation of the third. On this great contradiction, he triumphantly declared, the whole Marxian system foundered. A recent writer has said that "nowhere is there in print such a miracle of confusion" as the Marxian system.[2] Yet all deductive reasoning proceeds by a process of approximation; and similar "contradictions" could be demonstrated in all such cases between successive approximations, or between *any* approximation and the facts. It is a question of the *uses* to which an approximation is put. What is important is whether or not the corollaries, held to be deducible from the approximation, are invalidated by the qualifications which the closer approximation requires—whether the alterations introduced in volume III make any

---

[1] Since, if the "composition of capital" is equal in all industries, a change in wages will not affect the ratio of comparative costs. But if this assumption does not hold, a change in wages will affect the industries with a high proportion of labour to machinery more than those with a low proportion, and hence will alter the comparative cost-ratios.

[2] A. Gray, *Development of Economic Doctrine*, p. 301.

substantial difference to the conclusions developed from the assumptions made in volume I.

Like Ricardo, Marx attached chief importance to an analysis of the movements of the class revenues. So much, indeed, had Ricardo's interest lain in the distribution of wealth as to evoke the anger of a writer such as Carey, who declared that "the system of Ricardo is a system of discord . . . it creates hostility between classes . . . his book is a manual for demagogues who seek to gain power by the distribution of the soil, by war and by pillage".[1] Similarly, a recent writer has said of Marx that, weaving "a tissue of economic fallacy" on "a prophetic note of righteous indignation", he made it his purpose "to demonstrate that class-hatred is justified".[2] Such tortured verdicts may ring strangely. But what they emphasize is to this extent true: that Marx focussed attention on the class relation, expressed in class incomes, as the relation which defined the major rhythm of capitalist society and was crucial for any forecast of the future. At the same time, it would be wrong to say that his interest was confined to the sphere of distribution, and to treat his analysis as essentially a theory of distribution. Production, Exchange, Distribution, while they might be separate facets, could not be treated as separate categories of economic relations; and, as he insisted in his *Critique of Political Economy*, they had an essential unity.[3]

The law of value was a principle of exchange relations between commodities, including labour-power. It was simultaneously a determinant of the mode in which

[1] Carey, *Past, Present and The Future* (1848), p. 74, *cit.* in *Theorien über den Mehrwert*, Vol. II, p. 4.

[2] E. Hallett Carr, *Karl Marx*, p. 277.

[3] *Critique* (Ed. Kerr); p. 291, etc.

labour was allocated between different industries in the general social division of labour and of the distribution of the product between classes. To say that commodities had certain exchange-values was an alternative way of saying that the labour-force of society was divided between occupations in a certain way, and (included in the latter statement) that the social product was divided between subsistence for labourers and income for capitalists in certain proportions. (For instance, a statement concerning the values of corn and silk is at the same time a statement about the proportions in which labour is divided between the production of corn and of silk. If corn and silk were the only two commodities produced, the former being consumed by workers and the latter by capitalists, the statement that labour was divided between silk-manufacture and corn-culture in a certain ratio would be equivalent to saying that the social income was distributed between workers and capitalists in a corresponding way.) In his first volume Marx adopted the simplifying assumption of a "pure" capitalist economy: an economy of "pure competition," as did the classical economists, and a mode of production based on a simple relationship between capitalists and workers; the latter performing the sum-total of essential productive activities, the former figuring simply *qua* capitalist, as owners of property-rights and hirers of labour-power.[1] This was competent to provide the generalized type-form of

[1] In a letter to Engels in 1858 Marx stated the assumptions made for the purpose of volume I as follows: It is "assumed that the wages of labour are constantly equal to their lowest level. . . . Further landed property is taken as =o. . . . This is the only possible way to avoid having to deal with everything under each particular relation." On these assumptions value is "an abstraction", which figures in "this abstract undeveloped form" as distinct from its "more concrete economic determinations". (*Marx-Engels Correspondence*, p. 106.)

all existent capitalist societies (to which admittedly the concept of "pure" capitalism was only an approximation) as Euclidean lines and points and circles and cubes could represent the essential characteristics of all actual three-dimensional spatial relations. The guiding motive of this volume was to analyse the relation between the revenues of these two classes and to explain the origin and character of capitalist profit.

In the third volume Marx pointed out that, when account was taken of the fact that the ratio between labour and machinery (or, more precisely, between variable and constant capital) was different in different industries, it was seen that commodities exchanged, not according to the principle as enunciated in the first volume, but according to what he termed their Prices of Production (*i.e.* wages *plus* an average or "normal" profit). Nevertheless, he declared that the principle of the first volume was still the determinant of what the value of commodities was in the *aggregate*, and hence the determinant of the rate of profit and in turn of the Prices of Production themselves. In making this statement he was not guilty of the stupidity of asserting merely that a total equals a total, as Böhm-Bawerk charges.[1] Clearly what he had in mind was the relation between the value of finished commodities, treated as an aggregate, and the value of labour-power—the crucial relation on which, in common with Ricardo, he conceived profit to depend. He was stating that it still remained true that the distribution of the total product between workers and capitalists (and hence the volume and rate of profit) depended on the relation between these two quantities; and that (provided one could assume the "composition

[1] *Karl Marx and the Close of his System*, pp. 68-75.

of capital" in the group of industries producing subsistence to be not very different from the average of
industry as a whole) this crucial relation could still be
treated as determined according to the simple manner
of volume I. If this was so, the analysis of surplus-
value and of the influences which determined it was not
invalidated by the qualifications introduced in volume
III. The revenue of the capitalist class, and movements
in it, were still ruled by the same causes, even if this
revenue was differently distributed between various
industries from what had been envisaged in the "first
approximation".[1] To use an analogy, let us suppose
that one were to enunciate the theory of rent on the
assumption that all land was of homogeneous quality,
stating that rent would be equal to the difference between
the cost of production and the selling-price of corn (the
latter being determined by the cost of production at

---

[1] It is perfectly clear that Marx was fully aware of the nature and
significance of these qualifications introduced in vol. III and in what
measure they affected the corollaries to be drawn from the assumptions
of vol. I. Engels, in his Preface to the 1891 Edition of *Wage-Labour
and Capital*, says: " If therefore we say to-day with economists like
Ricardo that the value of a commodity is determined by the labour
necessary to its production, we always imply the reservations and
restrictions made by Marx." Much earlier than this Marx had taken
Proudhon to task for saying that a rise of wages would lead to a general
rise of prices. " If all the industries employ the same number of workers
in relation to the fixed capital or the instruments which they use, a
general rise of wages will produce a general lowering of profits and the
current price of goods will not undergo any alteration." "But the
relation of manual labour to fixed capital is not the same in different
industries, all the industries which employ a relatively greater amount
of fixed capital and less workers will be forced, sooner or later, to lower
the price of their goods ", and conversely in industries employing " a
relatively smaller amount of fixed capital and more workers. . . . Thus
a rise in the wage-level will lead, not as M. Proudhon declares, to a general
increase of prices, but to an actual fall of some prices, namely, to a fall
in the price of those goods which are largely manufactured with the aid
of machinery." *Misère de la Philosophie* (Ed. 1847), pp. 167-8.

the intensive margin). To introduce the fact of hetero-geneity of land (and hence of *different* costs of production on each farm and each acre) as a later approximation would then make no essential difference to the corollaries based on the simpler assumption, provided that the cost of production of corn on the average remained the same and bore the same relation to the price of corn. More-over, the corollaries of the earlier approximation would embody certain essential truths about the nature and determination of rent (those connected with what one may term the scarcity aspect of rent, as distinct from its differential aspect), which no formulation of the theory of rent.could imply without some reference to this relation between the average cost and the average selling-price.[1]

The corollaries which remained unaffected by these later qualifications were various and were among the most important for the main purpose which he had in hand: namely, to discover "the law of motion of capitalist society". Ricardo's doctrine that "if wages rise, profits fall", and with it the conclusion that a rise in wages will encourage capitalists to substitute machinery for labour, remained undisturbed. So also did the influences which caused the rate of profit to alter, including Marx's ex-planation of the "tendency of the rate of profit to fall", which will later be considered, and to which it is clear that Marx attached considerable significance in defining the long-term trend of capitalist society. But there is also a less familiar corollary, which to-day has more

[1] Curiously enough Böhm-Bawerk, in constructing his own theory of capital, makes use as a first approximation of what amounts to the same assumption as that which he condemns in Marx, namely, that "an equally long production-period would prevail simultaneously over all employments". (*Positive Theory of Capital*, pp. 382 and 405.)

central importance than when it was written; namely, that concerning the effect of monopoly. Marx had pointed out that monopoly cannot increase the rate of profit *in general* (as distinct from raising it for some sections and lowering it for others), except in so far as it has the effect of lowering wages. Unless monopoly affected the relation between the value of labour-power and the value of commodities (*i.e.* altered "the rate of exploitation"), it was powerless to raise the rate of profit as a whole. Apart from such an effect of monopoly in depressing real wages below their normal level, the growth of monopoly "would merely transfer a portion of the profit of other producers of commodities to the commodities with a monopoly-price. A local dis--turbance in the distribution of the surplus-value among the various spheres of production would take place indirectly, but they would leave the boundaries of the surplus-value itself unaltered." [1] In a later chapter we shall see that this conclusion has particular relevance to certain problems of Imperialism

The essential difference between Marx and classical Political Economy lay, therefore, in the theory of surplus-value. If its significance was not an ethical one, wherein then lay its practical importance? Clearly, its importance as basis for a critique of capitalism was in many respects parallel to that of the theory of rent for a critique of the landed interest in the hands of the Ricardian School. The theory of rent had formed the ground for maintaining that the very policies which would tend to the lowering of the rate of profit and the consequent retardation of capital accumulation and industrial progress would at the same time augment the

---

[1] *Capital*, Vol. III, p. 1003.

revenue of the landed class and swell the burden of unproductive consumption on the national wealth.[1] The theory of surplus-value implied that, since the two class-incomes of profits and wages were so contrasted in their essential character and in the manner of their determination, the relation between them was necessarily one of antagonism in a sense which made it qualitatively distinct from the relation between ordinary buyers and sellers on a free market. The capitalist class would have an interest in perpetuating and extending the institutions of a class society, which maintained the proletariat in a dependent position and created surplus-value as a category of income, as powerfully as the landed interest had formerly had in maintaining the Corn Laws; while the proletariat would have a corresponding interest in weakening and destroying these basic property-rights. Any change in profit, as the income of the class upon whose decisions and expectations the operation of industry depended, would have an effect on the economic system altogether different from a change in any other price or revenue—a difference which had particular relevance, as we shall see, to Marx's theory of crises. Moreover, it might well be in the interest of capital to retard the development of the productive forces and to promote policies which were detrimental to the production of wealth, provided that these policies tended to extend the opportunities of exploitation and augment its revenue. This possibility

[1] The Ricardian argument was that the fact of diminishing returns on land would, in the course of progress, cause rents to rise and by increasing the cost of subsistence for the workers cause profits to fall. The only way to avert this, and so to maintain the possibilities of capital accumulation and industrial expansion, was to throw open foreign trade and allow the competition of imported raw produce.

was converted into a probability by the very nature of the technical basis on which industrial capitalism had been built. Founded on power-machinery and large-scale technique, the process of progressive capital accumulation tended continually to extend and to enlarge this basis: a process which, by encouraging a progressive concentration and centralization of capital, increasingly prepared the ground for monopoly. The picture which Marx drew of these developments is a familiar one. With the growth of monopoly, class antagonism was rendered more acute, and not less; the income of the propertied class became with increasing openness the fruit of monopoly-policies and of little else. But the same process which established the growing "social character" of the productive process itself forged the instrument which was to break the fetters of "individual appropriation". "The productive forces developing within the framework of bourgeois society create at the same time the material conditions for the liquidation of this antagonism." It created also the homogeneity, the discipline and the organization of the factory proletariat as a class; until this class, finding itself in ever sharper antagonism to a system of property-relations which had grown so patently à fetter on production, should demand and enforce the emancipation of itself and of society by the expropriation of its exploiters. Since a regime of large-scale technique and complex productive relations could not revert to petty property and the small-scale production which this entailed, the negative act of expropriation must necessarily take the positive form of socialization, in the sense of the transference of land and capital into the collective ownership of the workers' State. This revolutionary

77

act of the organized workers which established collective property would in fact be the charter both of equality and of individual rights of which nineteenth-century liberalism had dreamed, but which it had been impotent to attain. It would be the only real charter of individual rights precisely because (in the words of the *Communist Manifesto*) "in bourgeois society capital is independent and has individuality, whereas the living person is dependent and lacks individuality"; because only by the suppression of the power of one class to exploit another through the suppression of private property in land and capital, which endowed this power, could the substance of liberty for the mass of the people appear.

CHAPTER IV

ECONOMIC CRISES

UNDOUBTEDLY for Marx the most important application of his theory was in the analysis of the character of economic crises. At the time serious study of this phenomenon was still in its infancy. There had been a few fertile but unsystematized observations by Sismondi as to the disrupting effects of competition and of production for a wide market; there had been the classic discussion between Malthus and Ricardo as to whether gluts and depression could be due to deficiency of consumption; in Germany Rodbertus had developed his under-consumption theory of crises. But so far as the Ricardian School and its legacy is concerned, it can be said that crises virtually held no place in their system of thought: if depressions occurred they were to be regarded as due to external interferences with the free working of economic forces or with the progress of capital accumulation, rather than as effects of any chronic malady internal to capitalist society. Even the successors to this school were sufficiently obsessed with this presumption to seek for an explanation either in natural causes (such as harvest variations) or within "the veil of money". But for Marx it seemed evident that crises were associated with the essential features of a capitalist economy *per se*. The two fundamental characteristics of this economy were what he termed the "anarchy of production"—the atomistic diffusion of productive decisions among numerous autonomous entrepreneurs—and the fact that it was a system of production not for consciously designed social ends but for profit. It was by virtue of the former that the classical laws of the market held sway and assumed the particular form which they did.[1] But for Marx this was responsible for the existence of tendencies disruptive of equilibrium as well as of the tendencies *towards* equilibrium which the classical economists had exclusively stressed. It was by virtue of the second feature of capitalist society that the pursuit of surplus-value, and circumstances which favoured its augmentation, assumed a dominating significance, so that a change in profit, as the revenue of the ruling class, was calculated to exert an influence on events quite unparalleled by a change in any other class of revenue. Moreover, Marx clearly regarded crises, not as incidental departures from a predetermined equilibrium, not as fickle wanderings from an established path of development to which there would be a submissive return, but rather as themselves a dominant form of movement which forged and shaped the development of capitalist society. To study crises was *ipso facto* to study the dynamics of the system; and this study could only be properly undertaken as part of an examination of the forms of movement of class re-

---

[1] It needs, perhaps, to be made clear that Marx, by terming individual production "anarchy", had no intention of using it as necessarily synonymous with chaos. He intended the term in its literal sense; and emphasized that while it was responsible for disrupting influences, it was also the medium through which the "invisible hand" of the market ruled. In a recent discussion between Mr. G. B. Shaw and Mr. H. G. Wells, the former declared that Mr. Wells could only see in capitalism a *lack* of system, which he itched to systematize; whereas capitalism was in fact very much of a system ruled by laws and compulsions of its own. Marx would, I think, have subscribed to this view. (Cf. *The New Statesman*, Nov. 3, 1934.)

lations (the class struggle) and of the class revenues which were their market-expression.

There was one aspect of the matter which had certainly exercised economic writers for some time, and had evoked a number of rival explanations. This was the alleged tendency of the rate of profit on capital to decline. With changing circumstances the attitude to this question had undergone an alteration. In the eighteenth century this decline was usually welcomed as a healthy sign, apparently because economic writers had viewed the matter primarily from the standpoint of the borrower of capital. But in the nineteenth century, with the flowering of bourgeois Political Economy *par excellence*, admiration was inclined to turn to apprehension. So prominent did discussion on the matter become that Marx went so far as to say that "the difference between the various schools since Adam Smith consists in their different attempts to solve this riddle ".[1]

Hume (who spoke both of the rate of interest on a money loan and of the wider generic term, profit) declared that "so long as there are landed gentry and peasantry in the State the borrowers must be numerous and interest high", by reason of "the idleness of the landlord" and his profligacy. In such a condition industry must stagnate and progress be small. *Per contra*, merchants constituted "one of the most useful races of men, beget(ting) industry by serving as canals to convey it t..-ough every corner of the State. . . . Extensive commerce, by producing large, diminishes both

---

[1] *Capital*, Vol. III, p. 250. In a letter to Engels in 1868 Marx referred to the problem of " the tendency of the rate of profit to fall as society progresses " as " the great *pons asini* of political economy to date ". (*Marx-Engels Correspondence*, p. 244.)

interest and profit, and is always assisted in its diminution of the one by the proportional sinking of the other. I may add that, as low profits arise from the increase of commerce and industry, they serve in their turn to favour its further increase, by rendering the commodities cheaper, encouraging the consumption and heightening of industry."[1] For Adam Smith, like Hume, a high level of profit was a sign of backwardness in capital accumulation; and a decline in the rate of profit was normally to be expected as a result of the progress of accumulation. The reason which he gave for this, in terms of supply and demand, came to be hotly disputed by the Ricardian School, and may have contributed not a little to the vehemence of their scorn for mere "supply and demand" explanations. "The increase of stock," wrote Adam Smith, "which raises wages, tends to lower profit. When the stocks of many rich merchants are turned into the same trade, their mutual competition naturally tends to lower its profit; and when there is a like increase of stock in all the different trades carried on in the same society, the same competition must produce the same effect in all of them."[2]

But by the time that the Industrial Revolution was in full cry the perspective had been shifted and the question came to be differently regarded. Conflict with the landed interest was reaching an acute stage in the controversy over the Corn Laws; and profit, the revenue of the capitalist class and hence both the source of capital accumulation and the incentive to progress and invention, came to receive an emphasis which it had not had before. With Ricardo and his school, Profit occupied the centre

[1] Hume, *Essays* (Ed. 1809), Vol. I, Pt. 2, Ch. 4, pp. 316, 318, 320.
[2] *Wealth of Nations*, Third Ed., p. 89.

of the stage. The question naturally presented itself: How can a fall in this revenue be a condition favourable to progress? If the system, by its own development, generates a tendency for Profit to fall, is there not something strangely contradictory about the system: is it not thereby defined as transitory, generating the seeds of its own retardation and decay? [1] Such questions, implicit rather than explicit, seem to have lain at the root of the strenuous criticism which developed of Adam Smith's interpretation of the matter. This criticism did not deny the tendency, but sought an explanation for it, not in some internal feature of the system or of the process of capital accumulation, but in an external factor. This explanation was found in the famous "law of diminishing returns".

This external limit to progress had been foreshadowed a decade before *The Wealth of Nations* by Sir James Steuart, who had stated that "the augmentation on the value of subsistence must necessarily raise the price of all work . . . so soon as the progress of agriculture demands an additional expence, which the natural return, at the stated price of subsistence, will not defray".[2] In 1815 this was used by West in a criticism of Adam

---

[1] Cf. Marx: "Those economists who, like Ricardo, regard the capitalist mode of production as absolute, feel nevertheless that this mode of production creates its own limits: and therefore they attribute this limit, not to production, but to nature (in their theory of rent)." (*Capital*, III, p. 283.) Elsewhere Marx said: "That the bare possibility of such a thing (progressive fall of the profit rate) should worry Ricardo shows his profound understanding of the conditions of capitalist production. . . . What worries Ricardo is that the rate of profit, the stimulating principle of capitalist production, the fundamental premise and driving force of accumulation, should be endangered by the development of production itself." (*Ibid.*, p. 304.)

[2] *An Inquiry into the Principles of Political Economy* (1767), p. 226. Turgot, the Physiocrat, had also, about the same year, drawn attention to this fact. Cf. Cannan, *Theories of Production and Distribution*, pp. 147-8.

Smith's theory, both to explain the fact of the more limited productive powers of agriculture as compared to industry (which Adam Smith had attributed to the smaller potentialities of the division of labour in agriculture) and the tendency of profit to fall. Adam Smith's theory that it was the competition of capital which reduced the rate of profit, not only in some trades but in all, he denounced as a fallacy. Nor did he think it possible "wholly to account for the progressive diminution of the profits of stock by any increase of the wages of labour". The fall was attributable, not primarily to the rise of wages with progress, but to the decreased productivity of capital in agriculture. "The principle is simply that in the progress of the improvement of cultivation the raising of rude produce becomes progressively more expensive; or in other words the ratio of the net produce of land to its gross produce is continually diminishing. . . . The proposition is that every additional quantity of capital laid out produces a less proportionate return, and consequently the larger the capital expended, the less the ratio of the profit to that capital." [1]

Ricardo was even more explicit, and developed the argument in a manner which made it the fulcrum of his critique of the landed interest. As we have seen, among the basic principles of his system was the contention that value depended neither on demand nor on the abundance of commodities (which he designated as "wealth" or "riches" as contrasted with "value") but on the "difficulty or facility of production"; from which it followed that profit, or the value of the "net produce", depended, neither on the size of the "gross produce"

[1] *Essay on the Application of Capital to Land*, by a Fellow of University College (1815), pp. 2, 3, 19-20.

nor on the productivity of capital, but on the proportion of the social labour which was required to procure the labourers' subsistence—that is, on the difference between wages and the value of the product.[1] Hence the dictum "when wages rise, profits fall",[2] which at first sight looks like a simple truism, is considerably more than a truism in its fuller implication that profit is uniquely determined by these two quantities (the cost of producing subsistence and the cost of producing products in general). Moreover, since capital was conceived as being essentially "advances of wages" to labourers, the dictum was further interpreted to mean that the *rate* of profit (that is, the amount of profit proportioned to the original outlay) must depend uniquely on the same two quantities. Any factor which influenced the rate of profit could do so only in so far as it altered this ratio of wages to the *value* of the gross produce. "No accumulation of capital will permanently lower profits unless there be some permanent cause for the rise of wages."[3]

Adopting, as Ricardo did, Malthus' law of population; there appeared to him to be no sufficient cause for a rise in the price of labour-power owing to a deficient labour-supply—at least, not as a long-run factor. The labouring population was only too avid to catch up with any expanded opportunities for employment which an increase of capital might afford. Hence there seemed to him no reason, within the capital-labour relation, why additional funds of capital, invested in additional supplies of pro-

---

[1] It was the onus of Ricardo's criticism of Say that he confused "riches" and "value", and a minor criticism of Smith that he "constantly magnifies the advantages which a country derives from a large gross, rather than a large net income". (*Principles*, Chapters xviii and xxiv.)

[2] Cf. above, p. 46.

[3] *Principles*, Chapter xix, p. 398.

ductive labour and in ever-widening cycles of production, should not continue to extract at least the same rate of profit as before. The only sufficient cause, therefore, of a *fall* in the rate of profit as capital accumulation proceeded could be the operation of some factor which tended to raise the price of labour-power by raising the value of the workers' subsistence; and such a factor he saw in the law of diminishing returns on land. In his *Principles* he wrote: "If the necessaries of the workman could be constantly increased with the same facility, there could be no permanent alteration in the rate of profit or wages, to whatever amount capital might be accumulated. . . . Adam Smith does not appear to see that at the same time that capital is increased the work to be affected by capital is increased in the same proportion. . . . Whether increased productions, and the consequent demand which they occasion, shall or shall not lower profits, depends solely on the rise of wages; and the rise of wages, excepting for a limited period, on the facility of producing the food and necessaries of the labourer. I say excepting for a limited period, because no point is better established than that the supply of labourers will always ultimately be in proportion to the means of supporting them." [1] In a letter to Malthus he wrote: "I contend that there are no causes which will for any length of time make capital less in demand, however abundant it may become, but a comparatively high price of food and labour—that profits do not *necessarily* fall with the increase of the quantity of capital, because the demand for capital is infinite, and is governed by the same law as population itself. They are both checked

---

[1] *Principles*, Second Ed., pp. 398-404. Cf. also pp. 133-4 on "the natural tendency of the rate of profits to fall".

by the rise in the price of food and the consequent rise in the value of labour. If there were no such rise, what could prevent population and capital from increasing without limit?"[1] From this he drew the conclusion on which rested the *onus* of his case against the landed interest: "I think it may be most satisfactorily proved, that in every society advancing in wealth and population . . . general profits must fall, unless there are improvements in agriculture, or corn can be imported at a cheaper price."[2] Since both these conditions are contrary to the landlords' interest, "it follows that the interest of the landlord is always opposed to the interest of every other class of the community. His situation is never so prosperous as when food is scarce and dear: whereas all other persons are greatly benefited by procuring food cheap."[3]

It was these strictures on the landed interest which roused the criticism of his friend Malthus, and it was this topic of the tendency for the rate of profit to fall which formed the central ground of their disagreements.[4] The contention of Malthus was that profit might fall not from a rise in wages but from a fall in the price of commodities due to a deficient demand; and that this was likely to occur if capital accumulation proceeded too rapidly, particularly if this accumulation occurred at the

[1] *Letters of Ricardo to Malthus, 1810–23*, Ed. Bonar, p. 101. When Malthus said that rapid capital accumulation must lead to over-production, Ricardo commented that in the specific circumstances described by Malthus (lowered profit and insufficient demand), "the specific want would be for population". (*Notes on Malthus*, p. 169.)

[2] *Essay on the Influence of a Low Price of Corn on the Profits of Stock* (1815), p. 22. This is what Marx described as an increase of "relative surplus-value" (a fall in the value of labour-power relatively to the value of the product).

[3] *Ibid.*, p. 20.

[4] Cf. Malthus, *Principles*, pp. 293-336, and *Letters of Ricardo to Malthus, 1810–23*, Ed. Bonar, pp. 186-91.

expense of a diminished consumption. In contrast to Say's Law of Markets, he declared it possible for production to outrun consumption, in the sense of causing a fall in price and in profit, and a consequent "glut" and depression in trade, if productive equipment was augmented at the expense of consumption. "Parsimony, or the conversion of revenue into capital, may take place without any diminution of consumption if the revenue increases first. . . . (But) no nation can possibly grow rich by the accumulation of capital, arising from a permanent diminution of consumption; because such accumulation being greatly beyond what is wanted, in order to supply the effective demand for produce, a part of it would very soon lose both its use and its value, and cease to possess the character of wealth".[1] In contrast to Say and Ricardo, he held it to be a natural tendency, with expanding accumulation, for all commodities to fall in value relatively to labour; although it is not clear how he reconciled this view with his own doctrine that population continually tended to expand up to the limits of subsistence. "It has been thought by some very able writers," he wrote, "that although there may easily be a glut of particular commodities, there cannot possibly be a glut of commodities in general. . . . This doctrine, however, . . . appears to me . . . to be utterly unfounded. . . It is by no means true that commodities are always exchanged for commodities. The great mass of commodities is exchanged directly for labour, either productive or unproductive; and it is quite obvious that this mass of commodities, compared with the labour with which it is to be exchanged, may fall in value from a glut just as any one commodity falls in value from an

[1] *Principles*, pp. 369-70.

excess of supply, compared either with labour or with money".[1]

This combined with the writings of Sismondi, who had advanced a closely similar criticism,[2] to become the fount-head of the various doctrines of under-consumption which again occupy the stage as a central controversy to-day. With the triumph of the Ricardian tradition in Victorian England this doctrine of Malthus for long fell into obscurity, save as illustration of the cardinal fallacy that luxury created employment and that it was better to spend than to save. In Germany, some thirty years later, it was advocated in a new form by Rodbertus, and through him and his influence on Lassalle and Dühring and the rising school of German Socialism it came to be implanted fairly firmly in socialist thought. By an ironic turn of the wheel a doctrine fashioned originally as an apology for landlords and bondholders as "unproductive consumers" came to be a weapon in the hands of the proletariat in criticism of a system which imposed poverty and restricted consumption on the mass of the producers.

[1] *Principles*, pp. 353-4. The disagreements between Malthus and Ricardo on the theory of value were closely related to this issue. Malthus wished to define value in terms of "the amount of labour which a commodity can command", whereas Ricardo insisted on his own definition that value consisted in the amount of labour required to produce the commodity in question. In terms of Malthus' definition, any fall in profit would show itself as a fall in commodity-values. But according to Ricardo's definition, the value of commodities would only fall if improvements caused them to be produced with less labour than previously; and such a fall would only result in a lower rate of profit if labour-power alone among commodities failed to fall in value. (Cf. *Letters to Malthus*, p. 233.)

[2] H. Grossman in his *Simonde de Sismondi et ses Théories Économiques* claims that Sismondi did not consider under-consumption as a *cause* of crises, but as the result (p. 55). But it is difficult to see that this interpretation is borne out by such passages as *Nouveaux Principes*, Vol. I, pp. 120, 329; and *Études*, Vol. I, p. 60 *et seq.*, Vol. II, p. 233. Cf. also the comments of M. Tuan, *Sismondi as an Economist*, p. 68 *et seq.*

In recent years it has had a revival, even to-day what one may call a vogue. Much of this has been due to the advocacy of Mr. J. A. Hobson over a number of years, who expounded the doctrine in a novel manner, but along lines which in essentials were traditional. More recently still it seems to have been espoused by Mr. G. D. H. Cole,[1] while Mr. J. M. Keynes has pronounced the "Principle of Effective Demand" of Malthus to be a neglected and fundamental contribution to economic understanding.[2] While repudiated (at least, in its Rodbertian form) both by Marx and by Engels,[3] it has had considerable popularity in Marxist circles, having been given a special "Marxist" variant by Rosa Luxemburg, who criticized Marx for neglecting this aspect unduly.[4]

[1] Cf. *Principles of Economic Planning*, pp. 50-1.
[2] Cf. *Econ. Journal*, June 1935.
[3] Cf. Engels, *Anti-Dühring*, pp. 319-21. Marx wrote as follows: "It is purely a tautology to say that crises are caused by the scarcity of solvent customers or of paying consumption. . . . If any commodities are unsaleable it means that no solvent purchasers have been found for them, in other words, consumers (whether commodities are bought in the last instance for productive or individual consumption). But if one were to attempt to clothe this tautology with a semblance of a profounder justification by saying that the working class receive too small a portion of their own product, and the evil would be remedied by giving them a larger share of it, or raising their wages, we should reply that crises are precisely always preceded by a period in which wages rise generally and the working class actually get a larger share of the annual product intended for consumption." A footnote to this passage adds: " Advocates of the theory of crises of Rodbertus are requested to make a note of this." *Capital*, Vol. II, pp. 475-6.
[4] *Die Akkumulation des Kapitals* (Ed. 1921), esp. p. 79 *et seq.* and p. 299 *et seq.* Luxemburg herself criticized some of the traditional formulations of the under-consumption theory; but claimed that Marx had given too little emphasis to what she termed the " realization of surplus-value " through sale in a market and hence to the consuming-power of society. This led her to her famous theory of the " third party "—that capitalism always required either an intermediate " middle " class or else colonies, in order to dispose of its surplus of commodities. Cf. J. A. Salz, *Das Wesen des Imperialismus*, pp. 40-4.

To plain common sense untouched by learned sophistries, there has seldom been much doubt as to whether the Ricardian doctrine or that of under-consumption was nearer to the truth. The end of production, presumably, was consumption. The producer's realization of profit depended on the existence of a market for sale. If disproportionate development between industries was possible—an expansion of productive capacity in certain directions in excess of demand—it seemed reasonable enough to assert, as Malthus had done, the possibility of a general disproportion between *all* consumable commodities in relation to "effective demand". The doctrine (to which we have referred)[1] that production and exchange, viewed as a *whole*, was properly to be treated as a continuous barter-process of goods against goods, and that consequently total demand would increase *pari passu* with total supply because they were identical, seemed an abstract evasion of the real problem. Total income might be sufficient to cover the total cost of all consumption goods produced if the whole of that income was in fact spent on consumption goods. But if part of that income was not spent, but saved, this saved portion of income went to purchase, not consumption goods, but producer's goods which would further augment the flow of consumption goods in the future. If saving continued, where was the market to be for this additional flow of final products, unless prices were to decline to a point where profit fell or even disappeared? Were not goods made ultimately to be consumed, however "long" and "roundabout" the process of production; and were not profit on capital and the wages of labour admittedly "derived" from the value of, and the final demand of

[1] See above, pp. 40-3.

consumers for, consumption goods? Only in an economist's fancy did it seem possible for a world to exist where (in J. B. Clark's unhappy phrase) [1] "they would build mills that should make more mills for ever" and have no glut.

To this the traditional view had two replies. The first was made by Ricardo in reply to Malthus. In his *Notes on Malthus*, in comment on the passages we have quoted, he wrote: "I deny that the wants of the consumers generally are diminished by parsimony—they are transferred with the power to consume to another set of consumers. . . . By increase of capital from revenue is meant an increase of consumption by productive labourers instead of by unproductive." [2] In a famous passage Adam Smith had said that "what is annually saved is as regularly consumed as what is annually spent, and nearly in the same time too; but it is consumed by a different set of people ". [3] This answer clearly depended for its force on the simplified conception of capital as consisting of "advances to labourers". If a capitalist or a landowner "saved" he could thus be conceived as handing over part of his income as wages to extend the process of production: the consumption which he had forgone the additional workers undertaking in his stead. Hence saving involved no absolute fall in consumers' demand. It was not so immediately clear that this result followed, if part of the investment took the form, not of "circulating capital" but of "fixed capital"— was embodied, not directly in the hiring of labourers,

[1] In his preface to the English translation of Rodbertus' *Over-production and Crises*.

[2] *Notes on Malthus*, pp. 164 and 174. Cf. also James Mill, *Commerce Defended*, p. 78.

[3] *Wealth of Nations* (Ed. 1826), p. 319.

but in the purchase and installation of machines. But on closer analysis it becomes clear that in this respect there is no fundamental difference between the two cases: that the purchase of a machine is as much a transfer of spending-power to others—in this case to labourers engaged in making the machine and to capitalists who employ them—as is an investment of capital which takes the form of hiring labour direct (although the circumstances would not be indifferent, as we shall see, to the effect of the investment on the demand for labour and on profit).

The second reply was to the other half of the under-consumptionists' riddle: what was to happen to the additional goods produced by the extra machines or the extra labourers? The answer here was that either the income of society was enlarged by the enlargement of the productive mechanism to embrace more workers than before (and hence to enlarge the revenue distributed in the form of both wages and profits); or else, if investment took the form of transfer of labourers to make machines, the resulting increase in the output of goods, being fruit of increased productivity of labour, was accompanied by lowered costs of production, so that while goods were more plentiful they could also be sold more cheaply without loss.[1]

What one may perhaps call the crude form of the under-consumption theory (that investment *per se* causes

---

[1] Cf. E. F. M. Durbin, *Purchasing Power and Trade Depression*, pp. 75-6, where this argument is emphasized. This argument provides an answer, for instance, to the contention of Malthus that " parsimony " so increases the output of commodities that these cannot find purchasers " without such a fall in price as would probably sink their value below their cost of production ". (*Principles*, p. 353.) Mr. Durbin points out that their cost of production is *also* reduced as a result of capital investment. Whether it is reduced *proportionately* is another matter.

a glut) as represented in the writings of Sismondi and Rodbertus, seems to have been regarded by Marx as too superficial to afford an adequate answer to the classical Law of Markets. In treating demand as though this were an isolated factor, they had neglected the relationship in which this stood to production: neglected the fact that society *qua* consumer, with a given aggregate of purchasing-power, was simply one facet of society *qua* producer. Of Sismondi Marx said that, while "he estimates very fully the contradictions of bourgeois production, he does not understand them and hence cannot comprehend the process of their solution": in particular he ignores the fact that "conditions of distribution are conditions of production viewed *sub alia specie*".[1] And he indicated the need for a much more rigorous analysis of the process of capital accumulation than had been attempted hitherto. Unfortunately his own analysis has been left to us in an unfinished state. But the torso that he left was sufficiently epoch-making, and has so much anticipated, indeed surpassed, the work of later economists on the same subject as to make the neglect that it has suffered at the hands of academic economists truly amazing.

The starting-point of Marx's examination of the problem can be said to have lain in two crucial, and neglected, notions: the one, an emendation, the other an extension of Ricardian doctrine. The first was his separation of capital into "constant" and "variable" capital; the second his concept of an "increase of relative surplus-value". The former was an important qualification of the notion of capital as simply "advances to labourers". In using this notion earlier economists had

---

[1] *Theorien über der Mehrwert*, III, p. 55.

been far from clear. True, they had a tolerably clear notion of the difference between fixed and circulating capital (corresponding, as Marx points out, to the Physiocratic *avances primitives* and *avances annuelles*), and of the fact that in different branches of production these two elements were differently combined; and Ricardo had appreciated the importance of durability in the case of fixed capital, having remarked that "in proportion as fixed capital is less durable, it approaches to the nature of circulating capital", since "it will be consumed in a shorter time". But when they passed from the single industry to the economy as a whole, they seem generally to have returned to the notion that all capital was ultimately reducible to "advances of wages" to labourers. The meaning of this view does not seem to have been clearly defined. Presumably they cannot have intended to mean by it that all capital was reducible to this form in a given cycle of production. Yet it led Ricardo apparently to identify the rate of profit (the ratio of profit to total capital) with the ratio of profit to wages, and J. S. Mill to state that the rate of profit depended *uniquely* on the proportion of the produce going to labour (McCulloch, however, had seen, not very clearly, as had also Longford more clearly, that it depended on the ratio of profit to *total* capital). Marx pointed out that the distinction between fixed and circulating capital properly turned, not on the time the capital took to circulate, but on the difference between the concrete rôle in production played by *instruments* of labour and *objects* of labour, the former circulating "piecemeal" in the course of wear and tear of machines, and the latter imparting themselves as a whole to the product in a single act. ("Cattle as beasts of toil are

95

fixed capital; if they are fattened, they are raw material which finally enters into circulation as commodities, in other words they are circulating, not fixed capital".[1]) But this distinction he considered to be less fundamental than that between "stored-up" or "dead" labour of both types and active "living" labour, since the latter distinction for the economy as a whole corresponded to that between productive powers inherited from the past and the current production of *net* or added value. Capital invested in equipment or in stocks of raw material Marx termed *constant capital*, and capital devoted to the purchase of labour-power as a current wages-fund he termed *variable capital*. This led him to point out that the rate of profit (ratio of profit in a given period to *total* capital) was not dependent solely on what by contradistinction he termed the "rate of surplus value" (the ratio of profit to wages, or of surplus-value to variable capital).[2] The former could change even though the latter remained constant, if a change occurred in the proportion in which the existing stock of capital

[1] *Capital*, II, p. 183. Cf. also: "The value thus fixed decreases constantly until the instrument of labour is worn out, its value having been distributed during a shorter or longer period over a mass of products which emanated from a series of currently repeated labour processes" (*Capital*, II, p. 179.) In the course of his discussion of fixed capital Marx spends some time in considering the maintenance problem, citing Lardner on railways to show that "the boundary between regular repairs and replacement, between expenses of repairing and expenses of renewal, are more or less shifting". (*Ibid.*, p. 203.)

[2] Marx was careful to show that it was not the ratio of profit to wages in each turnover, but the "annual rate of surplus-value" that was relevant to the determination of the annual rate of profit; the annual rate of surplus being related to the simple rate by the period of turnover of the variable capital. The period of turnover of the variable capital, therefore, became a separate factor in the determination of the rate of profit. (*Ibid.*, pp. 336–66; also cf. the chapter on "the effect of turnover on the rate of profit", *Capital*, III, 85–92.)

was divided between these two forms (what he termed the "organic composition of capital"). The influence of technical progress was to alter this proportion, generally (though not invariably) in the direction of raising the ratio of constant to variable capital. Hence the tendency of industrial progress was to lower the rate of profit, even though there was no decrease in the rate of surplus-value. This was his reply to Ricardo's contention that only the operation of diminishing returns on land was adequate to account for a tendency of the rate of profit to fall.

But Marx was quick to indicate that there were "counteracting tendencies", the influence of which was in a contrary direction. Chief of these was an "increase of relative surplus-value" to which we have referred. This occurred when an increase in the productivity of labour, being extended to the production of subsistence, resulted in a fall in the value of labour-power as well as in the value of commodities in general. The result was an increase in the rate of surplus-value, by reason of the fact that a smaller proportion of the social labour-force was required to be employed in producing the workers' subsistence, so that the "net produce" increased alike in value and in amount; or, as Marx put it more directly, by reason of the fact that a smaller portion of the labourer's working-day required to be employed in replacing the value of his own labour-power and a larger portion of the working-day remained to produce surplus-value for the capitalist. This possibility had been suggested by Ricardo, but had not been pursued by him. His obsession with the threat of diminishing returns on land had apparently caused him to belittle its significance, save as a consequence of the opening

POLITICAL ECONOMY AND CAPITALISM

up of foreign markets and the importation of cheaper corn. But this heightening of labour-productivity was itself one of the effects of technical progress; and the possibility of its extension to agriculture as well as to industry was a further reason for the denial by Marx of diminishing returns as a significant factor in influencing the rate of profit and the occurrence of economic crises. To this influence, and its relation to the "tendency of the rate of profit to fall", we shall presently return.

The notion of the "organic composition of capital", expressing as it did a relation between "stored-up" or past labour and "living" or currently applied labour, can be seen as the precursor of later Austrian notions of "period of production" or "capital intensity".[1] Yet Marx has often been criticized for having no conception of the rôle of time in production and for confusing a rate of flow with a stock of capital as though Part 2 of Volume 2 of Capital, which deals with these matters, had never been written. Marx made it clear that "the period of turnover of the invested capital" depended both on the length of time occupied by the "working process"—the time during which labour is being directly applied to working up a product—and also on the time during which "goods in process" are for technical reasons maturing. As examples he cites "winter grain [which] needs about nine months to mature", and timber-raising where "the seed may require one hundred years to be

---

[1] The sequence of dates is interesting, and has not, I think, been pointed out by historians of economic thought. Vol. 2 of *Das Kapital* appeared in 1885 and Böhm-Bawerk's *Positive Theorie* in 1889. The chief difference was that Marx did not deal with a connection between different periods of turnover and the productivity of labour, which was Böhm-Bawerk's main concern and one of his attempted "justification" of surplus-value. For Marx only the *value* of the constant and the turnover of the *variable* capital affected the rate of profit directly.

transformed into a finished product, and during all this time requires very insignificant contributions of labour". Moreover, he did not confine the concept to Wicksellian "working capital", but explicitly applied it to instruments of labour as well, indicating that, since fixed capital imparted its value to the product "piecemeal", it generally had a longer period of turnover than working capital; but not invariably so as the timber-example showed.[1] Where he differed from later economists was that he held consistently to the emphasis of Volume I that, despite the influence of capital-turnover on the *rate* of profit, *aggregate* surplus-value remained uniquely determined by the relation between the value of labour-power and the value of the product—the crucial exploitation-relation that was the foundation of his structure.

But these were no more than prolegomena to Part 3 of Volume 2 which he devoted to an analysis of the effect of capital accumulation on the division of the productive forces between the industries producing means of production and the industries producing consumption goods. The demand for the former depended on the current rate of renewal of constant capital and on the rate of addition to the existing stock of constant capital (or "stored-up labour"); so that any sudden change either in the rate of capital accumulation or in the proportions between constant and variable capital was likely to result in a disproportion between these two branches. To the process of exchange between these two departments he attributed crucial importance; and

[1] Cf.: "It follows . . . that according to the different length of the periods of turnover, money-capital of considerably different quantity must be advanced, in order to set in motion the same quantity of productive circulating capital and the same quantity of labour-power **with the** same intensity of exploitation". (*Ibid.*, 366.)

his analysis of it represents another notable contribution to economic thought. Indeed, what Quesnay's *Tableau Économique* had been to the agricultural and handicraft economy of the eighteenth century, Marx's departmental *schema* can be said to have been to the more complex economic processes introduced by the Industrial Revolution. Both were an attempt at a descriptive map of real processes as a basis for more developed analysis and generalization; and Marx clearly derived considerable inspiration from the *Tableau Économique* for the treatment of his own *schema*. It is interesting in this connection to note that already in a letter to Engels in 1863 he presented the essentials of these *schema* as his own *Tableau Économique*, applying them first to what he termed "simple reproduction", or static conditions of capital replacement without new capital accumulation, in order to disclose what balance was necessary between both departments and the various revenues in each, if the exchanges between them were to be effected without interruption.[1] In his years of failing health in the late 'seventies Marx developed the theme; but on his death left little more than notes and quotations: "a preliminary presentation of the subject", as Engels called it, "fragmentary" and "incomplete in various places". It was this unfinished manuscript that was posthumously pieced together by Engels to form the

[1] Cf. *Marx-Engels Correspondence*, p. 153 *et seq.* The condition laid down for equilibrium in the case of "simple reproduction" was that the constant capital used in a given period in Department 2 (producing consumption goods) should equal in value the variable capital plus the surplus-value during that same period in Department 1. This was a simple corollary of the principle that the total product of Department 1, expressed in value, must equal the constant capital used up or consumed in *both* Departments. The equilibrium conditions for "expanded reproduction" were similar but more complex. (Cf. *Capital*, II, p. 459 *et seq.*)

third section of *Capital*, volume II, in 1885. The manuscripts which were later published in volume III, and which deal with the tendency of the rate of profit to fall, were written earlier, in the middle 'sixties, but were again no more than "a first draft" and "very incomplete".

The main purpose of these *schema* was two-fold. First, they showed clearly the difference between the gross and the net product, between the total of commodity-transactions and the revenue or income of individuals. Following, as they did, upon a discussion of Adam Smith's proposition that "the exchangeable value . . . of all the commodities which compose the annual produce of the labour of every country must resolve itself into . . . three parts and be parcelled out among different inhabitants of the country, either as the wages of their labour, the profits of their stock or the rent of their land", Marx designed them, in part, to show how it could both be true that the value of each commodity was equal to the value of labour-power required for its production *plus* surplus-value *plus* the value of the constant capital used up, and that the net value produced by the economic system was equal simply to wages *plus* surplus-value.[1] Secondly, they postulated the relationships which would need to hold between the capital-goods industries and consumption-goods industries, on the one hand, and, on the other hand, the replacement-demand of industries for equipment and raw materials and the division of income of workers and capitalists between consumption and invest-

---

[1] *Ibid.*, 426 *et seq.* Mr. Fan Hung in *The Review of Economic Studies*, October 1939, has pointed out the parallel between Marx's analysis and Mr. Keynes' distinction between user-cost and factor-cost.

ment.[1] This implicitly afforded an answer to the crude under-consumption theory: it showed that capital accumulation could proceed without causing any problems within the sphere of exchange, provided that these relationships were observed.

Marx was quick to add, however, that under individualist production for the market these necessary relationships could only be preserved by an "accident"; and he made it clear that in a moving situation the process of exchange would be subject continually to danger of disruption owing to the absence of any sufficient mechanism in a capitalist economy whereby the requisite proportions could be maintained. Any change of a major order in the economic system, in particular a change in technique or the rate of accumulation, would tend as a normal, and not merely an accidental result, to a rupture of equilibrium. That this is so follows from the fact that production, which is interdependent in its various branches, is controlled atomistically by a number of unrelated and autonomous decisions, each taken in blindness to the related decisions that are simultaneously being made elsewhere.[2] These decisions the market is impotent to co-ordinate *before* the event, and can only do so *after* the event—can only so do precisely through the pressure of the price-changes which the initial rupture of equilibrium creates. A crisis appears as catharsis as well as retribution: as the sole mechanism by which, in this economy, equi-

---

[1] Dr. Kalečki has pointed out that Marx was here saying virtually the same thing as certain recent propositions about the identity of "saving" and "investment" *ex post*. (*Essays in the Theory of Econ. Fluctuations*, 45.)

[2] This matter, and its relation to the generation of economic fluctuations is more fully developed later. (Chapter VI and p. 274 *seq*.)

librium can be enforced, once it has been extensively broken.

It is evident that there are two forms which this break in the proportions between these two broad departments of industry may take in the course of a period of rapid capital-accumulation; and there is reason to think that Marx had both these forms in mind when he referred to "disproportion" in the development of the two branches. An increase in accumulation, if it is a discontinuous increase, will involve a period of transition during which demand for consumption goods (as a proportion of current purchasing-power) declines and labour and other resources are transferred to the manufacture of means of production. *A fortiori*, this will be so if the accumulation is accompanied by any sharp change in the organic composition of capital. As an expression of this fact, profits will tend to fall in the consumption-goods industries, and unemployment to result. At first sight it might seem that this is no reason to provoke a general crisis, and that the decreased profits and employment of one department will be offset by increased profits and employment in the other department —in the manufacture of means of production. Why, it may be asked, should a change of this kind have more than transitory and partial effects, any more than changes in consumers' demand which continually occur and shift the "weight" of different industries inside the group of consumption trades: changes involving, say, a transfer from cotton to artificial silk, from bricks to cement, from gas to electricity? But a fall in activity which is general to the consumption trades has special consequences, for this reason: that the trades which manufacture instruments of production are dependent on the trades which manufacture finished consumption goods and the demand for the former is, in a special sense, "derived" from the latter. This constitutes an important qualification of the dictum that "demand for commodities is not demand for labour"; and implies that, as Mr. Durbin has recently emphasized,[1] a change in the demand for consumption goods compared to means of production has more fundamental significance than any shift of demand between consumption goods themselves. When a fall in profit occurs in the consumption trades this is likely to mean a fall in the demand for instruments of production in a manner capable of resulting in a general crisis. This is the aspect of truth on which the underconsumption theory has seized. Here is an important form of disproportionate development which arises from the fact that in any concrete situation, at any given point of time, capital is crystallized in more or less durable forms, and adapted to particular uses and only to those uses. J. B. Clark's picture of building "mills to build more mills for ever" can never be actualized, since in the real world mills are always specialized to a particular current stream of demand connected with consumption in the near future, and not a stream of demand stretching to an infinite future. Hence when consumption changes, the effect is transmitted back along the stream of demand to all the intermediate and constructional processes connected with it and adapted to it.[2]

---

[1] *Op. cit.*, p. 83.

[2] It is true that what has been said here applies only to profit on existing capital. It is not to say that new capital, invested in the new and cheapened means of production (promoted by the extension of the industries producing means of production), might not earn the previous rate of profit (unless there were forces at work tending to lower the *general* rate of profit). But at the moment when the fall in demand for

But while this form of disproportion may be the originating factor in a general crisis, it need not necessarily be so. A break of equilibrium may come from an opposite quarter, and show itself first in a decline of profit and of activity in the industries which manufacture means of production. Indeed, there is a certain amount of evidence that this is the most frequent form in which a crisis occurs. Professor J. M. Clark, in reviewing the available American data, points out that "observations so far as they go tend to the conclusion that general consumers' demand does not lead, but follows, the movements in production of consumers' goods—that it moves up or down mainly because changes in the rate of production have increased or decreased the current purchasing-power of the workers. . . . It is at the stage further removed from the consumer that the initiatory movement takes place—that is, at the stage of production rather than retail selling." [1] "Pay-rolls" (*i.e.* wage-payments) seem to increase more rapidly in the later stages of a boom than in the earlier, while industrial production, and in particular the output of constructional goods, shows a slackening rate of increase as expansion proceeds. [2]

But to return to Marx's *schema* of "expanded reproduction": it is instructive to notice the assumptions that were implicit in his handling of them; since an examination of these assumptions leads at once to two other, and in some ways more fundamental, elements in Marx's theory of economic crises. Firstly, he seems to have

consumption goods takes place, these new methods of production *are not yet available*; and the depression in the consumption-goods industry will intervene to check demand and expansion in the capital-goods industry, and so to inhibit investment in these new methods of production.

[1] *Strategic Factors in Business Cycles*, pp. 48 and 53.
[2] *Ibid.*, pp. 50-3.

been assuming that the new investment was resulting in no change in the organic composition of capital—that investment was being devoted exclusively to what Mr. Hawtrey has recently termed a "widening", as distinct from a "deepening" of the capital structure.[1] It was the case where this condition did not hold that occupied him in the opening part of volume III. Secondly, he begins by assuming that "expanded reproduction" (or net investment) is proceeding at a *constant* rate. As soon as this assumption is dropped, and an example is chosen either of reproduction at an *increasing* rate, or of saving occurring on a general scale without any concurrent act of investment,[2] there arises the so-called problem of "realization" of surplus-value, which was Rosa Luxemburg's main theme. Marx put the matter in this form. If capitalists decide to accumulate (or to save) part of their surplus-value that they previously spent on the purchase of consumption goods, then the sellers of consumption goods will be left with unsold stocks on their hands. Whence, therefore, do these sellers of consumption goods acquire the money to invest? If by sale of these goods money cannot "be withdrawn from circulation to form a hoard, or virtual new money-capital", the demand for new capital-goods cannot occur, and the accumulation-process will be

[1] I am indebted to Dr. M. Kalecki for drawing my attention to this. This assumption is not *necessarily* implied by Marx's tables, since the ratio of constant to variable capital in these examples refers to constant capital *used up*, and not to the total *stock* of it. But when he gives numerical examples of how the newly invested capital is distributed between capital of these two types, it is clear that he is making this assumption.

[2] What he termed "one-sided sale without a compensating purchase" implying "withdrawal of money from circulation and a corresponding formation of a hoard". (*Capital*, II, 581 ; also 589.)

interrupted. "The impulse to save will have proved abortive", in the language of some modern economists. This is "a new problem, whose very existence must appear strange to the current idea that commodities of one kind are [always?] exchanged for commodities of another kind".[1] Marx reserved the answer to this riddle until the concluding paragraph of volume II: it was that the consumption-goods industries could find a market for their goods with the producers of gold in a one-sided transaction of goods against money. "Expanded reproduction" at an increasing rate could occur smoothly to the extent, but only to the extent, that new money was introduced into the economic system. While this answer bore a superficial resemblance to that of Rosa Luxemburg —that accumulation required some outside market to enable the surplus-value that capitalists wished to accumulate to be "realized" by an act of sale—it differed from her view in two crucial respects. The difficulty only applied, as we have said, to the case where the rate of saving increased; and Marx spoke of a sale of goods against *gold* as a solution of the problem, whereas she had spoken of an export of goods against goods, which would not necessarily have provided a solution to the problem of an unsaleable surplus of consumption goods.[2]

It was, however, a very abstract assumption that

---

[1] *Ibid.*, 593. Cf. also Sartre, *Esquisse d'une Theorie Marxiste des Crises.*

[2] It is to be noted that an export of capital (with a consequent export surplus of goods) would afford a solution of the same kind to that to which Marx was referring—a one-way act of exchange, in this case against securities instead of gold. Marx did not explicitly state the conditions for expanded reproduction at a constant rate to occur smoothly. But it seems clear from his tables that these were that the *spent* part of V + S in Department 1 should equal C + the *saved* part of S in Department 2.

accumulation could proceed for long without any change in the "organic composition of capital". For one thing, it implied an inexhaustible reserve army of labour, if variable capital was to grow at the same rate as total investment was proceeding; and in normal circumstances before this "widening" of capital had proceeded very far, the depletion of the labour-reserve would create a tendency for a sharp upward movement of wages, which would itself tend to precipitate a fall in the rate of profit.[1] Hence the normal accompaniment of capital accumulation was a rise in the organic composition of capital; and this change, unless it were offset by an increase in the "annual rate of surplus value", would precipitate a fall in the rate of profit. It seems clear that Marx regarded this falling profit-rate tendency as an important underlying cause of periodic crises, as well as a factor shaping the long-term trend: as a fundamental reason why a process of accumulation and expansion would be self-defeating in its effects, and hence would inevitably suffer a relapse.

But what of the counter-tendencies to which Marx himself alluded? It has been said that Marx's analysis provided no logical basis for postulating which of the two tendencies would prevail: that he did no more than

---

[1] Some modern writers hold the view that a rise of money wages as the labour reserve is depleted will cause a breakdown of the situation, not in this way, but by plunging the system into a state of violent instability and precipitating a "hyper-inflation". (Cf. Joan Robinson, *Essays in the Theory of Employment.*) But it seems clear that Marx held to the Ricardian view that a rise in money-wages would generally lead to a rise of *real* wages and a fall in profit; and in one passage he criticizes those who say that a rise in money-wages produces an equivalent rise in prices, and proceeds to argue that the higher demand for wage-goods will cause a transfer of resources from luxury-production, and hence an increased supply of the former and decline of the latter.

list the "counter-tendencies" and set them beside his previous analysis as reasons why in fact "this fall (in the profit-rate) is not greater and more rapid".[1] There seems little doubt that Marx fully expected that the rate of profit would in fact continue to fall as capital accumulation and technical change proceeded. But that he provided no *a priori* proof that one set of influences would necessarily surmount the other was an omission which, I believe, was made, not because volume III of *Capital* is unfinished, but advisedly: made advisedly because it would have been alien to his whole historical method to suggest that any answer could be abstractly given or that any conclusion of universal application could be deduced mechanically from data concerning technical change treated *in vacuo*. Marx undoubtedly conceived the situation as one in which the actual value-changes that emerged were resultant of an interaction of technical changes and the particular configuration of class relations which prevailed at the given time and stage. The whole emphasis of his approach was on the dominating influence of the latter in shaping the "law of motion of economic society". (Among the factors relevant to this determining class-relation were the conditions of supply of labour-power, whether workers were organized in trade unions, and so forth.) This law of motion could not be given a purely technological interpretation: could not be made a simple corollary of a generalization concerning

---

[1] *Capital*, III, 272. In addition to an increase of relative surplus-value, referred to above, Marx included among his "counter-tendencies" what he termed a "cheapening of the elements of constant capital", due to enhanced labour-productivity; also the creation of "relative over-population", which might have a depressing effect on the wage-level; and finally foreign trade (which will be considered in a later chapter).

the nature of changes in productive technique. The actual outcome of this interaction of conflicting elements might be different in one concrete situation from what it was in another and different situation. There is often a tendency (from which I do not feel Mr. John Strachey's recent work [1] on the subject is free) to give Marx's view of this matter a too mechanistic twist, depicting it as though it relied on the forecast of profit falling in a continuous downward curve until it reached a point at which the system would come to an abrupt stop, like an engine with insufficient pressure of steam behind the piston. The true interpretation would seem to be that Marx saw tendency and counter-tendency as elements of conflict out of which the general movement of the system emerged: this conflict of forces achieving a balance, and hence an even movement, only "by accident", and hence promoting those sharp breaks of equilibrium, and their accompanying fluctuations, which in the concrete circumstances of capitalist economy showed themselves as crises. The ground-pattern, the limiting factors on the course of events, might be the technical conditions, as bones are to a body; but they were not the whole shape.

Can one, then, say anything more precise as to the conditions under which the tendency is likely to prevail over the counter-tendencies?

Let us assume a condition of affairs where large "relative over-population" exists, i.e. a plentiful surplus of labour in excess of the existing numbers em-

---

[1] *The Nature of Capitalist Crises.* On the other hand, certain writers have depicted Marx's theory as though it were solely a theory of disproportion, ignoring the falling profit tendency. Cf. esp. J. Borchardt's note on crises in *The People's Marx.*

ployed.[1] This might be due to the fact that the natural rate of increase of the population was greater than the rate of capital accumulation, or that labour was being displaced by machinery faster than investment in new industries was absorbing it, or because certain areas of the economy were still at the stage of what Marx called "primitive accumulation", under which peasantry or small producers were being dispossessed and proletarianized. This situation would be that pictured by Ricardo as the golden road of capitalism: each new wave of capital accumulation could be invested in a repetition and enlargement of previous productive processes, drawing on additional strata of labour-power at no higher price than previously and exploiting these new strata at the same rate of surplus-value as before. In other words, the field of exploitation could extend *pari passu* with capital accumulation.[2] Consequently no fall in the rate of profit need occur; and for the same reason there would be no motive, *ceteris paribus*, for any alteration in the organic composition of capital.[3] Each cycle of production would be larger than the previous; but the proportion in which capital was divided between constant and variable capital would remain the same; while there

[1] This is what economists to-day would speak of as a condition of infinitely elastic labour-supply to industry in general. We are also assuming that raw materials and food are in perfectly elastic supply.

[2] Cf. Marx: "The creation of surplus-value, assuming . . . sufficient accumulation of capital, finds no other limit but the labouring population, when the rate of surplus-value, that is the intensity of exploitation, is given." (*Ibid.*, p. 285.)

[3] The reason of this is that presumably capitalist entrepreneurs had previously distributed their capital between purchasing labour-power and purchasing machines, raw materials, etc., in what they judged to be the most profitable proportions. Unless the price of any of these things had changed, there would be no motive for capital to be distributed in any different proportions.

would be no problem of "disposal" of products so long
as the proportion in which industry was divided between
making means of production and means of consumption
continued to correspond to the proportion in which the
money-income of society was devoted to investment
(including repair and replacement) and to expenditure
on consumption goods.

If there impinged upon this situation the invention
of some new technical process, which made machines
more efficient or created a new use for machinery,
there would now be a motive to change the organic
composition of capital in the direction of investing
proportionately more as constant capital and less as
variable—to substitute machines for men, or "stored-
up labour" for "living labour". But *in this situation*
the change would not necessarily result in a fall in
the rate of profit. If we assume that the new process
is capable of application to all industries, including
agriculture and the industries which manufacture means
of production, then the rate of profit may very well rise
and not fall. For, provided there is no influence tending
to raise real wages (a condition which is given *ex hypothesi*
by the surplus condition of the labour market), the value
of labour-power will fall along with the fall in the value
of subsistence, thereby increasing "the intensity of
exploitation or the rate of surplus-value"; [1] while the

[1] The argument of Tugan-Baranovski (*Theorie und Geschichte der
Handelkrisen in England*, pp. 212–15), which is quoted by Prof. K. Shibata
in *Kyoto University Econ. Review*, July 1934, to show that a raised
organic composition must result in a *rise* in the rate of profit, rests on
a special assumption: namely, that the rate of surplus-value (in the
example cited) is *doubled* as a result of the change. This result is
achieved by making the total real wage-bill *half* what it previously was
(with the same total output): a special assumption in which the conclusion is, of course, implied. The assumption is parallel to that made

increase of productivity will lower the value of machines and raw materials in greater or less degree. In other words, the counteracting tendencies towards an increase of "relative surplus-value" and to a "cheapening of the elements of constant capital" may overbear the tendency to a decline in the rate of profit latent in the initial change in the ratio of constant to variable capital. Moreover, the tendency of labour-saving innovations to increase the state of "relative over-population" may exert a still further effect in depressing wages below the level at which they previously were.[1]

Let us now assume, instead, a different state of the labour market: namely, one in which "relative over-population" is small and in process of being exhausted by the expansion of industry, and the process of proletarianization of intermediate social strata is slow or is arrested, or else one in which the workers are sufficiently strongly organized to resist any pressure to reduce money wages and even to increase them whenever the competition of employers for labour-power permits. In this situation, as capital accumulation expands and the surplus of labour-power available in the market

in the first of our two cases above; but it is inconsistent with the second of these two cases below, where the price of labour-power remains constant, the price of finished products falls *pari passu* with the increased productivity, and the rate of surplus-value remains unchanged. In an unpublished mathematical note on this question, which I have been privileged to see, Mr. H. D. Dickinson furnishes a proof to show that even in the former case the profit-rate may fall. The matter turns on the relation between the enhanced labour-productivity and the degree of change in the organic composition.

[1] If this additional effect is at all considerable it may, partly or completely, reverse the initial tendency to raise the ratio of constant: variable capital. In other words, it will shift one of the conditions of equilibrium (the price of labour-power), and make profitable a reversion, as Marx pointed out, to more primitive technical methods despite the new invention.

approaches exhaustion (this need be only approached, not reached), the competition of capital to obtain labour-power will create a tendency for the price of labour-power to rise: not necessarily to rise universally, but at least for certain types of labour and in certain industries. This is a familiar state of affairs which prevails near the "peak" of an industrial boom. In other words, in this case capital accumulation is tending to outrun any possible *extension* of the field of exploitation; and short of some means of *intensifying* the exploitation of the existing field, the rate of profit per unit of capital must fall. The new capital, meeting limited reserves of cheap labour-power, tends to go increasingly into the form of constant capital—into new technical processes which result in a raising of the organic composition of capital. In this case the change in the ratio of constant to variable capital *is* associated with a fall in the rate of profit, since this very change is prompted by a state of relative scarcity in the labour market which precludes any immediate or at least equivalent "compensation" for this fall, in the shape of an increase of "relative surplus-value".[1]

[1] The distinction which is being made here corresponds to Mr. J. R. Hicks' distinction between "autonomous" and "induced" inventions (*Theory of Wages*, p. 125); the former constituting a new piece of knowledge, the latter a technical method, previously known, but not previously profitable to utilize owing to the relative cheapness with which labour could be obtained. It is to be noted that the other type of "compensation", the cheapening of constant capital, cannot be sufficient to counteract the tendency to decline in profit in this case, because if this cheapening were equivalent to the change in the ratio of machinery, etc., to labour, then the ratio of constant: variable capital would *not* change in *value* terms, the invention would not strictly be of a "labour-saving" type, and if known would have been profitable to introduce previously. Mr. Durbin's argument (*op. cit.*) that the previous rate of profit will be maintained because increased productivity will be proportional to the increased investment seems to depend on making a special assumption in which this result is implied: namely, a "rate

The importance that Marx assigned to this falling profit-rate tendency can be judged by the emphasis that he placed in his answers to Say and Ricardo on their neglect of the fact that capitalism was a system, not of "social production" (motivated by social ends), but of production for profit. Hence it was not the abstract limits to exchange, but the limits to investment and production at a certain rate of profit that was the relevant consideration. He accused the classical Law of Markets of concentrating so exclusively on the interdependence of production and consumption, of supply and demand, as to treat them virtually as identities; and hence to omit the very factors that were capable of producing disequilibrium between these elements. In depicting exchange simply as a process of C—M—C (Commodities —Money—Commodities), they neglected the fact that capitalist production was characterized by the relation of M—C—M' (Money-Capital: The Commodity, Labour-Power: Money-Capital *plus* Profit), and that if the conditions for realizing the expected profit from this closed transaction were interrupted, the transaction would be suspended, with a resulting rupture of a wide circle of other and dependent exchange-transactions. "Ricardo", Marx wrote, "conceives capitalist production

of new invention" *proportional* to the "rate of saving". Hence, the proportional fall of costs he arrives at is a *joint* result of saving *plus* new inventions. What he says in the ensuing chapter of the results of an *increasing* rate of saving would surely apply equally to a constant rate of saving and static conditions of technique? Neither Mr. Durbin's assumptions, nor those of the former of my two cases above, are of course consistent with what is generally termed "full equilibrium". Moreover, if supply-conditions in the labour market were such as to keep real wages constant (elastic supply) and *also* conditions were such as to enable subsistence to be cheapened proportionately with other commodities, there would be no incentive to "induced inventions" at all.

as an absolute form of production, of which the particular conditions should never contradict or hinder the end of production in general: abundance. . . . When we speak of value and riches, we must conceive of society as a whole. But when we speak of capital and labour, it is clear that the gross revenue has significance only in order to create a net revenue." "To deny crises they (the Ricardian economists) speak of unity where there is contrast and opposition. . . . All the objections made by Ricardo, etc., to over-production have the same basis: they regard bourgeois production as a mode of production wherein there is no distinction between purchase or sale (direct exchange), or they see *social* production, in which society divides its means of production and its productive resources according to a plan, in the proportions in which they are necessary to the satisfaction of different needs." But precisely because capitalist production is production for profit, "over-production of capital" becomes possible in the sense of a volume of capital accumulation which is inconsistent with the maintenance of the former level of profit.[1] "There is periodically a production of too many means of production and necessities of life to permit of their serving as means for the exploitation of the labourers *at a certain rate of profit.* . . . It is not a fact that too much wealth is produced. But it is true that there is periodical over-production of wealth in its capitalistic and self-contradictory form. . . . The capitalist mode of production, for this reason, meets with barriers at a certain scale of production which would be inadequate under different conditions. It comes to a standstill at

[1] *Mehrwert*, Vol. III, p. 54; Vol. II, pp. 309 and 311; also p. 269 *et seq.*

a point *determined by the production and realization of profit*, not by the satisfaction of social needs." [1]

The tendency for the rate of profit to fall as the stock of capital equipment increases plays a prominent part in certain recent theories of the trade cycle (*e.g.* Mr. Keynes and Dr. Kalečki); and its connection with the causation of a crisis hardly needs elaboration here. But it has sometimes been supposed that Marx's theory was seriously incomplete because, in the absence of any proof that the rate of interest would at the same time rise (or at least be rigid) instead of falling, it did not explain why a fall in the profit-rate should cause investment to decline. Some have even suggested that crises are rather to be attributed to the failure of the rate of interest to fall than to the fact that profit falls; the practical implication of this emphasis presumably being that the trouble is not attributable to capitalism *per se*, but can be remedied by an appropriate monetary policy which, as investment proceeds, permits the rate of interest to fall *pari passu*. True, Marx nowhere explicitly refers to the relation between profit, the interest-rate and the volume of current investment-decisions. But he clearly distinguishes the separate influence of the two—a distinction which, as Prof. Hayek has remarked,[2] later

---

[1] *Capital*, Vol. III, p. 303 (italics inserted). Marx admitted that it might be proper to call such over-production relative rather than absolute—relative to certain class conditions and to a certain level of profit.

[2] *Profit, Interest and Investment*, 5. Marx regarded the rate of interest as partly governed (in the long run) by the rate of profit, but also as governed at any one moment by the supply and demand for money-capital, or loanable funds. (Cf. Fan Hung, *loc. cit.*; and S. Alexander, *ibid.*, Feb. 1939.) Marx denied that there was such a thing as a "natural rate of interest", *i.e.*, that it was determined by "real", or production, factors.

economists mistakenly abandoned—and in a subsequent chapter on the rate of interest he gives reasons for thinking that at the crucial period when a crisis is germinating the rate of interest tends to rise. On the question of whether Marx's emphasis was a correct one, let it suffice to say here that there is some reason to think that changes in the rate of interest play a much smaller rôle in curtailing a boom than many writers have previously thought,[1] and that there is strong ground for doubting the ability of monetary policy to influence the long-term rate of interest in any sufficient degree.[2]

If the theory of Marx was different in important respects from that of most versions of the underconsumption theory, what is the precise relationship of the former to the latter? Is there a sense in which his theory is to be interpreted as one of underconsumption, as is so frequently done? There is, I think, no easy answer to this question, since an answer would require a more rigorous analysis and classification of the numerous variations on the under-consumption theme than has hitherto been undertaken. Certainly his theory is not one of under-consumption either in the sense that investment necessarily causes over-production unless some new source of consumption demand appears, or in the sense that higher wages would suffice to prevent crises and cure depression, or in the sense that a deficiency of consumption is always the precipitating cause of a crisis, so that the crisis *starts* in the consumption-goods industries. At the same time it is clear that he was far from attributing to the level of consumption a negligible influence as a limiting factor on the realization of profit.

[1] Cf. Kalecki, *op. cit.*
[2] Cf. Harrod, *Trade Cycle*, 168–70, etc.

We have seen that there was one case where Marx treated the crisis as originating, not "within the sphere of production", but in an element of disequilibrium within the sphere of circulation, or exchange. This was the case of an increase in the rate of saving which caused a glut in the consumption-goods industries. But there are passages which sound as though he regarded consumption-demand as a limiting factor in a more fundamental sense than this. The two passages which are most frequently cited by those who interpret his theory as one of under-consumption are the following. "The last cause of all real crises always remains the poverty and restricted consumption of the masses, as compared with the impulse of capitalist production to develop the productive forces as if only the absolute power of consumption of society were their limit." [1] This occurs in the course of a criticism by Marx of the view that crises are caused by a scarcity of capital. Its immediate context is inclined to be obscure and does not aid in determining its meaning. If it stood alone, it would doubtless be open to a simple under-consumption interpretation, similar to Malthus or Rodbertus. But, in view of all that Marx has said elsewhere, particularly in view of his explicit repudiation of the Rodbertus view that "crises are caused by the scarcity of paying consumption" and that "the evil could be remedied by raising wages",[2] we clearly cannot give it this interpretation. The second passage is this: "The conditions of direct exploitation and those of the realization of surplus-value are not identical. They are separated

[1] *Op. cit.*, III, p. 568.
[2] Quoted above, p. 90 f. Moreover, this latter passage in Vol. II was written at a *later* date than the former passage from Vol. III. (See above, p. 101.)

logically as well as by time and space. The first is only
limited by the productive power of society, the last by
the proportional relations of the various lines of production and by the consuming power of society. The
latter is not determined either by the absolute productive
power nor by absolute consuming power, but by consuming power that is based on antagonistic conditions
of distribution, which reduce the consumption of the
great mass of the population to a variable minimum
within more or less narrow limits".[1] What it seems
reasonable to suppose that Marx had in mind in these
passages is the following proposition, which would, I
think, to-day secure fairly wide acceptance. The amount
of profit which can be realized on existing capital is
always dependent, not only on how perfectly this capital
is distributed between capital-goods industries and
consumption-goods industries in relation to prevailing
investment and consumption, but also on the *total*
volume of consumption *plus* investment at the time.
To increase consumption would be the most enduring
way of increasing profit, because in addition to its
momentary effect, it would increase the demand for
future capital-goods (affording room for a "widening"
of capital) and hence exerting a delaying influence on
the tendency of new investment (by exhausting investment-opportunities) to cause the rate of profits to fall.[2]
Any increase of mass consumption, however, *via* a rise

[1] Marx, *op. cit.*, Vol. III, 287.
[2] Since the level of consumption limits the size of the consumption
trades, and hence the amount of equipment of existing type in these
trades, a given volume of investment will necessarily result sooner in
a deepening of the capital structure, or a raising of the organic composition, the *smaller* is consumption. In the language of a later chapter,
"capital saturation" is sooner reached by a given rate of investment,
the smaller is the level of consumption.

of wages would merely take away on the swings what it contributed on the roundabouts: it would raise costs as much as it increased demand. Hence there was little prospect under capitalism of consumption increasing proportionately with productivity. On the other hand, increased investment, while it might temporarily have a*similar effect in increasing demand, precipitated the problem of changing composition of capital, and hence of a falling profit-rate in the near future. In this sense consumption was an incident—an important incident— in the total setting: and the conflict between productivity and consumption was one facet of crises and one element of the contradiction which found expression in a periodic breakdown of the system. At the same time, it remained *only* a facet; and it seems clear that Marx considered the contradiction within the sphere of production—the contradiction between growing productive power, consequent on accumulation, and falling profitability of capital, between the *productive forces* and the *productive relations* of capitalist society—as the essence of the matter.[1]

But if consumption may be a limiting factor on the "realization" of surplus-value, it is evident that the labour-supply is a crucial limiting factor in the creation of surplus-value in the first instance, and that as such Marx treated it as fundamental. Marx treated a crisis, not simply as a transitional dislocation, but as playing a positive rôle in shaping the long-term trend of the

[1] E. Varga, for instance, in his *Great Crisis and its Political Consequences*, interprets Marx as defining crises as the conflict between "productive power" and "consuming power", and so interprets it in an apparently Luxemburg-sense as a problem of *markets* and *commodity-disposal*. This he admits is to express the matter in "greatly simplified and incomplete manner". A similar tendency is apparent in L. Corey's *Decay of American Capitalism*, esp. pp. 66 and 71.

system—as reacting on the new equilibrium into which, after a crisis, the system tended to settle; and he did so largely because of the influence exerted by a crisis on what he termed "relative surplus-population" or the "industrial reserve army". "Crises are always momentary and forcible solutions of existing contradictions, violent eruptions which restore the disturbed equilibrium for a while".[1] A principal effect of a crisis will be to recreate or to swell this "industrial reserve army". This, in turn, will have the effect of cheapening the price of labour-power: how strongly and how rapidly the effect will operate depending on the various factors which determined the strength of the workers' resistance to falling wages. The immediate effect of such wage-reductions, it is true, may be to deepen the crisis by reason of the deflationary effects of reduced wages on the demand for and the price of consumption goods. But in so far as it represents a lowering of the real price of labour-power, it will create the condition for an increased rate of surplus-value and so will serve to prepare the ground for a resumption of the investment-process. This cheapening of labour-power will also react in some measure on the previous tendency to raise the organic composition of capital: it will serve to retard the process of technical change by making more primitive technical methods profitable once again.

This periodic recruitment of the "industrial reserve army", therefore, appears as the lever by which the system resists any serious encroachment on capital-values, and compensates itself for the tendency of capital accumulation to cause the rate of profit to decline. It is what Marx termed "capitalism's own law of popula-

[1] *Capital*, Vol. III, p. 292.

tion"; which explained unemployment and poverty as existing, not because human productive powers were insufficient to wrest a livelihood from nature, but by reason of the limits set to employment and to wages by the conditions for the extraction of surplus-value; not because population was redundant in any absolute sense, but because capital was redundant relatively to the possibilities of reaping an expected rate of profit. Crises, as the uniform reaction of capital to disappointed profit-expectations, accordingly seem to operate *as if* the capitalist class were to act in unison as a single monopolist *vis-à-vis* labour. We have this picture: that so soon as a condition approaching full employment is reached, so soon as investment extends the utilization of existing technical methods beyond a certain margin, so soon as thereby the mass of producers are on the threshold of receiving any considerable improvement in their share of the benefits of progress, the fruit is snatched from their grasp, and the inexorable law of the labour market batters them into humility once more.

A distinction has been made above between an *extensive* and an *intensive* development of the field of investment. This distinction is, I believe, of crucial importance, not only for the light it throws on the history of crises themselves, the circumstances out of which they develop and the new developments which they create, but also in relation to Marx's theory of wages and hence to the changing form which the proletarian struggle assumes at different stages of development. In the golden age of competitive capitalism, the periodic recruitment of the industrial reserve army was a sufficient method by which the field of exploitation for a growing capital accumulation could be maintained intensively. It can

be regarded, perhaps, as the classic method of capitalism
for preserving the rate of profit. But by the fourth
quarter of the nineteenth century, with the growing
strength of labour organization, and consequent "rigidi-
ties" in the labour market, this classic method was losing
some of its effect; and the advantages of falling prices
of imported foodstuffs in the 'seventies and 'eighties seem
to have accrued as much in rising *real* wages to the
workers as in a falling money-price of labour-power to
the capitalists. It is all too commonly assumed that
Marx rested his theory of wages on the Malthusian law
of population, as Ricardo had done.[1] But this Marx
explicitly denied. Moreover, it is clear that Marx treated
the assumption that wages stood at subsistence level as
no more than a "first approximation" and by no means as
a universal "iron law" which held true of every situation
in the labour market. Indeed, in his debate on trade
unions with a Mr. Weston at a session of the First International, he explicitly repudiated such an interpretation.[2]
If, then, his theory, unlike Ricardo's, rested on no such
law of population, it might seem that it furnished no
reason why the price of labour-power should not rise
till it equalled the value of the product. What was to
prevent capital accumulation, with the increasing demand
for labour which it engendered, from raising the wage-
level until surplus-value disappeared, so that capitalism
of its own momentum should extinguish the class inequality on which it was reared? This question, as we
have seen—the reason for the persistence of a surplus-
value—has been a central one throughout the history

---

[1] Bertrand Russell, for instance, makes this statement in *Freedom
and Organization*, pp. 231-2.

[2] Published as the pamphlet *Value Price and Profit*.

of Political Economy, and one for which so many shallow apologetic answers have been devised. The crucial factor which operated here—according to Marx's theory the defensive mechanism by which the system inhibited its own self-extinction—consisted in the double reaction whereby the industrial reserve army was periodically recruited: the tendency of capitalist economy to have a bias towards "labour-saving" changes [1] and the tendency for accumulation to be retarded and for investment to recoil when signs of any appreciable fall in the rate of profit appeared. On the one hand, this intensive recruitment of a labour-reserve—a factor operating, as it were, from the side of demand in the labour market— and, on the other hand, the extensive recruitment of new labour-supplies by increase of population, by proletarianization of intermediate social strata, or by the extension of investment to virgin colonial areas, were the factors which operated continually to depress the price of labour-power to a level which permitted surplus-value to be earned. The operation of one or both of these factors was the *conditio sine qua non* for the continuance of capitalist production. From the standpoint of capital, accordingly, progress is arrested, and crises occur, because wages are "too high"; and this is how the matter is traditionally expressed in economic literature. But such a statement is, of course, strictly relative to the assumption that a certain minimum return on capital is "necessary", and only retains any meaning in this context. Rather is it true to say that crises occur because profit and interest are too high; since such a statement draws attention to the fundamental fact that, by comparison with a system of "social pro-

---

[1] Cf. J. R. Hicks, *Theory of Wages*, pp. 123–5.

duction", "the real barrier of capitalist production is capital itself".[1]

In the early stages of capitalist development the "industrial reserve army" was more easy to recruit, without any great pressure on the labour market from the side of demand. The field of exploitation was continually being extended by the process of "primitive accumulation"—by the dispossession of small producers, of peasantry and artisans. Hence the crises of this early period, while they might be sharp and violent, were apt to be short-lived and easy of cure. But as capitalism developed to a higher stage, the easy situation of its infancy disappeared. The supply of labourers was no longer swollen by the expropriation of a *petite-bourgeoisie*, at least not on the same scale as before. With a growth of labour organization and a heightening of class tension, intensive cultivation of the field of exploitation met increasing obstacles. And it is the difference between the ease and difficulty of these basic forms of compensation for a falling rate of profit which seems to constitute the primary difference between the crises of the earlier and the later stages of capitalist economy. New methods of extending the field of exploitation—extending it to new and untapped strata beyond its former frontiers—had to be pioneered. When these fields too approached exhaustion, yet newer methods, coercive methods, of intensifying the development of the home field required to be invented, such as those which contemporary history is revealing with such ruthless logic. To-day capital sows dragons' teeth, alike in the home and in the colonial field; and the peoples reap the harvest.

[1] *Capital*, III, p. 293.

CHAPTER V

THE TREND OF MODERN ECONOMICS

ONCE the formal question of internal consistency is settled, the acceptance or rejection of a theory depends on one's view of the appropriateness of the particular abstraction on which the theory is based. This is necessarily a practical question, depending on the nature of the terrain and the character of the problem and the activity to which the theory is intended to relate. One frequently hears the claim made for a theory that it has a greater generality than some rival formula; and on the face of it this plea seems cogent enough. But one would do well to be somewhat sceptical of such a claim, at least until one was sure that the greater generality had not been purchased too dearly at the expense of realism. In making abstraction of particular elements in a situation, there are, broadly speaking, two roads along which one can proceed. In the first place, one may build one's abstraction on the exclusion of certain features which are present in any actual situation, either because they are the more variable or because they are quantitatively of lesser importance in determining the course of events. To omit them from consideration makes the resulting calculation no more than an imperfect approximation to reality, but nevertheless makes it a very much more reliable guide than if the major factors had been omitted and only the minor influences taken into account. So it is that one creates the abstraction of a projectile which moves in a vacuum—as it is never found to do in reality—in order to estimate what are the dominant factors which will govern the trajectory of an object propelled through a resistant medium. The correctness or otherwise of the particular assumptions chosen can only be determined by experience: by knowledge of how actual situations behave, and of the actual difference made by the presence or absence of various factors. The method as a whole yields valid results (provided the assumptions are rightly chosen), so long as the presence of the minor factors introduced in the subsequent approximations has the effect merely of adding certain additional parameters to the original equations, and not of altering the structure of the equations themselves.[1]

Secondly, one may base one's abstraction, not on any evidence of fact as to what features in a situation are essential and what are inessential, but simply on the formal procedure of combining the properties common to a heterogeneous assortment of situations and building abstraction out of analogy. This is akin to what an early scientific writer described as a "general definition of the things themselves according to their universal natures . . . (relying) on general terms which (have) not much foundation in knowledge", and used to "build most subtle webs" from "themes not all collected by a sufficient information from the things themselves".[2]

---

[1] This, I believe, is the case which J. S. Mill called one where the principle of the composition of causes applies. Cf. for further reference to this, below, p. 190.

[2] Sprat, quoted by Prof. L. Hogben in *Science and Society* (New York) Vol. I, No. 2.

Within limits, of course, such a method is not only perfectly valid, but is an essential element in any generalization: a generalization is no generalization but an imaginary hypothesis unless what it generalizes is something common to the phenomena to which it refers. The danger of the method is of its being pushed too far, beyond the point where the factors which it embraces cease to be the major factors determining the nature of the problem which is in hand. What the abstraction gains in breadth it then more than loses, as it were, in depth—in relevance to the particular situations which are the focus of interest. And the danger is the greater in that this point may be passed without any awareness that this is so. Frequently this method of progressive refinement of analogy has led to little but confusing sophisms. In a sphere where generalization can take a quantitative form the method can have a greater show of reason and is doubtless less subject to abuse. And it may be the case that, even in its more abstract forms, the method can yield some element of truth; since so long as the abstractions it employs retain any elements which are common to actual situations, the relations which are postulated must represent *some* aspect of the truth in each particular problem. One may instance, perhaps, the theory of probability applied to features which are common to all games of chance; or, as probably a more barren example, attempts which have been made to develop general rules of language which shall be valid for all particular languages. As a yet more barren example one might add the attempt of the economist Barone to frame a set of equations which would demonstrate that the same law must prevail in a collectivist economy as rules in a *laissez-faire* world.

But in all such abstract systems there exists the serious danger of hypostatizing one's concepts; of regarding the postulated relations as the determining ones in any actual situation, instead of contingent and determined by other features; and hence of presuming too readily that they, will apply to novel or imperfectly known situations, with an abstract dogmatism as the result. There is the danger of introducing, unnoticed, purely imaginary or even contradictory assumptions, and in general of ignoring how limited a meaning the corollaries deducible from these abstract propositions must have and the qualifications which the presence of other concrete factors (which may be the major influences in this or that particular situation) may introduce. All too frequently the propositions which are products of this mode of abstraction have little more than formal meaning, and at most tell one that an expression for such-and-such a relation must find a place in any of one's equational systems.[1] But those who use such propositions and build corollaries upon them are seldom mindful of this limitation, and in applying them as "laws" of the real world invariably extract from them more meaning than their emptiness of real content can possibly hold.

It does not seem a bad rule in a subject so wedded to complex practical issues as is Political Economy to keep one's feet firmly planted on the ground, even if this be at the sacrifice of some logical elegance of definition and of some of the impressive, but often misleading,

---

[1] Such pursuits are sometimes defended on the ground that they are " tool-makers " for subsequent analysis. Perhaps it is true that this is their principal use. But even tools are better made when their manufacture is fairly closely subordinated to the uses which they are intended to serve.

precision of algebraic formulation. In general the abstractions employed by the classical economists and by Marx were of the first of the two types that we have mentioned. The concept of the perfect market, of homogeneous labour, of equal compositions of capital were intended to generalize what were in actuality the most essential factors in determining exchange-values. Patten has remarked that Ricardo was essentially a concrete thinker,[1] and Marx was specially anxious that his theory should embrace those features which were characteristic of capitalist society rather than of any other. While a disturbing influence, even a reflex influence, was admittedly exerted by other and neglected factors in the situation, this was regarded as being of secondary importance in determining the larger shape of actual events. Interest was focussed on what was peculiar to a particular system of economic relations, even at the expense of a wider, but perhaps more barren, generality. Since their time, however, I think it is not incorrect to say that the efforts of economic analysis have been predominantly directed along the second road. In abstracting phenomena of exchange from the productive relations and the property and class institutions of which they are the expression, an attempt has been made to arrive at generalizations which will hold for *any* type of exchange economy. Marshall remarks of J. S. Mill that he seemed to attribute to the laws of exchange "something very much like the universality of mathematics", even while he admitted distribution to be relative to transitory institutions.[2] From the general relations of an abstract market we pass to yet more perfect abstractions, and to-day are introduced to the relations which

---

[1] *Quarterly Journal of Econ.*, 1893.   [2] *Principles*, p. 824.

will necessarily prevail in any situation where "scarce means which have alternative uses serve given purposes". Something of the real world doubtless still lingers even in this tenuous definition. But hardly enough to make one believe that the resulting propositions can hold anything at all imperative for the problems of the actual world. If an economic law is a statement of what actually tends to happen, and not a mere statement of a relation between certain implicitly defined variables, then such propositions can surely be precious little guide to the "laws of motion of capitalist society"—or, indeed, to any of the other matters on which they are intended to pass an economic judgment.

It was an important element in Marx's theory of ideology that in a class society the abstract ideas which were fashioned from a given society tended to assume a phantom or fetishistic character, in the sense that, being taken as representations of reality, they came to depict actual society in an inverted or a distorted form. Thereby they served not merely to hide the real nature of society from men's eyes, but to misrepresent it. The examples which he cited were mainly drawn from the concepts of religion and of idealist philosophy. Thus it came about that ideas and concepts, which in their day may have played a positive rôle of enlightenment as weapons of criticism turned against the system both of ideas and of institutions of a previous epoch, later became reactionary and obscurantist, precisely because they were treated as constituting the real essence of contemporary society, not merely its abstract and partial reflection; with the result that reality was veiled. In the realm of economic thought (where one might at first glance least suspect it) it is not difficult to see a parallel tendency at work. One might think it harmless enough to make abstraction of certain aspects of exchange-relations in order to analyse them in isolation from social relations of production. But what actually occurs is that once this abstraction has been made it is given an independent existence as though it represented the essence of reality, instead of one contingent facet of reality. Concepts become hypostatized; the abstraction acquires a fetishistic character, to use Marx's phrase. Here seems to lie the crucial danger of this method and the secret of the confusions which have enmeshed modern economic thought. Today, not merely do we have the laws of exchange-relations treated in abstraction from more fundamental social relations of production, and the former depicted as dominating the latter, but we even have the relations of exchange treated purely in their *subjective* aspect— in terms of their mental reflection in the realm of individual desires and choices—and the laws which govern actual economic society invertedly depicted as consisting in the abstract relations which hold in this ghostly sphere.

The dividing landmark in the history of economic thought in the nineteenth century is usually placed in the 'seventies with the arrival of the new utility theories of Jevons and the Austrian School. But if we fix our attention less on the change of form, and instead on the shift towards subjective notions and towards the study of exchange-relations in abstraction from their social roots, we shall see that essential changes came earlier in the century, or at any rate the commencement of tendencies which later assumed a more finished shape. Marx, indeed, mentioned 1830 as the year which closed the final decade of "classical economy" and opened the door to "vulgar economy"[1] and the decline of the glories of the Ricardian School. This was the period when the new industrial capitalism, both economically and politically, was coming into its own, and when at the same time (as the events of the 'thirties were witness) the proletariat and its criticism of capitalist society was emerging as a coherent social force for the first time. Thenceforward, no statement concerning the nature of the economic system could remain "neutral".[2] Economists, becoming increasingly

[1] This term, of course, was not used by Marx simply as a term of abuse, as is commonly supposed, but in a descriptive sense, familiar to continental philosophy, as contrasted with "classical". He states that "by classical political economy I understand that economy which, since the time of W. Petty, has investigated the real relations of production in bourgeois society, in contradiction to vulgar economy, which deals with appearances only . . . and confines itself to systematizing in a pedantic way, and proclaiming for everlasting truths the trite ideas held by the self-complacent bourgeois with regard to their own world ". (Capital, I, p. 53 f.) Marx seems particularly to have had in mind McCulloch, Senior, Bastiat, and if not Say at any rate Say's "interpreters" and followers. Professor Gray is clearly wrong in implying that Adam Smith and Ricardo were included under the title of "vulgar economy" (op. cit., p. 322).

[2] This, of course, was specially true of the theory of profit. Here it is interesting to note that Böhm-Bawerk refers to the position of Adam Smith on the subject of interest as one of "complete neutrality", and adds that "in Adam Smith's time the relations of theory and practice still permitted such a neutrality, but it was not long allowed to his followers". (Capital and Interest, pp. 74-5.) On the other hand, Cannan's statement that "James Mill . . . showed a desire to strengthen the position of the capitalist against the labourer by justifying the existence of profits" (Hist. of Theories of Production and Distribution, Second Ed., p. 206) seems more questionable. James Mill was capable of some exceedingly frank characterizations of the nature of capitalist production, which one can hardly imagine being made twenty-five years later. One of the best examples of the change was the subsequent attitude to Ricardo's "lapse" in his third edition. Ricardo was frank enough to add a chapter in this edition on "Machinery" in which he stated his conversion to the view that the introduction of machinery was capable of being harmful to the interests of labour. This shocked McCulloch, and his followers hastened (and for most of the century succeeded) to draw a veil over this breach of good taste.

134

obsessed with apologetics, had an increasing tendency to omit any treatment of basic social relationships and to deal only with the superficial aspect of market phenomena, to confine their thought within the limits of the "Fetishism of Commodities" and to generalize about the laws of an "exchange economy", until in the end these were made to determine, rather than be determined by, the system of production and of productive relations. In his Preface to the second edition (1873) of volume I of *Capital*, Marx speaks of English Political Economy as belonging "to the period in which the (proletarian) class struggle was as yet undeveloped". Of the period from 1820 to 1830 he says that it "was notable in England for scientific activity in the domain of Political Economy. It was the time as well of the vulgarizing and extending of Ricardo's theory, as of the contest of that theory with the old school. Splendid tournaments were held. The unprejudiced character of this polemic . . . is explained by the circumstances of the time." But this, though it was reminiscent of the intellectual vigour prior to 1789 in France, was no more than "a Saint Martin's Summer". After 1830 "the class struggle practically as well as theoretically took on more and more outspoken and threatening forms". This "sounded the knell of scientific bourgeois economy. . . . In place of genuine scientific research, the bad conscience and the evil intent of apologetic." Even honest inquirers were limited by the general atmosphere to evasive compromises, and to eclectic attempts "to harmonize the Political Economy of capital with the claims, no longer to be ignored, of the proletariat". The product was "a shallow syncretism, of which John Stuart Mill is the best representative". Of that new departure in economic thought which marked the last quarter of the century neither Marx nor Engels seem to have made more than cursory mention or to have taken much notice.[1] If they had done so, it seems probable that they would have regarded it as a continuation of tendencies already latent in the "vulgar economists", rather than as the revolutionary novelty in economic thought which it has generally been regarded as being. After all, the new departure consisted more of a change of form than of substance, as Marshall always emphasized. That so many of the economists of the last quarter of the century should have advertised their wares as such an epoch-making novelty, and tilted their lances so menacingly at their forebears, seems to have an obvious, if unflattering, explanation: namely, the dangerous use to which Ricardian notions had been recently put by Marx. It is, I think, significant of the temper of economists that Foxwell once declined to deliver a Presidential Address to the Royal Economic Society on Ricardo on the ground that his denunciation of the author of the heresy of a conflict of interests between capital and labour would have been too violent;[2] and among the leaders of the Austrian School the desire to refute the Socialists was a greater preoccupation than in England.

The essential problem for Marx, as we have seen,

---

[1] Engels, in his Preface to volume III of *Capital* in 1894, refers parenthetically to the new theory of Jevons and Menger as the "rock" on which Mr. George Bernard Shaw was building a new kind of Socialism and "the Fabian church of the future" (p. 20). But apart from this they seem to have made no mention of it. This would seem surprising in view of the importance it had for the new Fabian Socialism: a fact of which, as this single reference shows, Engels was perfectly aware. Jevons' *Principles* appeared in 1874; Marx died in 1883; *The Fabian Essays* appeared in 1888; Engels lived until 1895.

[2] Cf. J. M. Keynes in *Econ. Journal*, December 1936, p. 592.

was the explanation of surplus-value; and it was because the successors of Ricardo either evaded this problem entirely or provided quite inadequate solutions that they provoked his condemnation and his scorn. The "cost of production" theory of J. S. Mill he regarded as a superficial evasion of the issue. Treating value as being governed by the price of labour (wages) *plus* an average rate of profit, it was not a refinement of Ricardo's theory, but, since it included no explanation of profit, represented an abandonment of the crucial problem which Ricardo's system had presented without ever having solved. The "cost of production" theory of value solved nothing, because it left the determination of the "cost of production" unexplained.[1] But there were others who were less innocent of recognising the crucial difficulty than was J. S. Mill, and attempted to supply an explanation of profit, even if it was one which was shallow and untenable. These attempts fall broadly into two main types: on the one hand were those who sought to explain profit in terms of some creative property inherent in capital, namely, in terms of its productivity; on the other hand were those who sought to explain profit in terms of some species of "real cost", analogous to labour,

---

[1] With regard to J. S. Mill's attitude, Cannan has said: "Senior is at least entitled to the credit of having seen that profits had not been satisfactorily explained. . . . J. S. Mill, on the other hand, seems to have been totally unaware that anything was lacking." (*History of Theories of Production and Distribution* (Ed. 1893), p. 214.) Böhm-Bawerk classed J. S. Mill (along with Jevons and Roscher) among the eclectics in their interest theory, who did little more than add an element or two to Senior's unsatisfactory theory. (*Capital and Interest*, pp. 286, 498, etc.) To his credit, Mill rejected the productivity theory of profit, stating that "the only productive power is that of labour". (*Essays on Some Unsettled Questions*, p. 90.) In his *Principles* (Bk. 11, Ch. xv) he seemed to adopt Senior's abstinence theory without examination or further analysis of the problem.

which the capitalist contributed and for which profit was not a surplus-value but an equivalent.

The attempt to explain profit in terms of the "service" rendered by capital to production had already been made by certain of Ricardo's contemporaries, in particular by Lauderdale and Malthus and also by Say, "that master of polished and rounded sentences", as Böhm-Bawerk called him. Labour which was aided by machinery, said Lauderdale, could produce a larger sum of values in an hour than could labour which was not so aided. "The moment he places a portion of capital in the acquisition of a spade, one man must obviously, in the course of a day, be able, with his spade, to prepare as much land for receiving seed as fifty could by the use of their nails." [1] The difference represented the "productivity" of capital. The fundamental objection to this, as to any form of productivity theory, was that, as Marx pointed out, it included the illicit link of imputing to the owner the "productivity" of the things he owned. "A social relation between men assumes the fantastic form of a relation between things"; and the behaviour of things is not only represented animistically as due to some innate property in them, but imputed to the influence of those individuals· who exercise rights of ownership over them. On this level there could be no distinction between the "productivity" of a capitalist and of a landlord—to deny which, indeed, seems partly

[1] Lauderdale, *Inquiry into the Nature of Public Wealth*, p. 163. Lauderdale admitted, however, that profit may "in some cases be more properly said to be acquired than produced" (p. 161). Say said: "The capitalist who lends, sells the service, the labour of his instrument." (*Letters to Mr. Malthus*, Ed. Richter, 1821, p. 19.) In his *Treatise on Political Economy* (Vol. I, Ed. Prinsep, p. 60) he spoke both of "labour or productive service of nature" and "labour or productive service of capital"!

to have been the intention of the theory. But neither could there be any distinction between the income of the employer of "free" labour and the income of the slave-owner: the "productivity" of the latter, indeed, was presumably the greater of the two since it was derived from the productivity of his animate as well as his inanimate chattels. A further difficulty has been expressed by Cannan as follows: "If the income of England without any capital would be but one instead of a hundred, it does not necessarily follow that the whole ninety-nine hundredths is profits at present. The weak point in the explanation of profits given by Lauderdale and Malthus is that, while they show clearly enough that the use of capital is an advantage to production . . . they fail to show why the advantage has been paid for at all, why the 'services' of capital are not, like those of the sun, gratuitous." [1] Böhm-Bawerk trenchantly summed up the productivity theories of interest thus: "What the productive power can do is only to create a quantity of products, and perhaps at the same time to create a *quantity* of value, but never to create *surplus* value. Interest is a surplus, a remainder left when product of capital is the minuend and value of consumed capital is the subtrahend. The productive power of capital may find its result in increasing the minuend. But in so far as that goes it cannot increase the minuend without at the same time increasing the subtrahend in the same proportion. . . . If a log is thrown across a flooded stream the level of water below the log will be less than the level of water above the log. If it is asked why the water stands higher above the log than below, would anyone think of the flood as the cause? . . . What

[1] Cannan, *op. cit.*, p. 205.

139

the flood is to the differences of level, the productive power of capital is to surplus-value."[1] The truth is that if a number of factors are jointly necessary to a given result, there is as little meaning in comparing the degree of "necessity" of these factors in the creation of wealth as in asking whether the male or female is the more necessary to the creation of a child. Even if it were possible to give a meaning to such separate "productivity", it would have no necessary relation to the emergence of *value*. For the latter one must inevitably look to characteristics affecting the supply; and any differentiation between incomes must necessarily be sought, not in terms of "service", but in terms of cost.

The attempt to find an explanation of profit which would make it analogous to wages as payment for a necessary cost involved in production, and at the same time contrast it with the rent of land, is represented by Senior's notorious "abstinence" theory. This constituted an important landmark in economic thought, because it introduced a species of "real cost" which was purely subjective and so shifted the whole context of the discussion—shifted it more radically than was apparently recognized at the time or has been recognized since. "Abstinence" is capable of being defined, it is true, objectively in terms of the things abstained from; but such abstaining could have no significance as a cost—no more than any other act of free exchange—unless one were to suppose that some special "pain" to the owner was involved in parting with these things. And if "abstinence", as the subjective equivalent of profit, was to be conceived in a psychological sense, then so presumably must labour be: labour as a cost

[1] *Capital and Interest*, pp. 179-80.

for which wages were paid being regarded not as a human activity, involving a given expenditure of physical energy, but as the strength of the psychological disinclination to work. Abstraction was to be made of human activity, its characteristics and its relationships, and only the reflection of them in the mind to be taken as the data for economic interpretation.

Already among previous writers there had been signs of an inclination, if shown only in ambiguity, to conceive the notion of "real cost" as something subjective rather than objective. Adam Smith had used the phrase "toil and trouble"; while McCulloch referred to the fact that things which cost the same "toil and trouble" to acquire would involve "the same sacrifice" and hence be held in similar "esteem" and be "of precisely the same real value".[1] With the introduction of Senior's "abstinence" there could be no mistaking that such a shift of meaning had occurred. Both question and answer had thereby been subtly moved to a quite different context. But as an explanation of profits, even within its restricted sphere, the theory met with an essential difficulty. Marx was quick to point out that there was no discoverable connection between the capitalist's "abstinence" and the profit which he earned, and that if they were connected at all, it was apparently in inverse relation. He had only to contrast the profit and the "abstinence" of a Rothschild to feel that the so-called "explanation" required no further refutation.

This defect was one aspect of a fundamental dilemma which faces any attempt to cast a theory of cost in subjective terms, and to which we shall later return. Where was one to set the limit to such "abstinence", short of

[1] *Principles of Political Economy* (1825), pp. 216-17.

including in it the sale or hire of every sort of property, and so imputing a "real cost" to any means by which an income could be acquired in an exchange society? If "abstinence" was to be allowed to the capitalist who owned a factory which he had inherited, or owned a dock or a canal, how could it reasonably be denied to the owner of land who leased his property for a rent? Of this difficulty Senior was aware; since he pointed out that, if the revenue to the owner of a dock or canal is regarded as "the reward of the owner's abstinence in not selling the dock or the canal, and spending its price in enjoyment", the same remark applies to every species of transferable property and "the greater part of what every political economist has termed rent must be called profit".[1] Accordingly, he decided to exclude all *inherited* capital from his definition. But this, of course, is to leave one on the other horn of the dilemma: namely, that in this case abstinence could not be regarded as an explanation of profit at all. As Cannan has said, Senior's theory ended by "reckoning as rent 'the greater part of what every political economist has termed' profit".[2]

Marx's retort to Senior remained unchallenged until, towards the end of the century, the concept of marginal increments, a concept borrowed from the differential calculus, was introduced as an attempt to give greater precision to economic notions. Jevons' "disutility" and Marshall's "effort and sacrifice" were merely the subjective "real cost" of McCulloch or of Senior in a more finished guise. Marshall, it is true, was careful to discard the discredited term "abstinence" for the more neutral term "waiting"; but as a designation of a sub-

---

[1] Senior, *Political Economy* (Ed. 1863), p. 129.
[2] Cannan, *op. cit.*, p. 198.

jective real cost the concept would seem in essentials to have retained the character of its sire.[1] But with the introduction of the concept of marginal increments, the new treatment had this difference. A relation between "efforts and sacrifices" and their price only existed *at the margin*; and while interest paid and sacrifice involved were regarded as tending towards identity for the *marginal* unit of capital supplied, there was no necessary relation between the *total* income received by the capitalist and the *total* "sacrifice" incurred, either in any individual case or for the whole class. The rich man who inherited his wealth, and having more than he could conveniently spend saved it, might get an income quite dispropor-

---

[1] Marshall (*Principles*, pp. 232-3), noting Marx's objection to the abstinence-concept, defined the term "waiting" as applying, not to "abstemiousness", but to the simple fact that "a person abstained from consuming anything which he had the power of consuming, with the purpose of increasing his resources in the future". This seems to imply that the concept was not limited by Senior's qualification, excluding inherited property, and that it could equally well be applied to land—to the fact that a landlord leased his land for cultivation, instead of using it for his own enjoyment or subjecting it to "exhaustive" cultivation himself. In which case, as a category of "real cost", it was clearly so general as to lose any distinctive meaning. If it was *not* intended to imply the existence of any psychological "pain" associated with the act of postponement (as the remark about "abstemiousness" seems to suggest), then it seems to remain a mere description of the act of investment which adds little to our knowledge of the nature and cause of profit. Elsewhere, however, Marshall speaks of "postponement of gratifications" as "involv(ing) *in general* a sacrifice on the part of him who postpones, just as additional effort does on the part of him who labours", this sacrifice justifying "interest as a reward to induce its continuance". (*Ibid.*, p. 587.) A recent writer in the *Quarterly Journal of Economics* claims that Marshall identified "two wholly different things under the term real cost"; but considers that the hedonistic element—the positive "pain"—was not intended to figure prominently in either his concept of work or of waiting. (Talcott Parsons, Vol. XLVI, pp. 121-3.) Whether intended, however, to figure prominently or not, it seems, according to the evidence of several passages, to have been an important part of the background of Marshall's theory of value and of distribution.

tionate to any "sacrifice" that he incurred. But an equality, nevertheless, would *tend* to prevail between the price of capital and the disutility involved in the saving of the marginal £ invested and added to the existing stock of capital; since, if the former was greater than the latter, capital accumulation would increase, while if the former was less than the latter, capital decumulation would set in until equality was restored. Hence interest was a necessary price to maintain the requisite supply of capital. Labour and wages were treated by a similar method. Wages would tend to equality with the disutility involved in the most burdensome unit of a given supply of effort, even though the worker who loved work and hated leisure might be fortunate enough to suffer little psychic pain from his day's labour and yet received the normal wage for his work.[1]

---

[1] Cf. "The exertion of all the different kinds of labour that are directly or indirectly involved in making it, together with the 'abstinence' or rather the 'waitings', required for saving the capital used in making it: all these efforts and sacrifices will be called the *real cost of production* of the commodity. The sum of money that has to be paid for these efforts and sacrifices will be called either its money cost of production or its expenses of production; they are the prices which have to be paid in order to call forth an adequate supply of the efforts and waitings that are required for making it; or, in other words, its supply-price." (Marshall, *Principles*, p. 339.) The essential dualism of this theory of real cost was admitted by Marshall when, in an article in 1876, he referred to the fact that it was only possible to measure "an effort and an abstinence . . . in terms of some common unit" through the medium of some "artificial mode of measuring them"—namely, through their market-values. (*Fortnightly Review*, 1876, pp. 596-7.) This difficulty he considered to apply similarly to the measurement of "two diverse efforts". While the difficulty in this latter case is much *less* than in the case of two quite dissimilar things such as "effort" and "abstinence", it remains a much greater problem when effort is conceived in subjective terms than when it is conceived objectively in terms of output of physical energy. The ratio of different types of subjective real cost could only be regarded as equivalent to the ratio of their money measures, if the *same persons* supplied both types.

The landlord, however, remained in a different category, since no disutility presumably was involved, even at the margin, in the supply of land, since *ex hypothesi* land as a free gift of nature did not depend on any human will or action for its existence. Yet even the natural powers of the soil could be sapped by exhaustive cultivation and land be reclaimed from the sea; while, on the other hand, in the supply of capital there was room for a substantial element of what Marshall termed "savers' surplus". Hence, the difference between the reward of capital and the return to land was only one of degree. "Rent of land", in a famous phrase of Marshall, "is not a thing by itself, but the leading species of a large genus."

The influence of this theory over half a century has undoubtedly been to discredit the Marxian theory of surplus-value, and to imply that interest was as "necessary" a category of income as wages and essentially similar in its origin; even though a writer such as Mr. J. A. Hobson attempted to give a different twist to the theory by making it the basis for an elaborated concept of "social costs" and "surpluses" which has been hailed in some quarters as an attempt to dress Marxian "surplus-value" in up-to-date clothes. But the dilemma which confronted Senior's theory is not avoided by this more generalized concept of disutility; and only some vagueness in its enunciation seems to have prevented its inadequacy from being appreciated much earlier and more widely than has been the case. Either the concept is too narrow, if strictly defined, to afford any complete explanation, or else it is too wide, if more generally defined, to give much meaning to subjective "real cost". If the "sacrifice" involved in "waiting" is to have any meaning, at least a meaning analogous even to the subjective cost involved in work, then it must apply only to acts of postponing consumption with which is associated some positive psychological loss or pain over and above the temporary loss of the goods the consumption of which is forgone. It may well be said that some such additional loss is involved for the man who starves himself in order to educate his children, or in any case where a *greater* present utility is sacrificed for a *smaller* future utility. But how it can be said to be involved in most ordinary acts of saving and investment, where an act of exchange of utilities to-day for at least an equal quantity in the future is generally involved, is hard to see. To do so is to assert that there is some unique loss attaching to postponement, which attaches only to choices made in time and to no other choices. But does one's experience suggest that mere waiting for one's fruit ever causes positive discomfort unless one is either uncertain of getting it or one is suffering pangs of hunger in the interval?[1] Unless "waiting" does indeed imply "abstemiousness" one finds difficulty in discovering what, positively, it means. On the other hand, if *mere* postponement is all that "sacrifice" is held to represent (as Marshall's statements in *some* places suggest), then it is hard to see where to draw the line short of any and every act of choice involving alternatives, one of which must be "sacrificed" whatever choice is made. As Marx retorted to Senior and Mill, "every human action may be viewed as 'abstinence' from its opposite".[2]

---

[1] The answer to this question is not necessarily the same as the answer to the question: Would one decide to have the fruit now or to wait for it, if the free choice were offered?

[2] *Capital*, I, p. 6o8 f.

At any rate, if postponement of consumption occurs in an act of *new* saving, it must surely be held also to occur in the postponement of consumption of existing and of inherited capital; and if in the case where the property is inherited from history, why not also in the case where property is inherited from nature as well as history, namely, in the case of land? (For the landowner to sell his land and live on the fruits of this sale as much reduces the total capital of society as for a capitalist to live on his capital, even though the supply of land itself is unaffected.) Marshall, indeed, seems here to have adopted the empirical solution of taking all cases of postponement for which a recompense was in fact demanded by individuals as identical with cases where a "sacrifice" was involved in the act—taking individual attitudes towards saving at their face-value, and assuming the empirical fact of resistance to the act of postponement as evidence that a real "sacrifice" attaching to the act existed and was a fundamental cause.[1] This line of distinction may be both convenient and plausible. Nevertheless, the crucial dilemma remains. If a "something more" is postulated as lying behind the mere empirical fact of resistance to postponement, one finds difficulty in giving it any precise meaning or even in believing that it exists. If, on the other hand, no more than the empirical fact of resistance is postulated, then this solution rids the notion of "real cost" of any content: it is to make it indistinguishable from what later came to be called "opportunity cost"— the cost of sacrificed alternatives (that "arithmetical

---

[1] Marshall admitted, however, that there was no reason to suppose that the ratio of real cost in two cases was identical with the ratio of their money measures, or even to suppose (as we have already noted) that there was any meaning to be attached to a *quantity* of "real cost". (*Fortnightly Review*, 1876, pp. 596-7.)

truism", as Mr. Durbin has called it).[1] Such a quantity by itself affords no explanation, because it is itself not independent, but something dependent on the total situation; and all that has been done by this definition is to shift the inquiry back to the nature of the total situation of which both profit and this so-called "cost" are simultaneously resultant. Whether a person *does* demand payment for a certain act (*i.e.* whether it has a "supply-price") depends on whether he *can* demand payment; and this depends on the total situation of which he is a part. To adopt this criterion is to make the existence or non-existence of a "sacrifice" depend, not on the nature of the action, but on the nature of the circumstances surrounding the individual or the class in question. A "sacrifice" can only be incurred in the measure that one has the luxury of alternatives to forego. No opportunities, no sacrifices! Only Lazarus can sacrifice nothing; while Dives, with the world and its fullness before him, can sacrifice daily enough to wash away the sins of mankind. Conceived subjectively, any cost-concept must lose its identity amid a world of choices and alternatives, where one facet of every choice is a utility and the other facet a "sacrifice" or "opportunity cost", and disutility retains no meaning except as utility foregone.

Let us, however, suppose a subjective loss or pain to be assumed to attach to the mere act of postponement.

[1] It remains formally distinguishable from the doctrine of "opportunity cost" as customarily stated to the extent that the latter usually represents the supply of factors of production as given quantities, while the former postulates that the supply of them is (in part) a function of their price (and hence that they have a "supply-price"). But in neither case is a more fundamental cause of their supply or non-supply (in the shape of a real cost "inevitably" requiring reward) any longer postulated.

Even so, there seems no convincing reason for identifying such a real cost with the receipt of interest: no reason to presume that the incidence of this cost rests (save in a sense so superficial as to rid it of meaning) upon the class to which interest accrues as income. The reason by which this identification is customarily defended is that the recipients of interest are those who take the immediate decision on which the act of "saving" depends. Yet it is by now a commonplace that the *ability* to save (in the shape of an income of a certain size) is the major factor in determining the volume of saving; while it is frequently those who claim the rich to be the bearers of abstinence that are the loudest in their assertions that if incomes were less unequally distributed, and the consumption of the poor were raised, capital accumulation would decline. If the latter be true, then it would seem that the final incidence of this cost of saving must lie, not upon the rich, but upon the restricted consumption of the poor, which alone permits those high incomes to be earned from which the bulk of investment is drawn. If we were defining the result of investment in an egalitarian socialist economy, we should have no doubt what to say: we should say that one of its results was a relative restriction of present consumption, the incidence of which fell on the community at large. Yet in the unequal society of to-day the pedlars of abstinence theories would have us believe that the restriction of present consumption which results from this investment falls upon the rich and not upon the poor, upon whose restricted consumption the high saving-ability of the former depends. If abstinence can be held to exist as a "real cost" at all, it must, surely, be regarded as being borne by the proletariat which receives no recompense for its pains, rather than by the capitalist who draws interest as price of the restricted consumption of others? To assert the contrary is, surely, to be guilty of the circular reasoning of assuming the income of the capitalist to be in some sense "natural" or "inevitable" in order to show that what he invests of this income is the unique product of his individual abstinence in refraining from doing what he likes with his own?

Apart from these fundamental difficulties in the concept of subjective real cost, there is a further reason why any cost-theory of this type is incompetent to explain interest as a concrete phenomenon in the actual world. The actual world is one in which capital accumulation is a continuing process, and not one in which production is carried on with a constant stock of capital, the interest earned on which is in "equilibrium" with a certain "supply-price of waiting". If there were, indeed, such an equilibrium, then no *new* capital accumulation would take place. Hence the "surplus" element in interest, even in the restricted sense in which the term "saver's surplus" is employed, is actually much greater than Marshall's theory on the face of it represents: for any existing stock of capital there is, in fact, not even an equality between the reward of capital and the "supply-price of waiting" *at the margin*.[1]

[1] Cf. F. P. Ramsey: If the rate of interest exceeds the rate of discounting the future "there will not be equilibrium, but saving, and since a great deal cannot be saved in a short time, it may be centuries before equilibrium is reached, or it may never be reached, but only approached asymptotically. . . . We see, therefore, that the rate of interest is governed primarily by the demand price, and may greatly exceed the reward ultimately necessary to induce abstinence." ("A Mathematical Theory of Saving" in *The Economic Journal*, December 1928, p. 556.) Cf. also Pigou, *Economics of Stationary States*, pp. 259-60. Of course, there is *an* equilibrium at the margin; but this applies only to *new* investment, current income being eaten into by "saving" until

Neither these ambiguities nor these special difficulties were involved in the interest-theory of Böhm-Bawerk. He had explicitly abandoned any attempt at explaining values in terms of cost, and for him a cost was always a determined, not a determining, element, representing simply an opportunity-cost or displaced alternative, dependent on the strength of competing demands. Thereby costs were all ultimately traceable back to demand and to utility. He was not concerned, therefore, with what he regarded, in that form, as the meaningless question as to whether any subjective real cost was involved in the supply of capital. He was concerned only with the question, on the one hand as to whether the act of postponing consumption, in other words an act of choice through time, had any peculiarity attaching to it which would cause a given quantity of present utility generally to be treated as equivalent to a *larger* quantity of utility in the future, and, on the other hand, whether the fact of time had any significance for the productivity of labour. He concluded that there was this peculiarity attaching to choices made through time: that the dimness of will and imagination, which was a general psychological trait of human beings, caused objects and events at a distance in time to be permanently discounted when balanced subjectively against equivalent objects and events which were close at hand; while, on the other hand, time had a significance for production in that labour expended on productive processes which took time ("roundabout" or

equilibrium is achieved (at the margin) between the restricted present expenditure and the (discounted) anticipated future income. This is what Prof. Pigou calls a "subordinate equilibrium". But there is never an equality between the interest currently received and the "marginal supply-price" of the existing stock of capital—if there were, there would be no *new* investment.

long or indirect methods of production) was generally more productive than labour expended directly to produce immediate output. These two influences were principally responsible for the fact that a competitive market always placed a premium on present goods as against future goods, both because in the individual estimation the former were valued more highly, and because the possession of goods in the present (*e.g.* subsistence for labourers) enabled labour to be employed on "roundabout" or long processes of production which would yield a larger final product than labour employed at short notice on immediate and current production. The one factor operated on the side of supply, and the other factor on the side of demand, to produce a permanent discount, *ceteris paribus*, of the "future" price of anything over its "spot" price. This premium or *agio* on present goods was the phenomenon of interest, which had given rise to the problem of "surplus-value". Not "human prospectiveness", as Marshall put it, but the prevailing weakness of human prospectiveness—or what Professor Pigou has aptly termed a deficiency of the telescopic faculty — was the explanation of the mystery which had perplexed economists for half a century.

It can hardly be denied that this ingenious theory contained positive elements which afford insight, descriptively and analytically, into certain aspects of the process of capital accumulation. Even though time or "roundaboutness" was clearly not the only, or even major, condition of the productivity of technical processes, it was clearly an important element; and since time was irreversible, the time-dimension of different productive processes assumed a particular significance in determining the order in which such processes were successively adopted. Moreover, the concept of "stored-up labour", as represented by an additional time-dimension (the length of time over which it was designed to be stored), was an objective one which was independent of the subjective theory of value in which the remainder of the theory was cast. But, viewed as a whole, as an explanation of surplus-value, the theory depended for its validity on the subjective theory of value of which it was simply a part and a particular application. Given the adequacy of this wider theory, its own adequacy seemed to be implied; since it showed that interest was simply the product of a general subjective estimation, as was any other value: in this case a subjective estimation of things separated through time. If the former was valid as a general explanation of value, so was the latter as the explanation of a particular value; if the former is invalid, then so also must the latter be.[1]

Yet, after his impressive critique of previous theories of interest, it is strange that the weakness of his own theory

---

[1] True, Böhm-Bawerk claimed that each of the factors of which he treated was alone sufficient to explain the phenomenon of interest. For this reason it might be held that his theory did not depend upon the subjective theory of value, since subjective under-estimation of the future was only *one* of the reasons for the emergence of interest. Without the influence of this subjective factor, however, the mere "technical superiority of roundabout methods" would clearly be incapable of explaining interest as an *enduring* phenomenon, and hence as a necessary consequence of permanent elements of the economic problem. By itself, it would rank no higher than any other of the productivity-explanations which Böhm-Bawerk himself condemned. The higher productivity of "roundabout methods" would not suffice to explain why labour applied to this particular use yielded a surplus-value, in the absence of some additional reason to explain why the application of labour to this use was restricted, and hence was relatively scarce. It might suffice to explain the surplus-value as a temporary and disappearing phenomenon due to the time required for the construction of these more productive "roundabout methods", but not as a phenomenon consistent with full equilibrium.

—its inability to answer essential questions—should not have been plain to its author, and particularly strange that he should have imagined that it afforded a sufficient answer to the problem as it was posed by Marx, and hence a refutation of the answer which Marx gave. In what sense did this theory explain the phenomenon of interest? Hardly in any sense which could assimilate interest to wages in its origin or in the character of its determination or in its universal "necessity" as a category of income. It amounted to an explanation in terms of the relative scarcity, or limited application, of labour applied to particular uses—namely, in the form of stored-up labour embodied in technical processes involving a lengthy "period of production": a scarcity which persisted by reason of the short-sightedness of human nature. As a result of this under-development of the productive resources, the ownership of money-capital, which in existing society provided the only means by which lengthy production-processes were able to be undertaken, carried with it the power to exact a rent of this scarcity. As a landlord could exact the price of a scarcity imposed by objective nature, so, it would seem, the capitalist could exact the price of a scarcity imposed by the subjective nature of man. If there was any significance in such analogies within the limits of this theory, it was, surely, between interest and rent, rather than between interest and wages? Like Ricardo and Marx, Böhm-Bawerk had condemned the inadequacy of mere "supply and demand" explanations.[1] But, confined as it was in the main within the limited circle of

[1] "The man who, when asked what determines a certain price, answers 'Demand and Supply', offers a husk for a kernel." (*Capital and Interest*, p. 66.)

exchange-relationships between factors of production abstracted from more fundamental social relationships, was his own theory any more competent to explain? True, he introduced into his theory one significant assumption about production: a technical fact, associated with the dimension of time. But why should he have chosen this technical fact in isolation from the rest and neglected the social relations which determined the place of man in production and his association with technique? The decisive factor in the supply of capital, according to his theory, was the subjective under-estimation of the future. Not only is this a factor which would not necessarily exist outside an individualist society, and the existence of which even in an individualist society has been denied by some; but the degree of this subjective under-estimation is itself dependent on the distribution of income, and hence on the class relations in society. Interest is, therefore, dependent on the latter in a double sense: in that the size of incomes among the capitalist class, relative to their accustomed standards of consumption, determines their attitude to saving and investment, while the poverty of the masses determines the price at which they are willing to sell their labour-power in return for immediate income. Hence, interest depends for its determination precisely on the type of social relations and institutions, historically determined and not universal, with which Marx was concerned. As will be seen in a subsequent chapter, in a socialist society there would be no reason for the under-estimation of the future which gives rise to interest as a persistent phenomenon to prevail, and no reason for the emergence of interest as a category of income at all. As a solution of the interest-problem in any sense which would be relevant to questions such as these, this theory is empty and deceptive. Moreover, it is not possible to say that its author had no intention of claiming it to be a solution in this more fundamental sense, and that he merely intended his theory to assemble descriptively some of the relevant variables of which any determinate explanation would have to take account. In his *Positive Theory of Capital*, he explicitly adduces as important corollaries of his theory that "the essence of interest is not exploitation", but that, on the contrary, interest is "an entirely normal phenomenon; is, indeed, an economic necessity", is "not an accidental 'historico-legal' category, which makes its appearance only in our individualist and capitalist society" and "would not disappear even in the Socialist State".[1]

But in this very application of the notion of utility a strange contradiction appears which takes us at once to the centre of the problem of the subjective theory of value. To be sufficient anchorage for a determinate theory of value, even formally viewed, it was necessary that utility should be conceived as an expression of some fairly permanent and consistent aspect of human psychology. This is not to say that human preferences had to be assumed to be unchangeable; but that they must not be so contingent and fickle as to make it improbable that they were independent of other variables in the system which they were intended to determine.[2] In so

[1] Pp. 361 and 371.
[2] Prof. J. M. Clark states his belief "that this type of theory acquires meaning just so far as there is attached to it some premise as to how choices actually do behave". (*Essays in Honour of J. B. Clark*, p. 54 f.) But it is not sufficient, for this purpose, to premise merely their behaviour: it is necessary to premise that this behaviour (or certain determining elements underlying it) is independent of the movement of market-prices.

far as utility could be hedonistically treated as a fundamental "satisfaction", then, as we have seen, it could reasonably be held to fulfil this condition. A process of rational selection among the objects of choice could then be held to make economic choice conform to certain fundamental traits of human psychology. Even though the *translation* of such choices into economic action was dependent on the distribution of income, the actual choices themselves might be treated as independent of market-prices. But if one can no longer link "desire" (the immediate volition or act of choice) with "satisfaction" (the more fundamental psychological event), then the validity of such an assumption of independence becomes very doubtful. Why should we not regard such "behaviour-reactions" as continually conditioned and modified by the market conditions which they meet? Böhm-Bawerk makes no attempt to maintain that the preference for present goods which lies at the basis of his theory of interest represents any superior "satisfaction" attaching to present goods: a holiday next year will give us as much happiness when it comes as a holiday next month, only we see the former more dimly in our imagination. If we grasp the present in preference to the future, it is a matter simply of the imagination, of defective rationality and ephemeral desire. Professor Pigou has indeed singled out this case of subjective overestimation of present utilities as the most important instance where "desire" and "satisfaction" diverge, to the detriment of economic welfare. In a very direct sense this subjective attitude to present and future is dependent on, and not independent of, the structure of market-prices: namely, that it admittedly varies with the income of the individual or class in question, since the latter will condition the degree of urgency of present wants and the strength with which they excite and obsess the imagination. An example of this is the fact that a group or a community may become cumulatively poorer because, having a high preference for the present, it becomes progressively less capable of providing for the future. In terms of its subjective attitudes, therefore, nothing determinate can be postulated or forecasted. Moreover, this attitude may vary in such a number of ways with such a number of influences as to throw almost as many doubts on its universality as on its constancy. It clearly may vary with the type of commodity offered for sale and the manner in which commodities are sold; it may vary according as the person is an impressionable youth or of more mature experience; it may vary according as the individual is making his choice *qua* isolated individual, or *in loco parentis familiae*, or *qua* collective person in the capacity of a member of a college, a club or a business company. Yet it was an application of subjective notions where their weakness was most evident that Böhm-Bawerk chose in order to provide a solution for the crucial problem of surplus-value. But the weakness which is specially manifest here serves to draw our attention to a defect which attaches to the whole structure.

When Bailey had said that value implied "a feeling or a state of mind which manifests itself in the determination of the will", he was expressing a notion which by the end of the century was to be woven into a system. The utility-theory interpreted the value of a commodity, and by derivation that of all the constituent factors required to make it, in terms of the service rendered in satisfying consumers' desires. But the relation was not directly between value and *aggregate* service (or total utility): these stood frequently in inverse ratio, as the early economists had observed. The direct relation was between value and utility *at the margin*; the crucial factor being the increment of satisfaction rendered to consumers by the final or marginal increment of a given supply. A housewife who pursued the motive of maximum satisfaction would achieve her aim by distributing her money so that the satisfaction yielded by the final penny spent in every direction was equal; since, if this equality was not achieved, she would have gained by spending less in one direction and more in another. This is a case of what Jevons called the Principle of Indifference. There can be seen to follow from this simple principle another one: namely, that the prices of various commodities on a market must stand in the ratio of their marginal utilities —of the satisfaction yielded to consumers by the final or marginal unit of each. If prices do not stand in this ratio, it will profit consumers to demand more of some commodities (those where the ratio of marginal utility : price is relatively high) and less of others (those where this ratio is relatively low), until equilibrium is achieved.

But this leaves the question: What fixes the position of the margin itself? To this the answer is that it is fixed by the available supply; which in turn raises the further question: What determines the limitation of supply? If the supply of all things was unlimited, there would be no unsatisfied desires, no marginal utility and no price. A price can, therefore, only arise because of the limitations imposed on the supply of commodities by the limitation of the factors of production required to produce them—a limitation expressing itself in the form of costs.

In the manner in which they have assumed these limits to be determined, two variants of the subjective theory of value are distinguished. On the one hand, the Austrian School assumed that, in any given set of conditions, the supply of such ultimate productive factors was fixed.[1] Being limited by an unalterable (for the moment) scarcity, these factors, like any commodity, would acquire a price equal to the marginal service which they could render in production; these prices formed the constituent elements of cost. On the other hand, Jevons and Marshall assumed that (with the exception of natural resources) these basic factors of production could be varied in supply, but that their variation was conditioned by the disutility, or the "effort and sacrifice", which their creation cost. Hence in equilibrium they must receive a price equivalent to the disutility (at the margin) involved in the supply of them. As Jevons put it: "Cost of production determines supply; supply determines final degree of utility [or 'marginal utility']; final degree of utility determines value"; and again, "Labour is found to determine value, but only in an indirect manner, by varying the utility of a commodity through an increase or limitation of the supply."[2] Pareto has summarized this notion in the phrase that value is the resultant of a conflict between desire and obstacles—obstacles which preclude the full satisfaction of desires. But the ultimate determinants

[1] Strictly speaking, the Austrians did not assume, or need to assume, that the supply of basic factors of production was unchangeable: merely that the quantity of them was determined by conditions external to the market, and hence could be treated as independent.

[2] *Theory of Political Economy*, p. 165.

of both sets of forces—both "blades of the scissors", in Marshall's phrase—are conceived as subjective in character, product of states of mind.

This structure seems to rest on a crucial assumption: namely, that the individual will is autonomous and independent, in the sense that it is not influenced by the market relations into which the individual enters or by the social relations of which he is part. No one, of course, would deny at least some influence of this kind. If it is of a minor character and confined to a few special types of influence, this can easily be allowed for without impugning the validity of treating the individual will and its characteristics as the determinant of economic relationships. But if this influence of social interaction is considerable, the validity of the assumption is shaken; and this atomistic treatment necessarily breaks down. Not only is it then likely that the fallacy of composition will be involved in any attempt to pass from the individual to the whole; but states of will or of mind will be incapable of being treated as "independent variables" in the determination of events.

Doubtless such an assumption seemed natural enough to a century of individualism, and may to-day seem natural enough to the isolated bourgeois individual, priding himself on his independence from social influences and social dependence. But anything more than a superficial analysis of the texture of society will show in what numerous ways the individual will, on the contrary to being autonomous or independent, is continually moulded by the complex of social and economic relations into which it enters. In the first place, the actual nature of the preferences which the individual exhibits, as well as the form in which they are translated into money, will be influenced by his position in society and the income he receives. For instance, his preference for present against future, as we have seen, or for leisure as against commodities, and hence the "sacrifice" which he incurs in working or saving, will depend upon his income; with the circular result that the nature of the fundamental costs which affect both the values of commodities and the rewards of the factors of production will be determined in turn by the distribution of income. A man who is landless will estimate the "sacrifice" or "disutility" involved in hiring himself to a master at much less than will a peasant farmer possessed of land and instruments of his own, since the destitute position of the former causes him to place a lower subjective valuation on his own labours in terms of the necessaries of life. The same will be true of workers backed by a trade union, as contrasted with unorganized workers with a traditionally low standard of life. Hence to postulate any normal values requires the prior postulation of a certain income-distribution and hence a certain class structure. To give a precise form to the exchange-relationships of a given society requires as data not merely the mental disposition of an abstract individual, but also the complex of institutions and social relations of which the concrete individual is a part. In the search for a spurious generality, such factors are "taken for granted" in the modern theory of value: in a formal sense you are at liberty to assume about them whatever you please. At best this seems akin to framing the laws of physics or astronomy without the "gravitational constant". But in practice a more positive error emerges, when the assumption as it stands is taken to be a description of actual economic society. As a positive descriptive statement, it is false by reason of its very partiality. It implies that economic phenomena are ruled by a series of contractual relations freely entered into by a community of independent individuals, each of whom knows well what he wants and has access to and knowledge of all the available alternatives. And since by unnoticed sleight of hand harmony has been introduced into the premise, harmony emerges in the conclusion.

As we have said, however, it may be maintained that the essential elements out of which human choice is constructed are capable of being postulated independently of the distribution of income and of the social position of the individual. The actual schedule of preferences— the fundamental "indifference-curves" of Pareto—are not affected by the state of the individual, whether he be rich or poor, starving or satisfied. Hence subjective attitudes, in this sense at least, are capable of being postulated as an independent basis for a determination of the value-problem. But, firstly, it is to be remarked that, even if this is so, such factors are not sufficient of themselves to determine the problem; and something additional requires to be postulated concerning the *position* of the individual if we are to know how these basic attitudes will be translated into actual choices and actual demands—what sort of demand-curves are constructed from given sets of indifference-curves.[1] Secondly,

[1] This is simply an example of the fact, expressed in Marshall's famous barter-case, that, given a system of indifference-curves, it is necessary to postulate the *position* in the plane from which each individual commences to conduct exchange-transactions before one can construct the actual demand- or offer-curves which will shape the course of the bargaining. Marshall defines this position in terms of the *stock* of each commodity held; but the principle has a wider application than to this simple case.

it is precisely these basic mental attitudes which it seems impossible to postulate, short of a hedonistic definition of utility or of some similar assumption. Otherwise what meaning can be given to these schedules of preferences which define the individual's attitude to any conceivable set of alternatives whether he may ever have experienced these alternatives or not—preference-schedules written presumably somewhere on the mind which would tell us, if we could discover them by introspection, how the millionaire would value leisure and income if he happened to be beggared, or how the means-test victim would behave if he suddenly acquired a fortune? If, as earlier notions of utility implied, "desires" which prompt immediate acts of choice coincide with some more fundamental "satisfaction" yielded by the object of choice, then probably some meaning can be given to the assumption of a constant set of mental attitudes of this kind. But if "desires" diverge from "satisfactions", the latter, even if they exist, will not rule behaviour, and so will have little relevance to the economic problem; while "desires" alone, divorced from any deeper roots that they may or may not have, can certainly not be held to display any such constancy or independence.

This brings us to a second reason which impugns the assumption that the individual will is independent: namely, the influence of convention and of propaganda. Both of these factors, to judge by the powerful influence which they so evidently exert on acts of choice, seem to be responsible for considerably greater divergence between "desire" and "satisfaction" than has been traditionally admitted by economists. Among the former are to be included all those complex influences which the desires and tastes of others exert on the individual, including the influence of class standards and of social emulation, to which Thorstein Veblen so forcibly drew attention. Among the latter are to be included all those devices of advertisement, suggestion and selling-artifice, which have become such a dominant characteristic of the present age. Their success depends on the extent to which they can mould and create desire; and in the degree of their success consumers' choice becomes a variable dependent upon the actions of producers. Moreover, consumers' desires are clearly open to the influence of suggestion in a variety of ways. The mere existence of a supply, if appropriately brought before the public gaze, may create a desire which did not exist before; while the amount and cunning of the sellers' propaganda may be decisive in determining whether people give books at Christmas or gloves or handkerchiefs or umbrellas; whether the public diet shall be composed more largely of bananas or fish or milk; whether the "drier side of England" or the Cornish Riviera is preferred as a holiday centre. When such propaganda can influence group-conventions, the marriage of these influences can exert redoubled power in shaping individual choice, as is fully exemplified in the slavery of fashion, where least of all can the individual be said to have a will of his or her own. In the sphere of world-trade to-day one can see the rising influence, both direct and indirect, of propaganda upon demand. "Buy British", "Buy Empire", "Buy German" campaigns shape consumers' preferences to moulds into which they would not otherwise fit. Apparently a paramount, and neglected, economic influence of the spread of national cultures beyond national frontiers is to create the taste for those things which bulk large in that nation's habitual consumption because that nation has some special facility in producing them. When one takes full account of the extent of such influences as these in the world to-day, there seems to be little doubt that they are a significant factor in the determination of demand in the case of nearly every commodity other than the prime necessaries of food and shelter.

Nor can the influence of convention be regarded as of minor importance. Human taste, beyond the most primitive level, has clearly been developed by a process of education in which custom and convention have played a principal rôle, together with other factors in the social environment. The most that can be postulated as innate to the "natural" individual is certain primary desires or tendencies of a not very differentiated kind. In the history of each individual, the precise configuration of that complex scale of preferences (even assuming such an entity) with which he is supposed to embark on life as an adult is clearly acquired from the influence of the society around him, and is afterwards subject to continual modification by such influence. Artificial silk becomes cheap and every girl factory-worker finds silk stockings to be a necessary element in her life because others wear them. The tailored suit becomes a necessity for the gentleman, who would suffer much loss of satisfaction if deprived of it, because a given station in life is conventionally marked by a given standard and style of dress. Most of the expenditures on house-decoration, furnishings and social entertainment are clearly controlled by the exactions of certain social standards. People drink afternoon tea or cocktails, and would be deprived of satisfaction if individually they had to abstain from them. Men enjoy the austere discomfort of the boiled shirt and starched collar because emulation demands. Their wives collect silver for the sideboard, and, a few years back, muslin curtains, palms or aspidistras for the parlour, as symbols of bourgeois respectability. Even a motor-car seems often to be desired as much for the status as for the use it gives. Some years ago a discussion took place in the pages of *Economica* as to whether any meaning could be given to the "total utility" of boots as measured by what a gentleman would pay if compelled to—perhaps £10 or £20 or £30—rather than walk barefoot to his office or his club. The answer was given that the question had no meaning, since, if boots were universally priced at £10 a pair or more, none but the very rich would wear them, and the average man would find little hardship in being seen in sandals, or even barefoot, when all his neighbours and equals were accustomed to do likewise.

That this assumption of the autonomous individual will, independent of social relations, was fully intended to be taken as a descriptive statement about economic society is evidenced by a significant corollary which the utility-theory was held to imply. And the evident zeal with which this corollary was emphasized reveals how far from innocent of apologetic obsessions the economists' choice of assumptions clearly was. This corollary was hailed as a decisive reinforcement of the case for *laissez-faire*, and consisted in the demonstration that a regime of free exchange achieved the maximum of utility for all parties. The argument was a plausible one, given its concealed assumptions; and even to-day, when part of its fallacy has been frequently pointed out, the fallacy seems to die hard and continually to reappear in altered guise. The clearest form of its demonstration is in the simplified case of the exchange between two sellers of two commodities, A and B. It follows as an alternative version of the principle which was referred to above that exchange between them will continue up to that rate of exchange at which the utility of *both* commodities (the amount of the commodity parted with and the amount of the commodity acquired in exchange) is equal for *each* of the two parties. Up to this point each party will gain more utility than he parts with by continuing to exchange A against B. Beyond it any rate of exchange must deprive one or both of the parties of more utility than he acquires in exchange, and consequently there can be no agreed rate of exchange which will satisfy both. The point of equilibrium, therefore, in the bartering— the rate of exchange which will be established on a free market—will be the point (as Jevons put it) where "both parties rest in satisfaction" and where "each party has obtained all the benefit that is possible". If this price is one which brings the greatest benefit to each, it must, therefore, be that which brings the greatest benefit to all: prices established under conditions of a free market maximize utility for all concerned. This corollary, which is implied rather than explicitly enunciated in Jevons' presentation of the theory, is emphasized more clearly by Walras and Pareto and by Auspitz and Lieben in their *Récherche sur la Theorie du Prix*.[1]

Some doubt should have been cast on the significance of such a maximum when subsequent discussion elicited the fact that there was, not one, but a number of rates of exchange where this condition (the equal utility of

---

[1] Walras' interest in economic theory, indeed, appears to have been prompted by discussion with a Saint-Simonian and the consequent desire to furnish a simple proof that free exchange on a competitive market yielded an *optimum* result. (Cf. Wicksell, *Lectures*, Vol. I, pp. 73-4.)

TREND OF MODERN ECONOMICS

both commodities to each of the two parties) was fulfilled. Under the simple barter conditions cited by Jevons equilibrium might be reached at any one of these points, according to which party secured the advantage in the preliminary stages of the bargaining; and any one of these points could equally well be a position of "satisfaction". But any such position of "satisfaction" is clearly relative to the situation of the individual at the time when the bargain is undertaken. In any given situation the resources and the choice of alternatives which lie before the individual are restricted, and in a capitalist society most notably restricted by the class to which the individual belongs. In this given situation in which the individual finds himself there may be one path consistent with his best advantage, which it will profit him to take; but that path is determined for him by external circumstances, and is not the path he would have trodden had his situation been different. A relative maximum of this kind could only approximate to a *maximum maximorum*, possessed of any absolute significance, on the assumption that each individual had free range of opportunities, and had only taken the road he had after surveying and estimating the range of extant alternatives. This is what can*not* be postulated of capitalist society; and it is the absence of this assumption—indeed, the existence of the direct opposite, namely, class division—which forms the necessary starting-point for any understanding of the specific character of capitalist society. Yet this was precisely the assumption which the originators of the Utility School had illicitly introduced. That the assumption is still apt to pass unnoticed is indicated by the fact that it still forms the tacit basis to-day of most of the comparisons of the effects of a competitive and of a monopoly regime, or of a capitalist and a socialist regime, which are made in economic writing.[1]

Aware of the difficulties in the conception of utility, economists have been increasingly inclined in recent years either to abandon the concept of utility or else to define it anew in a purely empirical sense. The empirical fact that individual desires express themselves in observable *choices* on a market is postulated, and equations to determine economic events are constructed with such choices as the given data; irrespective of what either the psychological or the social roots of these choices may be. Thus Pareto started with the use of the concept of *Utilité* and later abandoned it for *Ophélimité*;[2] and Cassel, who was fond of parading familiar ideas in novel wording, eschewed the word utility altogether. Professor Robbins denies that utility can ever be compared for two individuals (characteristically using the denial to rebut certain implications of the Law of Diminishing Marginal Utility as to the damage done to economic welfare by inequalities of wealth), and asserts that all that economics as a "positive science" is right in assuming is that each individual arranges the objects of choice according to a certain scale of preference.[3] Economics becomes a sort of theory of "catallactics", in

[1] Professor Pigou states that "all comparisons between different taxes and different monopolies, which proceed by an analysis of their effects upon consumers' surplus, tacitly assume that demand-price is also the money measure of satisfaction". (*Econs. of Welfare*, p. 24.) Cf. also *Collectivist Econ. Planning*, Ed. Hayek.

[2] Cf. *Manuel d'Econ. Politique* (Ed. 1909), p. 157.

[3] *Essay on the Nature and Significance of Econ. Science*, Second Ed., p. 137 et seq. Professor Robbins claims for modern economic theory this superiority over the Ricardian system, that the former has "press(ed) through to the valuations of the individual". (*Ibid.*, p. 20.) Can one not complain of it that it has pressed through *no further* than the valuations of the individual?

which "there is no penumbra of approbation round the theory of equilibrium. Equilibrium is just equilibrium."[1]

It might appear as though this was to evade the essential problem by retreating into pure formalism, and that a theory defined in this way, and so emptied of real content, had reached a level of abstraction at which it was impotent to deliver any important judgment on practical affairs, at any rate on the problems peculiar to a particular system of economic society. If all that is postulated is simply that men *choose*, without anything being stated even as to how they choose or what governs their choice, it would seem impossible for economics to provide us with any more than a sort of algebra of human choice, indicating certain rather obvious forms of inter-relationship between choices, but telling us little as to the way in which any actual situation will behave. Moreover, as we have already seen, if the "demand schedule" of individuals is not conceived to rest on something ultimate or fundamental, it cannot be very solid anchorage for a system of market-equilibria. If demand may change with every wind that blows over the face of the market, as it may if we postulate nothing but empirical desires, what entitles us to assume that such desires are not entirely creatures of price-movements? Indeed, if for this theory "equilibrium is just equilibrium", it looks very much as though a mere generalized definition of equilibrium is all that we are pro-vided with. Such a clarification of definitions may be a highly useful, indeed an essential, task. But can it pro-vide any more than the empty shell of a theory of *Political* Economy, in the sense of a study of the problems of actual

[1] *Essay on the Nature and Significance of Econ. Science*, Second Ed., p. 143.

economic society and the type of question which they raise? In the first edition of his *Essay*, Professor Robbins, indeed, declared that the corollaries of economic theory depended, not upon facts of experience or of history, but were "implicit in our definition of the subject-matter of Economic Science as a whole":[1] a statement which seemed sufficiently to characterize the theory as a system of tautology. In his second edition this reveal-ing admission is abandoned: instead, it is pleaded that economic theory is by no means "merely formal", that it rests on postulates which are, in fact, elementary generalizations about any and every type of economic activity, and that its corollaries represent "inevitable implications", which, far from being "historico-relative" in character, hold true of any and every type of economic society.[2] But it must be difficult for many to be re-assured by this re-statement when they learn that the slender substratum of fact on which these laws of universal application are made to rest still consists simply in the postulate of individual choice. Choice is, of course, not confined to the type of activities which are traditionally known as "economic"; and it transpires that we are being furnished with an abstraction so general as to embrace features common to *any* type of human activity. This, indeed, Professor Robbins frankly admits. "Every act which involves time and scarce means for the achievement of one end involves the relinquishment of their use for the achievement of another (and) has an

---

[1] *Essay on the Nature and Significance of Econ. Science*, First Ed., p. 75.
[2] *Ibid.*, Second Ed., pp. 80, 105, 121. Mr. H. D. Henderson has also claimed that economic theory postulates laws which rule whether "merchant adventurers, companies and trusts; Guilds, Governments and Soviets may come and go", operating "under them, and, if need be, in spite of them all". (*Supply and Demand* (Ed. 1932), p. 17.)

economic aspect."[1]   Professor von Mises is even more definite: "It is illegitimate to regard the 'economic' as a definite sphere of human action which can be sharply delimited from other spheres of action.   Economic activity is rational activity. . . . The sphere of economic activity is coterminous with the sphere of rational action."[2] The principles here enunciated, and their "inevitable implications", consequently refer, and refer only, to *an* aspect of every type of human activity—to cooking and housekeeping, to games and recreation, to the planning of a holiday, to the choice between being a philosopher or a mathematician, as well as to what are usually known as the specific problems of production and exchange. But if this is the case—if economic principles are admittedly so tenuous an abstraction of one aspect of human affairs from all the rest—one is surely justified in doubting whether the imperative character of the corollaries which such a theory is competent to yield can be of any high order of importance for the specific problems to which the specific characteristics of this or that type of economic society give rise.

The search for logically concise definitions of one's subject-matter, which is so popular to-day, must generally be barren, and when pushed to an extreme must result in emptying ideas of real content and attaining little but an arid and scholastic dogmatism.   This tendency would seem to be product, not merely of a passing fashion, but of a more fundamental defect. What so many apparently ignore to-day is the lesson which Marshall was primarily concerned to teach in the Hegelian Principle of Continuity which he reiterated

---

[1] *Essay on the Nature and Significance of Econ. Science*, Second Ed., p. 14.   [2] *Die Gemeinwirtschaft*, Eng. trans., p. 124.

in the classic Preface to the first edition of his *Principles* (by comparison with which so much modern economic writing appears shallow and unsophisticated): [1] that in the real world there are no hard and fast boundary lines, as there are in thought, and that discontinuity and continuity are inevitably entwined. It is doubtless true that in Marshall's work certain aspects of continuity received exaggerated and one-sided emphasis—that his motto, *Natura non facit saltum*, was given a conservative emphasis. Yet by comparison with most modern writing, his approach to intellectual problems at least bore the stamp of a healthy realism: a virtue to which is, I think, traceable much that has appeared as eclecticism and obscurity to his critics; and which owed its origin to the fact that he had sufficient philosophic background to appreciate something of the complex character of the relation between abstract ideas and reality and to be anxious to keep his feet planted on the ground. It is only at the sacrifice of any comparable realism that precise definitions of the type which is fashionable to-day can be attained. Clearly, any realistic definition of a study like economics must run primarily in terms of the concrete problems which it adopts as its subject-matter (as is the case with any science): it must be a

[1] "If the book has any special character of its own, that may perhaps be said to lie in the prominence which it gives to . . . applications of the Principle of Continuity. . . . There has always been a temptation to classify economic goods in clearly defined groups, about which a number of short and sharp propositions could be made, to gratify at once the student's desire for logical precision, and the popular liking for dogmas, that have the air of being profound and are yet easily handled. But great mischief seems to have been done by yielding to this temptation, and drawing broad artificial lines of division where nature has made none. The more simple and absolute an economic doctrine is, the greater will be the confusion . . . if the dividing lines to which it refers cannot be found in real life." (*Principles*, First Ed., viii-ix.)

definition by type rather than by delimitation. The definition of economics must be given by the slice of the real world which it handles, and the generalizations it creates, to be adequate, must represent the essential features of its real terrain. Whether it is successful or not in achieving this appropriate blend of generality and realism is a question of *fact*: through worship of epigram to abstract certain *aspects* only of events and enshrine them in isolation from the rest may win an appearance of superb generality, but only at the expense of reality. Precision may be a most desirable, even an essential, ingredient of the process of thought, as is sharpness of steel in cutting. But when sharpness of the tool and of its product are confused, when precision is sanctified as the end of thought and made the touchstone of truth, thought is rendered flat and sterile, and ideas become husks lacking the substance of life.

But the most abstract of economists, of course, intends to state considerably more about the real world than simply that human beings make choices. As Professor Robbins tells us there are "subsidiary postulates"; and these postulates, as he admits (a trifle reluctantly), are "drawn from the examination of what may often be legitimately designated historico-relative material". The truth seems to be that it is with these "subsidiary postulates" that Political Economy properly begins. At any rate, it is on such postulates that the realistic corollaries drawn by economists depend. Least of all could one charge Professor Robbins with a disregard for the practical implications of economic theory, however abstract his definition of the latter may be. But it is precisely with these "subsidiary postulates" that assumptions about economic society are implicitly introduced

which are substantially similar to those of earlier economists, and which are of the type that we have referred to
as that of the autonomy and independence of the individual
will. Indeed, the very form in which abstract postulates
about individual choices are put constitutes them a distorted description of the actual forces which control
economic phenomena in capitalist society, unless they
are radically qualified by statements concerning the
social relations by which individual choices are governed
and the choices of *classes* are differentiated in capitalist
society. The mere absence of any such qualification
means that the statement that individuals *choose*, as soon
as it is made concrete in the form that individuals choose
in a particular way, becomes the false statement that
individuals choose *freely*, and that the events which are
the outcome of these individual actions are unaffected
by those basic productive relations—class relations connected with ownership of economic property—which are
the distinguishing characteristic of capitalist society.
Assumptions which are concealed are stubborn; and
despite Wicksteed's hope that mathematical statement
might serve as a reagent to "precipitate the assumptions
held in solution in the verbiage of our ordinary disquisitions", the increasingly mathematical economics of
to-day still rests substantially on the same basic premises.
The difference, so far as its apologetic influence is concerned, is that the conjuror's skill is now improved, so
that the corollaries which he produces with much patter
about "ethical neutrality" and with considerable elegance
of technique seem to his audience to be created *a priori*
from scientific principles of universal validity. Yet the
secret assumptions are there all the time, implicit in the
very formulation of the question; and even though out-

moded "utility" may be banished from the forestage, the desires of a free-acting individual are still conceived as ruling the market, and this "sovereignty" (as one writer has recently called it) [1] of the autonomous consumer is still the basis of any laws that are postulated and any forecasts that are made. So it is that economists will continue to contrast the autonomy of the consumer under capitalism with the "economic authoritarianism" of a socialist economy. [2] The fact is, of course, that the valuations of the market under capitalism represent a very high degree of authoritarianism. This assumption which rules subjective economics to-day—rules it, not simply as an incidental "additional assumption", but by virtue of the very form in which the whole problem is necessarily set—is parallel to a similar assumption which underlies the traditional theory of politics and of the State: namely, that the State is the expression of some kind of general will constructed out of the multi-

[1] Professor W. H. Hutt in *The South African Journal of Economics*, March 1934; where he declares that the principle is fundamental to economics. Cf. also his *Economists and the Public*, p. 257 *et seq.*

[2] A particularly naïve example of this occurs in the following passage: "That the consumption of the rich weighs more heavily in the balance than the consumption of the poor . . . is in itself an 'election result', since in a capitalist society wealth can be acquired and maintained only by a response corresponding to the consumers' requirements. Thus the wealth of successful business men is always the result of a consumers' plebiscite, and, once acquired, this wealth can be retained only if it is employed in the way regarded by consumers as most beneficial to them." (Mises, *op. cit.*, p. 21.) If in a certain community where plural or proxy voting was permissible a group of ambitious gentry managed to accumulate, by fair means or foul, a majority of the votes, and at successive elections thereafter proceeded to vote the retention of plural voting, Prof. Mises would presumably pronounce this a consistent democracy since the whole process was an "election result", and approve the actions of the self-appointed rulers on the ground that they reflected the decisions of a plebiscite as to what was beneficial to the majority.

tude of autonomous wills of free and equal individuals. In the economic sphere, as in the political, the facts of a class society belie the idyllic picture. What the power of a capitalist Press is in the one case, that of the advertiser is in the other. What class influence is in the one, class convention is in the other. In both spheres, differences of economic status, and the economic dependence of ownerless upon owners, are dominating factors. Moreover, in the economic realm "plural voting" is the rule, and not an exception; and it is a plurality which extends to some casting a thousand or ten thousand votes to another's one. Yet the majority of economic writings refer to the rule of the consumer because there is a market as naïvely as Herr Hitler will speak of his Totalitarian State as product of popular will because he has held a plebiscite.

As one might be led to expect, it is in the so-called Theory of Distribution that the most direct evidence of abstract concepts framed to apologetic purposes is to be found. It would hardly be incorrect to say that modern economics contains no theory of distribution worthy of the name. But that is not to deny that there have been pretentious claimants to this office. Outstanding among these has been the theory of marginal productivity. What is instructive is that this theory, which most strikingly bears the stamp of the mathematical method, has seen most practical service as a reply to critics of the capitalist system; and while the significance of the theory, when properly stated, is generally admitted to-day to be purely formal in character, it has been and continues to be used as an answer to the type of problem to which Marx's theory of surplus-value was framed as an answer, and hence as a refutation, or at least a sufficient substitute, for the latter. This theory is clearly a lineal descendant of the older theories of productivity of capital; but rid of the more obvious crudities of the older theories by the application to the "productivity" of different factors of the concept of differential increments. Yet it was this very refinement which, in fact, robbed it even of the slender claim to answer the practical problem of surplus-value which the crude productivity theory had had. By stating that the price of a factor of production (whether land, labour or capital) tended on a competitive market to equal the difference made to the total produce (measured in value) by the addition of a marginal unit of that factor (as the price of a final commodity was equal to the utility of a marginal unit), it was providing no more than a more precise formulation of traditional supply and demand explanations. And as Marshall hastened to point out, it could not constitute "a complete theory of distribution", since it left unanswered the problem as to the nature and determination of the supply of the various factors of production. Virtually it represented a further step towards treating not only commodities, but also the animate and inanimate instruments of production, simply as objects of market exchange, in complete abstraction from even the concrete activities of production, not to mention the basic social relations of which they were part. Yet the theory was immediately hailed as a complete reply to the classical problem of profit, rendering Ricardo and Marx obsolete. J. B. Clark hailed it as a newly discovered "law of nature"; and although few economists to-day are to be found to agree with him in so rash a statement, an important number of them, I believe, would subscribe to the view that there is some significant sense in which the theory could be said to show that the rule of competition "gave to each factor of production the equivalent of what it created". At any rate, whatever the private beliefs of professional economists, it seems not untrue to say that ninety-nine per cent. of their audience understand some such conclusion to be implied.

The action of critics of the new doctrine at first tended to greater confusion rather than to clarity, owing to their concentration on what proved to be a purely formal problem—the so-called "adding-up problem". The question which they asked was whether, if each of the factors was priced according to its "marginal productivity" as defined, the price of all of them when added together would equal the total product, no more and no less. In pursuing this largely scholastic inquiry they implied that, if this condition could in fact be fulfilled, the theory would have significance as a theory of distribution. This was the line of criticism adopted by Mr. J. A. Hobson, when he claimed that a factor of production could not be rewarded at a value equivalent to its *marginal* productivity, but must be rewarded at its *average* productivity. Unless the latter were true, the sum of the earnings of factors of production could not equal the total product. The reply to this criticism was simply to define the situation in more precise, and more abstract, terms; and to show that when competition was fully defined "normal equilibrium" must imply that marginal costs for each enterprise were equal to average costs (at a point where average costs are a minimum), so that the crucial condition was accordingly fulfilled by the very definition of competitive prices.

It is not, I think, without significance that Wicksteed, to whom so much of the mathematical refinement of this theory is traceable, principally used it to attack the Ricardian theory of rent and to demonstrate that any concept of surplus-value was untenable. What he failed to emphasize, or apparently to see, was that the very form of statement which made a concept of surplus meaningless in terms of this theory, simultaneously rendered meaningless any of those practical corollaries which justified its claim to be a realistic theory of distribution, and which he apparently held to be implicit in the theory. Wicksteed pointed out that the Ricardian theory of rent, formally regarded, was a "residual theory". Expressed in mathematical terms, it stated that "the whole produce being $F(x)$, and $F'(x)$ being the rate of remuneration per unit which satisfied capital-plus-labour, the whole amount which capital-plus-labour will draw out will be $x . F'(x)$, and the remaining $F(x) - x . F'(x)$ will be rent. Now this is simply a statement that when all other factors of production have been paid off, the 'surplus' or residuum can be claimed by the landowner."[1] If $S = x + y + z$, and $x + y$ are given, it must necessarily follow that z is determined as equal to $S - (x + y)$. Such a mathematical truism, said Wicksteed, could equally well be applied to x and to y, as to z. On the same line of reasoning the price of capital or the price of labour could be treated as a "residual surplus": it was all a matter of which factor was taken as "given" and which as the residual variable to be determined. But Wicksteed (like his present-day disciples) failed to notice that what renders the theory of rent a mathematical truism is the purely formal mode of stating it which he adopted; and that this formal mode of statement also makes the whole

---

[1] P. H. Wicksteed, *Co-ordination of the Laws of Production and Distribution*, pp. 17-18.

theory, as a theory of distribution, a truism, once the concept of competition is fully defined.[1] Naturally, no distinction between factors of production can exist on the purely formal plane: x, y, z are symbols which have no differentia except their notation. Rent and Profit are not differentiated from Wages by the rules of algebra: if they are to be distinguished it must be by characteristics introduced from the real world—characteristics associated with the actual activities which lie behind these price-phenomena. Wicksteed, indeed, declares that the theory as he expounds it seeks the laws of distribution "not in the special nature of the services rendered by the several factors, but in the common fact of *service* rendered"; [2] which apparently amounts to an admission that the principal differentiating qualities in factors of production have been, *ex hypothesi*, excluded and the theory erected simply on the premise that the factors in question are essential to production and hence are in demand. On this basis, to affirm an essential harmony of interests between classes, to deny the existence of "surplus-value" and "exploitation", and so forth, is a simple case of *petitio principii*.[3] To inquire whether a

[1] Wicksteed clearly thought otherwise. He thought that the theory could furnish "suggestions as to the line of attack we must follow in dealing with monopolies, and with the true socializing of production"—suggestions "magnificent in their promise". (*Ibid.*, p. 38.) Elsewhere he considers it a significant criticism of monopoly to say that it gives the monopolists "more than their distributive share in the product as measured by their marginal industrial efficiency". Actually, as "marginal industrial efficiency" is defined by this theory, the statement is equivalent to saying that the monopolists receive more than they would receive under competition, and is capable of meaning no more than this.

[2] *Ibid.*, p. 7.

[3] How purely formal the difference between factors of production has become is well expressed by the fact that Wicksteed, in addition to suggesting that ploughs, manure, horses, foot-pounds of power must be treated as separate factors of production, also suggested the inclusion

factor of production is being paid more or less than its "marginal productivity" has substantially the same meaning (and no more) as to ask whether conditions of competition prevail in the market or not. Moreover, by appropriate re-definition the concept can be made to apply to the pricing of factors of production under conditions of monopoly.[1]

What has here been said in criticism is not intended to deny that mathematical economics may have much to contribute to the refinement of implications and the clarification of assumptions. Nor is it to deny that the subjective attitudes of individuals play a rôle as links in the chain of economic events, and hence have a place in any complete analysis of economic phenomena. But it is to say that so long as mathematical technique retains its servitude to a particular mode of thought, the concepts which it fashions are calculated to veil rather than to reveal reality. For this mode of thought, which is enshrined in the subjective theory of value, first creates for us a realm where disembodied minds hold communion with etherealized objects of choice, and then, unmindful of the distance between this abstract world and reality, seeks to represent the relations which it finds in this realm as governing the relations which hold in actual economic society and as controlling the shape which

(for purpose of formal completeness) of "the body of customers and their desires" and even "commercial pushing", "goodwill" and "notoriety" as factors of production, each priced according to its marginal productivity (*op. cit.*, pp. 33-5). Mrs. Robinson has defined a separate factor as anything which has any technical difference at all from any other requisite of production, *i.e.* something which has no perfect substitute— a definition applauded by Professor Robbins for its formal elegance and economy. (Cf. *Econs. of Imperfect Competition*, pp. 108-9.) Such definitions are certainly elegant, but they are also very attenuated.

[1] Cf. Joan Robinson, *The Economic Journal*, September 1934.

events must have under any and every system of social institutions. This is to confuse thought and to distort reality. It is to have everything standing on its head. To emancipate economic thought from this heritage is a task that is long overdue.

CHAPTER VI

CONCERNING FRICTIONS AND EXPECTATIONS: CERTAIN RECENT TENDENCIES IN ECONOMIC THEORY

ONE of the marked features of economic thought in recent years, and in particular in the last decade, has been a decline in the older dogmatism, a quickening of scepticism and a reawakening of controversy. What a few years back was treated as settled doctrine, requiring only refinement of its implications and application to special problems, is to-day questioned in its basic assumptions. Systems of thought whose final shape was regarded as perfected, save for a few trifling elaborations, are thrown back into the melting-pot. In these movements of thought it is not hard to see reflected the startling events of the real world of affairs in the last two decades. On its practical side this deepening of scepticism has consisted in the virtual break-up of *laissez-faire* as a body of doctrine: one might almost say that it is of this that the shift of doctrine has essentially consisted— a change which has followed and not preceded the decline of *laissez-faire* in the real world. To-day this doctrine, at least in its traditional form, retains relatively few, if noteworthy, defenders. But it can hardly be said that where the old faith and certainty has been supplanted much beside confusion and eclecticism at present reign.

These recent shifts of perspective mainly centre, I

believe, in two significant modifications of traditional assumptions. Both of these seem to be connected with the characteristics of a new age of monopoly, the one directly, the other only indirectly. The first of these consists in a criticism, or at least reconsideration, of the traditional concept of competition and an attempt to restate the conditions of equilibrium in terms of monopoly or the presence of monopolistic elements. The second consists in an emphasis on the qualifications which have to be introduced into traditional equilibrium-analysis— into the statement of economic laws and tendencies— in situations where the expectations of individuals can exercise a significant influence on events. The traditional doctrine of *laissez-faire*, as we have seen, was based on the harmonious and self-regulating effect of competition, whether this was stated in the form of the classical law of cost or according to the subjective theory of value in the form of the equality of marginal utility and cost. If, in fact, not this but a different equilibrium rules, the results of actual *laissez-faire* must be different from those which have been imagined. Again, the essence of the classical theory had been that what ultimately occurred was independent of the subjective wishes or expectations of the individual entrepreneur. If this was not so, and subjective expectations became an independent determining factor in the result, the "invisible hand" was to that extent thwarted, and again the outcome of actual *laissez-faire* must be different from what had previously been deduced.

Both innovations were concerned with the significance of factors which are usually referred to as "frictions". Traditionally it had been admitted that where competition was displaced by absolute monopoly, or something approaching it, the price was determined (within limits) by the will of the monopolist, and the cost-principle no longer applied to what was now a situation of deliberately contrived scarcity. But in all intermediate situations where sellers (and buyers) were numerous, elements which rendered the market "imperfect" and caused it to depart from the abstract ideal of competition were treated simply as frictions which either delayed the attainment of the equilibrium-position, without altering the nature of the position which would eventually be reached, or else introduced definite spatial differences in price—differences which were themselves a simple and direct function of the frictional element. For instance, ignorance of the market or inertia of producers was held to delay the operation of competitive forces, and so to allow any departure of price from normal to be longer sustained, but not to alter the fact that, given time for adjustments to be made, equilibrium would again be reached, even if more tardily than would otherwise have been the case. On the other hand, costs of movement between different parts of a market, separated in time or in space, would introduce definable differences in price as one moved away from the source of supply, these differences varying in precise ratio to the costs of movement translated into terms of price. The novelty of more recent theories lies in this: that the presence of certain of these factors, such as ignorance, inertia or costs of movement, are treated as having not merely this type of frictional effect, but of altering the nature of the equilibrating forces and of the equilibrium eventually reached.

What, then, is the criterion of when a friction is not a friction—or, rather, is something more than a friction?

How are we to tell whether certain "disturbing influences" are likely merely to disturb the "fit" of an approximation by a certain minor and calculable amount, or whether their presence transforms the situation in a qualitative sense? It might seem at first sight as though this would be wholly a matter of degree—of the magnitude of the disturbing friction compared to the strength of the other forces at work. But there is also a difference of kind involved—a difference in the nature of the frictional element in relation to the situation into which it is introduced.

The introduction of a new element into a situation may affect that situation in a number of ways. First, while it may have the effect of weakening or delaying the operation of certain of the determining influences, and so of retarding the working of the equilibrating forces after an initial displacement has occurred, it may be held to be irrelevant to the ultimate equilibrium that is reached because it leaves unaffected the nature of the determining forces. Of this type is the influence of ignorance and inertia according to the older theory. In this case the new element is such that it can be considered as leaving unaltered any of the variables in the equations which define equilibrium. Thus, a narrowing of the pipe connecting two cisterns will not alter the fact that the water will find the same level in the two, even though it will delay the process by which this equality is achieved

Secondly, the new element may cause a displacement of the situation by a simple and determinate amount. The friction in this case not merely delays, but shifts, the equilibrium which is reached. But its effect in doing so is simple and additive. Here the new factor in the situation is treated as though it were an additional constant, altering by a given amount the value of one or more of the variables in the governing equations; as the effect of costs of movement on price, according to the older view, was virtually treated as an addition to the supply-price or a subtraction from the demand-price. Its influence is thus of the same kind as that of any other of the data. If its quantitative importance is small relatively to that of the other factors which the theory in its first approximation had embraced, then it can properly be regarded as a mere disturbing factor, weakening the precision but not damaging the essential correctness of the previous generalization. At any rate, while its presence or absence may alter the values which the equations yield, its presence or absence leaves the essential form of the equations unchanged.

Thirdly, the introduction of the new element may transform the situation in a much more radical manner, in the sense of altering the character of the actual relations which hold between various quantities. Its influence can then no longer be properly regarded merely as that of a retarding or displacing friction: it is rather that of a new chemical element, the presence of which alters the character and action of other elements and so transforms the whole composition. Its effect is no longer simple and additive; and its presence can only be properly treated as actually changing one or more of the equations (expressing given conditions or postulating relations between quantities). But the new situation is capable of being rendered determinate, like the old, provided that the number of equations (or separate relationships which are known about it) can be made equal to the number of dependent variables. It is this type of influence which factors such as inertia or costs of movement have in certain recent theories of "imperfect competition." [1]

The difference between the first two of these types would seem to be partly one of degree. It is often a matter of one's time-reference—whether one is referring to events at a near or a distant period of time, to the equilibrium of a short period or a long period—whether a given frictional element can be regarded as merely retarding or as displacing. Moreover, if one's statements are dynamic in character and refer to a path of movement and not merely to a static position of rest (that is, if certain of one's equations express variables as a function of time), any friction that weakens and delays the action of any forces will *ipso facto* modify the subsequent path of events.

The essential difference for our present purpose is between cases of the first and second types, on the one hand, and of our third on the other. The simplest example of a transition from the former to the latter is where the influence of the retarding or displacing friction is sufficiently strong to eliminate entirely the influence of one or more of the main determining factors; as an obstruction in the connecting-pipe between two cisterns, which, if sufficiently small, may merely retard the flow between, if it grows important enough to inhibit the

---

[1] Cases of this third type seem to be those to which J. S. Mill's principle of "composition of causes" would fail to apply. They would also seem to be cases to which Prof. J. M. Clark refers as those where the introduction of change produces differences which are "qualitative or chemical in character" as distinct from being purely "quantitative". (*Econ. Essays in Honour of J. B. Clark*, pp. 46-7.) But I fail to understand what he means when he states that in equilibrium-analysis the "adaptive forces" need to be confined "to those which are self-limiting and not cumulative in character" (p. 48). Surely "self-limiting" or "cumulative" can only be applied to the nature of the total situation, and not to individual factors in it?

flow altogether may render the level of water in each of them entirely independent of the level in the other. What is of crucial importance in recent criticisms of the older concept of competition is that the presence in the market of frictions, such as ignorance, inertia or cost of movement, even in a small degree, is treated as introducing a change of our third type. Not only may their presence cause prices in different parts of the market to diverge from "normal" by an amount equivalent to the size of the friction, but it may cause the level of "normal price" throughout the market to be different from what it would otherwise be. The effect of the friction on price will be a double one—one direct in permitting spatial differences to occur, one indirect in changing the equilibrium-level itself. The traditional statement of "normal price" in a perfect market rested on the assumption that, since the individual was one among many, any action of his own could exert only a negligible influence on the market-price. The individual had to take the market-price as he found it and to treat it as independent of any action of his own in expanding or contracting sales or purchases. Hence, as a seller, he could never gain larger total or net receipts by restricting output (so long as price was higher than his marginal cost), and it would always profit him to expand output up to the point where the selling-price (and hence his additional receipts from extended sales) was equal to his marginal cost. Analogous considerations would apply if he were an entrepreneur buying factors of production in a perfect market. This is equivalent to saying that the demand for what the individual sold and the supply of what the individual purchased was infinitely elastic. If certain types of frictional element were present, however, this assumption would no longer hold; since the presence of the friction would have the effect precisely of rendering the demand for what the individual sold, or the supply of what he purchased, in some degree inelastic. For instance, the cost of visiting a rival retailer half a mile distant, or even inertia or ignorance as to the facilities he offered, would create a preference for buying from the near-by and familiar grocer, even though his price were higher; and similarly with workers accepting lower wages from an employer rather than move and seek employment in another district or town. If this inelasticity were at all appreciable, it would create a range within which the possibility was created for the individual seller to increase his net receipts by *restricting* his sales, even when price ruled at a level *above* his marginal cost; and analogously for an individual buyer in restricting his purchases. Hence the competitive principle that price would tend to be equated with marginal cost was replaced by the principle which Mrs. Robinson has termed [1] the equality of marginal revenue and marginal cost. In other words, each individual will base his action on the monopolistic principle of contracting output to the point at which his profit is a maximum. As a subsidiary principle it will follow that producing units, as represented by the scale of operations of an individual entrepreneur, will tend to be smaller than the most efficient size, instead of equal to the most efficient size (estimated in terms of current market-values) as the traditional theory of competition implied. To this view, therefore, the competitive principle will apply *only* in a market where frictions are completely absent—in other words, only in the rarest, and in a sense the most "arti-

---

[1] In *The Economics of Imperfect Competition.*

ficial", of cases in the real world (*e.g.* in organized produce markets). Where frictions are present in any noticeable degree, not only may prices diverge between different parts of the market, but the equilibrium-level itself will be differently determined, and determined according to the principle of monopoly.[1]

Thought appears to have been directed along these lines, so far as this country is concerned, by a path-breaking article by Mr. Sraffa in *The Economic Journal* for 1926; although for some time the significance of the hint contained in it does not seem to have been fully appreciated.[2] This article suggested that since most markets for the products of industry were in fact broken up into more or less separate "private markets" for each firm, the situation was properly to be treated in terms of the theory of monopoly rather than of the classical theory of competition. It was further suggested that this prevalence of monopolistic restriction, as a general and not merely an exceptional feature of capitalist industry, even where apparent competition prevailed,

---

[1] A good example of the change of treatment would seem to lie in the significance attached to Marshall's "marginal mobility". It was formerly asserted that obstacles to movement did not obstruct the ultimate attainment of competitive equilibrium so long as some mobility existed at the margin (*e.g.* a *few* sharp housewives in a market, and a *few* alert and mobile workers). The new view seems to imply that this marginal mobility would be impotent to prevent the fixation of a monopoly-price throughout the market if the mobility of the rest of the buyers or sellers was nil or very small.

[2] In 1925 the present writer cited the manuscript of an earlier article by Mr. Sraffa for an Italian journal, with its reference to the "private market" of each producer, and indicated its relevance to the part played by "goodwill" in the theory of profit. (*Capitalist Enterprise*, p. 88.) But he was far from appreciating, still less emphasizing, its fuller significance. Marshall, it is true, referred to a similar consideration as a limiting factor on price-cutting on a falling market. But he would seem to have attached to it no more than a short-period significance.

was a factor which accounted for a failure by industry to take full advantages of large-scale economies or of "increasing returns", and for a chronic under-utilization of productive resources. This point of view was developed in later work, in particular by Mrs. Robinson and by Professor Chamberlin, who advanced independently a theory of what the former termed "imperfect competition" and the latter "monopolistic competition" to supplant the traditional analysis of competitive equilibrium.

The practical implications of this new generalization were clearly of great importance. Profit was seen to contain always an appreciable element of direct monopoly-gain (*i.e.* a gain acquired by *restriction*): indeed the important element of "goodwill" in all business valuations was seen largely, if not entirely, to represent simply a capitalization of such monopoly-elements. *Laissez-faire*, when applied to the world of fact instead of to the ideal world of abstract competition, was found to sanction a state of affairs where productive resources might chronically remain under-utilized, available economies be ignored, and production-units be maintained at an inefficient size even according to its own restricted definition of economy and efficiency.[1] But once this position had been reached, larger vistas, even more disturbing to accepted notions, were immediately opened up. If the presence of these "frictional" elements in the market created opportunities for monopoly-profit and could be capitalized as business "goodwill", they

[1] The analysis of Professor Pigou and others had already made a breach in the traditional case for *laissez-faire* by establishing that even on the assumption of "pure competition" production was restricted below the *optimum* in certain cases of "increasing returns" where "external economies" prevailed. But the theory of "imperfect competition" added a further "exception", and moreover implied that the "exception" became virtually the general case.

could, surely, themselves be created by the entrepreneur? In the strange Alice-through-the-Looking-Glass sort of world which was opening to the economists' gaze, "frictions" almost became a species of commodity which could have a cost of production, yielded a profit and hence could acquire a price. Whether, even if they could masquerade as commodities, they could be said to be utilities was exceedingly doubtful. Indeed, from the standpoint of society and not of the individual, they seemed properly to be treated as elements of "illth" rather than of wealth—as Lucifers of restriction rather than Gabriels of creation. Yet they seemed to surmount this contradiction by possessing the convenient property of bludgeoning the other party to the transaction either *qua* consumer or *qua* worker into paying the price of their existence in the form of a monopoly-price (either in money or in labour-power) for real utilities.

It was this aspect of the problem to which Professor Chamberlin devoted particular attention in his analysis of the significance of advertising and selling-costs and their effect upon price. Advertising and selling-devices generally are the methods which can be used to work upon factors in the market such as ignorance or inertia or short-sightedness in space or time, and from these raw materials to create more spectacular attachments and preferences on the part of the consumer for the products of a particular firm.[1] Of this the modern vogue of

---

[1] Parallel to this in the labour market we find various devices for attaching the worker more firmly to a particular firm, ranging from types of welfare work, etc., designed to lessen "labour turnover" to "company unionism". The significance which this has is to combat the influence of trade union organization and collective bargaining on wages, or, in Marx's phrase, to increase the "rate of surplus value" by "depressing wages below the value of labour-power".

branded goods and proprietary articles is a special case; while the increasing rôle played in the modern world by the distributive apparatus and by distributive costs is its inevitable product. In other words, "forces of competition", which in the classical theory performed a positive and a social function as the instrument by which social interest dominated individual interest, cheapening products and promoting innovation, to-day appear primarily as a costly apparatus for resisting the operation of "the unseen hand" of social interest and for the manufacture of restrictive monopoly-rights.

The significance of all such devices of monopolistic competition is that they are designed to raise and render less elastic the demand of particular individuals or even of a whole market by a mixture of coercion, cajolery and propagandist suggestion.[1] To the extent that they do this, and thereby create a privileged market for a particular seller or group of sellers (or buyers), such methods "pay". Here we seem to have a new bewildering sort of "supply and demand" apparatus by which supply can create demand as well as demand evoke supply.

---

[1] It is frequently argued in defence of such propaganda that it may serve a constructive function in informing the consumer of alternatives of which he was not aware. (Again, it may encourage expansion in cases of "increasing returns" and so encourage economies in production, although there is no reason at all to assume that it will in general encourage those industries where "increasing returns" prevail most strongly: it may equally well encourage other industries at their expense.) Certainly, a substratum of such "information" doubtless results from most advertising. But "information" (*i.e.* of the kind which renders a market *more* and not less "perfect") has to be general and all-inclusive to be such (like lists of hotels and hotel-prices issued by certain foreign tourist agencies). But the essence of advertising is that it is *not* all-inclusive, but exclusive, crying a particular ware with intent to distract attention from the rest. Among instruments of coercion which have parallel aims and effects are to be classed such things as "tying-contracts", boycott and the various types of political influence.

We have here apparently a new type of expense, which so soon as it has become general becomes "necessary"; which is indistinguishable from any other form of cost of production but yet is entirely relative to the monopolistic competition which produces it and to the particular policy in this matter which the competitors decide to adopt.[1] As Professor Chamberlin has said: "Wherever selling-costs are incurred—and they are incurred in some measure for almost all commodities—to cast the price problem in terms of 'competitive' demand and cost curves is not merely inaccurate; it is impossible. . . . Under conditions of pure competition there would be no selling-costs. . . . The position of the demand curve shifts with each alteration in total selling-expenditure. In summary, the 'competitive' cost curve which includes selling-costs is inconsistent with itself, it is useless, it is misleading, and it is of very limited meaning." [2]

Here it would seem that we had again lost solid anchorage; and that in face of such a bewildering complex of dependent variables, nothing determinate could result. The classical theory of competition would appear to founder on this basic contradiction: that when competition is concretely defined as operating amid the sort of frictions which the real world must necessarily contain, the "competitive equilibria" cannot define the situation even as approximations. Are we really left, as it might appear, with a situation where an indefinite rise in prices may be engineered if selling-expenditures are sufficiently increased, and the capitalist system may raise itself indefinitely by its own bootlaces? True, it is

---

[1] Cf. Prof. F. Zeuthen, *Problems of Monopoly and Economic Welfare*, p. 60: "The *actual* possibilities of a monopoly-profit will thus help to constitute the costs of other enterprises."

[2] Chamberlin, *Theory of Monopolistic Competition*, pp. 175-6.

possible to produce some order from the apparent chaos if one can postulate certain relationships between the expenditure to be incurred on selling-devices and the concrete results which they yield in shifting demand curves and opening opportunities for increased profit [1]— if a sort of cost-of-production-cum-productivity theory of friction-creating can be evolved. But such constructions, while they are ingenious and elegant, seem to have limited validity when applied to actual fact; and for anything but isolated problems of limited dimension to meet serious difficulties. Doubtless they may provide a useful and valid method for analysing particular markets for a special range of products on fairly rigid assumptions of *ceteris paribus* with regard to other industries, other prices and other selling-expenditures. But for making statements in terms of the general equilibrium of the system as a whole—for the macroscopic problems of economic society—their validity seems to be more dubious. It is easy enough to assume a knowledge of certain relationships to be given: it is more difficult to see these assumptions translated into something tangible. The relevant relationships seem here to be themselves dependent on so many other variables in the situation as to raise doubts whether one can generalize at all widely on the basis of them without becoming involved in contradiction. For instance, a large part of the effect of advertising methods depends on their *differential* character—on their absence among rivals. If such devices have become general over an industry, and *a fortiori* over the whole of industry, then an undefined part of them will presumably have the effect (like pushing in a crowd) of merely counteracting

[1] *Ibid.*, p. 130 *et seq.*

the influence of the devices employed by others. While this selling-expenditure will be necessary for each if he is to retain his existing share of the market, it will not necessarily yield him any additional profit as distinct from maintaining the *status quo*. The influence of a given selling-expenditure on demand in any particular case will then be a complex function of the amount and form of selling-expenditures on all other commodities and of the change in the marginal utility of income to consumers as a result of the price-changes consequent on such selling-costs, as well as on the "suggestibility" of consumers in face of the particular selling-devices in question. The fundamental question remains as to who pays for the additional selling-costs which have now become general, and hence "necessary"—where their incidence falls. Will it fall on existing monopoly-profit as part of the cost of maintaining "goodwill"? If so, it must apparently have the effect of causing entrepreneurs to reduce either their output or their expenditure on such selling-devices, or both; unless each entrepreneur can hope to acquire a new differential advantage by pushing his selling-expenditure ahead of his rivals, on the assumption that the latter will not follow suit; in which case a new round in the selling-war will start. If the general inflation of selling-expenses results in reduced output, the burden will fall in restricted consumption on the community. What has really occurred may then be one (or both) of two things. It may be that profits are no larger, or even smaller, than before, but a proportion of labour and other resources has been transferred from normal productive activity to the unproductive activities of competitive marketing—to furnishing the accoutrement of economic racketeering. Alternatively, what may have occurred is that entrepreneurs as a class have increased their exploitation of other factors of production by forcing the latter to accept a lower real return. In other words, profit in general will have been raised by a lowering of the price at which workers are willing to supply their labour-power to the employer, or else by similar pressure on some intermediate section of society. Whether this is the final result, and if so of what magnitude it is, will depend on the social relations which determine how far exploitation of this type can be intensified.

In any attempt, therefore, to generalize about such a situation as a whole, we are apparently brought back to the type of determining relation with which classical Political Economy dealt. And this in a realm where it might seem that the greatest conquests of modern methods of analysis had occurred! We seem to be driven back to these simpler and original formulations precisely because, so soon as we admit the possibility of consumers' choices themselves being moulded by the actions of sellers, it becomes clear that a subjective theory of value is incapable of furnishing stable anchorage from which determinate statements may be made about the system as a whole. "Consumers' desires" are both constituted as the starting-point for a theory of value and at the same time are admitted to be themselves "dependent variables", determinable by the scale and nature of selling-expenditure on the part of producers. To revert to speech in terms of some simpler relationship, such as Marx's "rate of surplus-value", is, of course, to utter no magic formula which can deduce for us any fact about the effects of monopolistic competition that we did not otherwise know. Such knowledge is not given *a priori*, but is a matter of experience. But unless we cast our analysis in terms of certain fundamental relations of this kind, and relate more complex considerations to them, we seem unlikely to obtain any complete picture of the situation or to be able to see the wood for the trees.

The recent emphasis given to the effect of expectations on price-formation, if it can be given a genealogy, seems to have two lines of descent. On the one hand, it seems to have arisen from a study of short-period problems with special reference to the effect of the existence of large overhead costs; on the other hand, from a closer analysis of the causes of movements in the *general* price-level, as distinct from the problem of the *relative* prices of particular commodities. As we have seen, classical Political Economy was inclined to treat movements in the general price-level as a distinctly monetary problem, irrelevant to the determination of relative exchange-values and to problems of production. Renewed attention was attracted to the question by the large price-movements of the last quarter of the nineteenth century, and again by the price-phenomena of the war and the post-war period. What gave this study a new interest and a new direction was the view which developed that, on the one hand, changes in the general price-level could not occur except in the form of a change (at least temporarily) in relative prices (and hence with effects on production and on distribution) and that, on the other hand, expectations were competent to be an originating cause of a permanent change in the price-level. Interest in the former problem was largely stimulated by the publication of Professor J. M. Clark's work on *The Economics of Overhead Costs*. The study of this type of problem was not only a contributory stimulus to the interest in a new analysis of competition and monopoly, but sowed doubts as to the validity as well as the relevance of traditional analyses of long-period equilibrium. Such analyses depended in some form or another on costs as a determining factor. But where a large proportion of costs represented "overhead costs" of durable plant and equipment, costs were to this extent irrelevant to the fixation of price over considerable periods of time.[1] At any given moment of time, and over any concrete "short period", price might diverge very widely from "normal". This "short period" price was seen to be in part dependent on expectations in two ways: on the expectations as to the future which had prompted the original investment in the fixed plant and so determined its present amount, and on the contemporary expectations of entrepreneurs as to the course of prices in the immediate future which determined how intensively the existing plant was utilized to produce current output. How could it be certain that these short-period divergences of price would ultimately tend to return to the long-period "normal"? How could one be sure that those long-period forces of which Marshall spoke, working in the background to pull things back to predetermined equilibrium, would work entirely undeflected by any reciprocal influence of the short-period situation on themselves? Was it not possible that the events of the short-period situation helped to shape the very factors on which final equilibrium depended? If so, the real world was not only a succession of short periods where

[1] Overhead costs "introduce doubt and ambiguity into the most essential economic service of costs" so that the economist "is deprived of one of his ready-made yardsticks of economic soundness". Hence "private enterprise and private accountancy" can no longer be completely trusted. (J. M. Clark in *Econ. Essays in Honour of J. B. Clark*, p. 64.)

the long period was never reached; but even the long-period tendencies which continually strove to operate might be moulded by short-period happenings and hence be servant instead of master. It would be like a game of musical chairs where, not only was sitting equilibrium never reached so long as the music continued, but the players were allowed to move the chairs about the room. Expectations, if they could affect what occurred in the short period, could also influence the permanent shape of events.

Some element of retarding friction seems necessary to the operation of competition at all. As Professor Maurice Clark has pointed out, there seems to be an Hegelian contradiction in "perfect competition" as a concept, since, if competition worked perfectly and without friction, it would never be in the interests of a seller to cut his price, knowing as he would that all competitors would immediately follow suit and deprive him of all gain in so doing.[1] But in the real world, of course, competition can never work instantaneously. The essence of the matter is that the existence of delay introduces uncertainty for the individual as to the future course of prices arising from uncertainty as to the action of his rivals. At any rate, if he is one among many, it is natural for him to assume that their action and hence the future price will be unaffected by his own action. Consequently, he will base his present decision as to output

---

[1] J. M. Clark, *Econs. of Overhead Costs*, pp. 417 and 460. Prof. Chamberlin adds: "*Perfect* competition, it would seem, gives the same price as perfect monopoly." (*Op. cit.*, p. 4.) This is correct, if one imagines that equilibrium is reached *from* a price *higher* than the monopoly-price. Then it is true that the situation described by Prof. Chamberlin (where no individual anticipates any gain from initiating a price-reduction) will preclude price-reduction. But the situation will not hold any tendency to *raise* price from a previously *lower* level, except by agreement.

and sales on a consideration of the prices ruling at the moment modified by a more or less blind guess as to the course of future prices. Whatever action he decides on can have only a negligible influence on the total market situation; and the expectations of any single individual are, therefore, irrelevant to the final outcome. But what of the effect of the combined expectation of a collection of individuals (supposing that they are influenced by similar expectations)? Were the classical economists right in supposing that even this is irrelevant to the determination of price?

Clearly, an expectation which is common to a whole market, or to a substantial group of buyers or sellers, can influence the price of the moment or of the immediate future. Every fluctuation in the market bears witness to this fact. Moreover, where decisions bear fruit a long time ahead (as with lengthy production-periods) or are embodied in very durable objects, as occurs especially in decisions relating to capital accumulation and investment, such expectations may exercise an influence on the situation far into the future, extending over years or even decades. But this is not to say that their influence can be more than a temporary one, even if the temporary period be fairly long in duration: it is not to say that they can necessarily alter the nature of the long period "normal" to which exchange-values will ultimately tend to conform.

The reason for which the classical theory considered that subjective expectations, even when they were general, were irrelevant to the determination of long-period equilibrium lay in the objective nature of its theory of value. The factors which determined "normal value" were not such as were capable of being influenced by expectations or by any of the effects of short-period price-fluctuations. Thus there was no possibility of expectations bringing about a displacement of values which was permanent, still less a cumulative displacement. "Normal values" represented that arrangement and distribution of labour and resources which, in the existing state of demand and with the existing supply of labour and resources, constituted the most profitable position for the individual entrepreneur. If there was any movement away from that position by one individual separately, he would be involved in losses (or at least would fail to secure as much profit as he otherwise could have done). If there was any general movement away from that position, either in the direction of contraction or expansion, then either losses would be made all round or abnormal profits, or some industries would make abnormal profits and others would be involved in losses, with the result that forces would be set in motion to reverse the tendencies to contraction or expansion and to bring things back to the "normal" position once again. Given that fundamental cost-conditions and demand-conditions remained unaltered, expectations which did not conform to the objective situation were automatically checked and revised by the price-changes which the actions consequent on these expectations provoked.[1] Subjective expectations bred from ignorance of the general situation, while they were not irrelevant to the creation of economic fluctuations, were irrelevant to the final career of each

---

[1] Of course, under conditions where the buyers also base their actions on expectations of future prices (*e.g.* a purely speculative market), since they buy merely with the intention of selling again, there is a possibility of indefinite price-movement in either direction, prompted by an initial expectation on one side or the other. But the early utility-theorists, at any rate, implicitly ruled out this possibility from the consumers' market by their assumption that consumers' demand was related to a calculus

such fluctuation and to the tendencies to equilibrium which ruled the long-period trend of events.

It is clear, however, that this view must be subject to modification in two essential respects.

First, in so far as any of the governing conditions either contained a conventional element which was capable of being influenced by changes in the income of a certain class or was in any other way dependent on the income of a group or a class. Clearly, none of the determinants of value in the labour-theory of value were capable of being so influenced. But certain of the determinants of Marx's prices of production might be. For instance, in so far as the value of labour-power is partly determined by what one may call the conventional or social element embodied in the conception of a necessary standard of life, a change in wages brought about by temporary circumstances may itself alter the supply-price of labour-power or its "normal value" for the future.[1] For example, the change might be brought about in the one case by trade union action at a time of expanding demand for workers, or in the other case by the lowering of wages consequent on unemployment. Such a change in the supply-conditions of labour-power would react on the equilibrium-position to which things would later tend to return: it would alter both the

of utility, which could not itself be influenced by expected price-changes. Even so, of course, consumers may temporarily postpone consumption in face of an expected price-fall and so aggravate the latter; but probably only in order to purchase equivalently more at a later date. The fact that the larger the element of *speculative* exchanges in the system the *greater* is the instability of prices is a consideration which has been ignored by traditional theories of speculation, which have mainly concentrated on an apologetic for speculative dealings.

[1] This conventional element is what Ricardo referred to as the factor of "habit" and Marx as the "social" element in determining the "cost of production of labour-power".

aggregate and the rate of profit (and likewise rents) and hence would establish a new set of normal exchange-ratios. In Ricardo's theory this consideration received scant consideration, presumably for the reason that he thought the law of population to be powerful enough to make wages conform to a subsistence level after a sufficient lapse of time. But in the theory of Marx it had much greater importance. It was precisely because an alteration of wages could modify the future equilibrium on the basis of which capitalist production and expansion would continue that Marx attached so much importance to crises and to the "industrial reserve army" as shaping the future course of capitalism. For him, the law of motion of this society was not a law of nature which could be deduced mechanically from a few simple data and then forecasted for a century ahead: it was something which was itself shaped by the class relation between Capital and Labour and by changes in this relation.

Similar considerations apply to the supply of capital. The volume of capital accumulation is clearly dependent in a very direct manner on the income of the capitalist class. Hence any short-period change which affected the income of this class would react on the volume of capital accumulation during this and the immediately succeeding period: for instance, an expectation on the part of entrepreneurs which induced them to take action which actually resulted in losses.[1] This has an import-

---

[1] It might seem as though expectations as to the future of relative prices will also exert a *direct* and immediate influence on the volume of capital investment, and that this influence should be classed under the above head. But the significance in this case is different: it is the type of action which *ceteris paribus* will be subject to revision because actuality does not correspond with expectation; whereas changed investment which is the product of changed income, and hence of a changed "supply-price" of capital, will not.

ance in the case of capital without any close parallel because capital accumulation and the innovations which go with it is so essential and continuing a process of capitalist production. On it the amount of constructional work and the balance between different lines of production not merely temporarily, but also permanently, depends.[1] As will be seen, monetary changes may also have an effect on the supply of capital, and so leave the technical state of industry, the balance between industries and the configuration of relative prices permanently different from what they previously were.[2]

Secondly, it is clearly possible for subjective expectations to affect the general level of prices, if they can influence either of the two monetary factors which (given the commodity transactions) determine this level—namely, the volume of money and its velocity of circulation. How far they can affect the amount of money in circulation depends, in part, upon banking policy. But the velocity

---

[1] If we regard what the Austrians term the "time-structure of production" as lengthening continuously with time, then any short-period change which alters the rate of investment must alter the speed of this lengthening process and cause this "time-structure" to be different at any point of time in the future from what it otherwise would have been. This fact that capital accumulation is a continuing process has always constituted one of the difficulties of the view which treated capital as an ultimate factor of production. Capital is both a stock and a current flow of additions to that stock; the "supply-price" of these two things is different, only one of which can ever be said to be equal to the current return; and on the contrary to being independent of the latter this supply-price is continually changing with it. Cf. Armstrong, *Saving and Investment*, pp. 247–8; and above, p. 150.

[2] This is apparently the phenomenon to which Swedish economists have referred when they have pointed out in emendation of Wicksell that a change of prices (produced by a divergence between the "natural" rate and the money rate of interest) may bring about a shift in the "natural rate" itself. Cf. Lindahl and Myrdal *cit.* Brinley Thomas, *Monetary Policy and Prices*, pp. 78–9 and 85; and Myrdal, *Monetary Equilibrium*

of circulation of existing money they can clearly influence immediately and directly in so far as the first effect of such expectations is likely to be on the use of existing money-balances, in the one case by causing a drawing upon existing money-balances to finance optimistic expectations, in the other case by causing the proceeds of commodity-sales to swell idle balances as a result of pessimistic expectations. The expectation, if it is general, will tend to produce the very price-change which it hoped for or feared.[1]

This, however, is not to say that the price-change will necessarily be permanent, still less a continuing one. It all depends on whether the expansion (or contraction) of expenditure results in changes which confirm or which disappoint the original expectation. If the result is to yield losses to entrepreneurs (or in the converse case abnormal profits) then the movement will be self-defeating, and the contradiction between expected and realized gains will be the corrective that produces a return to the original position. If in the new position the profits that were considered normal in the old position are still realized (although not those abnormal profits, or losses, the expectation of which prompted the original movement), then there will not necessarily be any tendency to return to the old position: merely a tendency, having reached the new level, to stay there. But if the result of the original movement is to produce the very profits (or losses) that were expected—to yield a coincidence of realized with expected gain—then the movement, once started, will continue. In the first of these three cases the original position was one of stable equilibrium; in the second case, both the old and the

---

[1] Cf. Wicksell, *Interest and Prices*, p. 97.

new are positions of neutral equilibrium; in the third case the original position was one of unstable equilibrium.

A situation where the initial movement is likely to be self-defeating in its effects is where people wish and try to maintain their money-balances at the same size as before (measured in terms of real values). In this case an initial price-rise (or fall) will tend not only to be checked but reversed (*e.g.* through a rise in interest-rates). If, however, a continuing influence on the velocity of circulation is exerted by the fact that a price-change itself creates the expectation of a continuing rate of change in the same direction—the process of what Wicksell termed a rise of prices "creating its own draught"—then the change is likely, not only to persist, but to continue.

In recent years there has been an increasing emphasis placed by economists on the possibility of a change in the price-level, initiated in this way, becoming cumulative, because a price-rise itself breeds expectation of a further rise and the expectation each time tends to produce the very rise that had been expected. Hence a picture has emerged of the economic system as being unstable in a high degree. Professor Hicks has recently pointed out that this instability arises from the fact that under dynamic conditions one can no longer·hold to the crucial assumption that "the individual's scale of preference is independent of the prices fixed on the market" [1] —the tacit assumption underlying all versions of the subjective theory of value which we have had occasion to call in question in previous chapters of this book. So soon as we admit the effect of price-changes in the immediate past on expectations in people's minds as to

[1] J. R. Hicks, *Value and Capital*, p. 249.

what will occur in the future, and hence on their preferences spread out over time, this assumption of independence breaks down: cumulative movement in the direction
either of continuous inflation or deflation of all prices
becomes possible. In fact, we are faced with a situation
quite opposite to that which economics has traditionally
envisaged. Instead of the traditional picture of an
economic system possessed of such a high degree of
stability as to make a trade cycle scarcely explicable,
save in terms of some special disequilibrating influence
external to the system, we have the picture of an economic
system that is much more unstable even than the capitalist
system clearly is—moreover, a system about the larger
movements of which there is very little that one can say
by way of deterministic forecast.

One reason why in the past this instability has been
denied has presumably been the belief that a change in
the general price-level, of the kind to which we have
been referring, cannot occur without some change also
in *relative* prices, and a shift of relative prices of a kind
that disappoints the original expectation of which the
price-movement has been the consequence. Hence the
shift away from equilibrium tends to be self-corrective
because it results in price-changes that prompt a revision
of the original action. The chief way in which expectations influence the situation in a capitalist economy is
through the expectations and actions of *entrepreneurs*.
Consequently this influence will operate through the
medium of changes in investment; and since the originating act takes this shape, it will represent a changed demand
on the part of entrepreneurs for a particular class of
goods. The additional demand will represent a demand
for labour-power, raw materials and instruments of

production, and not *in the first instance* a demand for consumption-goods. The result of this will be that (if there is a state of full employment, or approaching full employment) the prices of the former will tend to rise. The initial price-rise, therefore, takes the form of a rise in the price of things which figure to the entrepreneur as costs; and in so far as this set of prices rises *relatively* to the price of his finished product, the margin between them will be narrowed and, not only his recent and "abnormal" profit-expectation, but even his "normal" expectation of profit will, *ceteris paribus*, be disappointed. True, it will subsequently [1] happen that the prices of finished goods will rise as wage-earners and others come to spend their increased purchasing-power. But even if these prices rise by the same absolute amount as costs have. risen, the margin between them will be smaller *proportionately* to the higher level of costs and of selling-prices; so that the rise in the latter will not prove sufficient compensation to the entrepreneur, seeing that his total outlay (in money terms) has increased.

To illustrate this argument, let us suppose, for example, a community where the sole product, and also (by a stretch of imagination) the only finished commodity which its inhabitants buy, consists of boots. Let us further suppose that the expectation of improved profit results in the decision of entrepreneurs in the boot industry to draw upon their money-balances in order to purchase more leather and equipment with which to expand output. The result is that the new demand for resources (constructional materials, labour-power,

---

[1] It is to be noted that our argument here is independent of whether this time-lag is long or short, or whether there is even any time-lag at all. If there is, then the argument of the text will be reinforced.

leather, etc.) competes with existing demands and so raises the price of these resources.[1] Eventually the price of boots will rise by an equivalent extent (as the wages, etc., come to be spent). In other words, receipts from boot-sales will increase by the same *amount* as costs have risen. But they will increase in smaller *proportion*. Meanwhile the capital outlay is larger than it was before, having increased to the extent of the rise in costs; so that the profits which can be realized will suffice only to yield a *smaller* ratio of profit to outlay and hence to disappoint the expectation on which the original investment was made.[2] The very rise in costs will, of course,

[1] If reserves of these things exist, then the price-rise of these resources is smaller, or even, in the event of infinitely elastic supply of such resources, nil. In this case the increase in the aggregate boot-output will be in proportion to the increased money-expenditure, and no rise in selling-price will occur. Here it is true that the rate of profit will not fall as a result of the expectation-fed expansion of output. But if there is any inelasticity in the supply of resources costs will be raised in some degree relatively to the selling-price of finished goods (given the assumptions referred to below).

[2] The matter can be put in this form. Investment in the industry is increased by x. For simplicity let us neglect the fact that part of the investment will take the form of durable plant, and assume that investment entirely takes the form of leather. Then the increase of investment will be equivalent to an increase of current cost-outlay on boots. Then if originally costs in leather and labour were X, receipts from boot-sales Y, and the resulting profit $Y - X = y$, the *rate* of profit was $\frac{y}{X}$. Now both X and Y are increased by x, leaving the difference between them still $= y$. But the *rate* of profit will now $= \frac{y}{X+x}$.

The result will be *as if*, in a community of barter, a farmer, in expectation of an improved harvest, decided to lay out more corn in return for labour, or contracted with labourers so as to promise them a larger claim on the contents of his barns when the harvest was in. The harvest then turned out to be no better than the previous year, with the result that he found himself worse off by reason of the optimistic contracts he had made, while the labourers in that year consumed a larger proportion of the current produce.

The result (to revert to our boot example) will not be substantially

in large measure have frustrated the intention to create new plant, or even to acquire more labour and materials. But it is this very frustration which precludes that increase of output which might have enabled the investment-intention to realize its expectations of profit.

Of course, it may be that the effect of an expectation-prompted movement towards expansion or contraction is modified by the rigidity of certain elements in the situation. This rigidity may be of money-wages, which may fail to rise in face of an increased demand for labour, or it may be of certain long-term contracts that are fixed in money: for example, loan-contracts, where the effect of the initial price-movement may be merely to "squeeze" (or, conversely, confer a bounty upon) *rentiers*. To the extent that this is the case, it might seem at first sight as though the profits realized in the upswing would be larger than would otherwise be the case; and conversely in the downswing. (It would, indeed, seem to be on some such conclusion as this that the traditional view has been based which favoured plastic rather than rigid money wage-rates in the face of changes in the general price-level.) But this conclusion does not necessarily follow, if the expenditure of these fixed-income groups is correspondingly smaller than it would otherwise have been. This consideration,

---

different if part of the increased investment is directed towards new and additional plant. Then, *either* the price of machinery and equipment will be raised (with comparable effect to the rise of price of leather and labour in our simpler case), *or*, if labour is drawn towards the constructional trades so as to change the technique of industry in the direction of a raised ratio of capital to labour (Marx's higher "organic composition of capital" or the Austrian's "more roundabout production"), then the rate of profit will fall for this reason. The actual outcome may well be a mixture of these two phenomena, the occurrence of the former promoting and leading to the latter.

accordingly, indicates that 'no answer to this type of question can be sufficient unless something is known of the reaction of consumers themselves to the price-rise; and to this we have paid no attention hitherto.

It should now be evident that underlying this whole argument about 'the movement of relative prices is the assumption that it is the expectations of entrepreneurs that play the active rôle, while the actions of consumers remain unaffected, or little affected, by price-expectations. And it is apparently on some such assumption as this that the traditional pictures of a stable system depend. For, in this case, as soon as prices start to rise, those persons whose money-incomes have not yet risen (*e.g.*, non-wage-earners) will curtail their purchases, with the intention of postponement. If, however, this is not the case—if consumers, like entrepreneurs, are influenced by a price-rise to believe that the rate of change is likely to continue, or at least that the new and higher level will be permanent [1]—then consumers will expand their *money*-expenditure in an attempt to purchase at least as many commodities as before. The result will be that consumption-goods will rise in at least the same proportion as costs have risen; there will be no shift of relative prices, no narrowing of the profit-margin and hence no necessary disappointment of entrepreneurs' expectations.

[1] This is the case that Professor Hicks describes as one of "elasticity of expectations" being equal to or greater than unity. (*Op. cit.*, p. 205.) It was this case (where "the demand of non-wage-earning consumers is quite inelastic") that I stated to be highly unlikely in a lengthy footnote on p. 112 (and again in a footnote on p. 213) of the original edition of these essays, in discussing the views of Mr. Keynes, Mr. Harrod and Mr. Lerner. I am now convinced that this case is not so unlikely as I then thought: that, in fact, it may correspond closely to reality at important phases of the trade cycle. At the same time, I still think that it cannot necessarily be regarded as *generally* true to reality, as some writers seem to have assumed without much question.

Consumers and entrepreneurs alike, by expanding their money-outlay, will have caused the price-change that they expected, and their money-incomes will have risen along with prices generally and with their own expenditure. The movement will have been self-justifying, not self-defeating.

If, however, we take into account the fact that the normal state of the system is one of unemployment and unused capacity, there is a further factor which makes for a high degree of instability in the rate of investment, and hence in the activity of the economic system and the volume of employment. The difference which this consideration makes is that, if there is a reserve both of labour-power and of other resources in the system, we have to deal with fluctuations, not only of investment-outlay of entrepreneurs in terms of money (which in a state of full employment can only lead to *price*-fluctuations) but of real investment-activity (*e.g.*, the output of capital-goods) as well. Such fluctuations of real activity introduce a cumulative factor, which reinforces what has been said above. The cumulative influence resides in the fact that the profit that is earned on existing capital equipment will depend on the level of demand and hence of activity: consequently it will depend, *inter alia*, on the rate of investment itself. A rise in the rate of investment (or *mutatis mutandis*, a fall) will increase the inducement to invest, thereby encouraging a further rise in the rate of investment. That this will be the case depends on the assumption, first that selling-price bears some definite relation to marginal cost, and secondly that, as existing equipment is more intensively utilized, the productivity of labour that is using this equipment will fall and marginal costs will rise. This rise of price (consequent on the rise of marginal cost [1]) will cause a fall in real wages [2] and a "shift to profit". Such a cumulative tendency, however, is unlikely to be of permanent duration, for the reason that, as investment proceeds, it leads to an increase in the actual stock of capital equipment (without any equivalent increase of Marx's "variable capital"), and hence eventually to a fall in the *rate* of profit yielded by a given *mass* of profit.[3] Hence at some point the eventual operation of the tendency for the profit-rate to fall is likely to counter-balance the tendency for total profit to rise, so that the inducement to expand investment will at first tend to be retarded and then reversed. (The converse will happen as investment falls off cumulatively in a slump.) What this factor is likely to produce, therefore, is a fluctuating movement· of considerable amplitude, with the upward and downward movement

[1] It is to be noted that this rise is independent of (and additional to) any rise of cost that may occur owing to the rise in the price of factors of production due to increased demand by entrepreneurs, to which reference was made a few pages earlier.

[2] If in face of this situation wage-earners demand a compensating rise in their *money*-wages, the possibility of profits nevertheless increasing will depend on whether this rise of money-wages does or does not result in a proportional rise of selling-prices; and this will depend on the conditions discussed in the previous paragraph. I have discussed this point at greater length, in its special application to a socialist economy, if this were to operate a similar pricing-system to capitalism, in *The Economic Journal*, December 1939.

[3] Professor Hayek has emphasized another influence which he suggests will operate in a similar way to reverse the expansion before long—probably before "full employment" is reached: namely, the fall of real wages and rise of profit will tend to discourage investment in the more labour-saving methods and encourage a shift to more labour-using forms of production (a "shortening" of the production-period in his terminology; a *lowering* of the composition of capital in Marx's). Hence investment will ultimately decline, because of *smaller* inducement to lock-up capital in expensive and very durable equipment. (Cf. *Profit, Interest and Investment*.)

at first "creating their own draught" with quickening pace, but in the course of doing so germinating a counter-influence, which eventually overpowers its predecessor and reverses the direction of movement.

The outcome of this analysis would seem to be that expectations, at any rate business-expectations on the part of entrepreneurs, play a dominant rôle in the causation of fluctuations, both in price and in industrial activity, and hence can exert an important, if strictly circumscribed, influence on the determination of long-period equilibrium. This represents a significant modification of classical theory and its statement of economic laws, and leaves little standing of the "economic harmonies" of *laissez-faire*. Of particular significance is the emphasis that it places on the tendencies away from equilibrium which lie inherent in an individualist economy, as they were stressed by Marx, by contrast with the tendencies *towards* an equilibrium which the Ricardian school had emphasized; and further on the fact that such ruptures of equilibrium themselves play an active and not merely a passive rôle with regard to the future. We are left with the picture of a highly unstable system, very different from the nicely equilibrated system that it has been traditional for economists to depict. We are, in fact, very far from the classical notion of economic movement as a simple product of certain mechanical motive forces (like growth of capital or of population), and much nearer to a conception of economic movement in terms of conflict and interaction.

So far the partial breakdown of the mechanical determinism of classical doctrine has a positive value: it clarifies our vision of reality. But there is another side to it. Subjective economics, resting as it does on an attempt to interpret economic events in terms of the psychological behaviour of individuals, finds itself faced with a chaos of indeterminacy, where almost anything is possible. Having crowned expectations, it finds itself ruled by them; and where expectation is king, his every mood is law. It lands us in a world of cumulative movement and unstable equilibria, where large-scale or long-distance forecast is impossible—a world in which a campaign of economic "ballyhoo" could exert, not merely a defined and limited, but illimitable influence.

Clearly we cannot rest content with such a situation, if only because the nihilist view in which we appear to be landed would, if it were true, make the economic system much more unstable than it actually is. Economists seem to-day to be at times in danger of imposing by thought an indeterminacy on reality, just as previously economists imposed on reality their own conceptions of mechanical equilibria. We clearly cannot be content to displace the proud structure of classical Political Economy with a groping subjectivism which (as Professor J. R. Hicks has cautiously said), while it may be "admirable for analysing the impact effect of disturbing causes, is less reliable for analysing the further effects", and may well run the "danger, when it is applied to long periods, of the whole method petering out".[1] The precise extent and nature of the instability to which the capitalist system is so evidently subject is, of course, a practical question, to be decided by the study of actual situations, and by comparative study of situations as they change and differ. Reasoning on the basis of known general characteristics of the system can never give us more than a provisional answer: nevertheless, this answer may

[1] *The Economic Journal*, June 1936, p. 241.

have great importance for practice, and in default of completer inductive studies may be the reasoning with which we have to be content. To generalize more confidently on the matter, and to see some pattern in the chaos of indeterminacy to which subjective economics threatens to lead us, we clearly need to go outside the narrow circle of exchange-relations—of what to-day has come to be narrowly defined as "economic" factors— within which the economists' problem is now usually set. We look like being more usefully employed in studying the connection between the economic and social conditions in which individuals are set—institutional and class conditions and the concrete relationships of social groups to the process of production—and the motives and actions to which these conditions give rise than in further complicating the algebra of the impact of expectational-systems on the constellation of prices.

One thing, at any rate, seems clearly to emerge; and it is of fundamental importance. What gives to expectations the influence that we have been discussing, and hence cradles the tendency of the system to violent fluctuation, is the particular type of uncertainty that is characteristic of a society of individual (as distinct from social) production. It is the atomistic diffusion of economic decisions under a system of individual production for a market that gives to expectations their rein. Connected with this is a distinction that would seem to be crucial for the methodology of economics: a distinction between the type of law that it is possible to postulate of a world of perfect foresight, and that different type of law, and degree of determinism, which operates where various types of uncertainty prevail. Of course, economic systems differ only in degree in the foresight of which those who take the ruling decisions are capable; although in this respect (as is suggested in a later chapter) the difference between a capitalist economy and a planned socialist economy is sufficiently large to justify one in treating it as a difference of kind.

What is significant here for the causation of fluctuation is the blindness of the individual entrepreneur—the man who takes the decisions which control production and investment—as to the course of events in the immediate future so far as these affect himself. It is quite another matter as to whether the situation is such that the economist or the scientist, standing outside the system, as it were, and observing it as a whole, can estimate the future. Even if such a scientific observer could foretell the outcome, given the relevant data, it does not follow that the entrepreneur could do so; since it is the essential nature of the latter in an individualist economy that he is in a situation where he is of necessity ignorant as to the current actions of his rivals. In the degree that he is thus in "blinkers", his and others' expectations will exert an influence in producing fluctuations—fluctuations which will be greater and their effects more lasting the more durable the form in which the decisions are embodied. The generation of such fluctuations is, accordingly, part of the essential nature of an individualist economy, not an accidental derivative. We are confronted with this paradox. If the entrepreneur could foresee the actions of his rivals, he would not act in the manner in which the theory of competition assumes him to act, and the laws of Political Economy in their traditional form would cease to hold true. Yet it is the existence of this essential blindness which gives scope to the influence of expectations, with the departures from equilibrium which this influence engenders and the element of indeterminateness which it introduces. Only by virtue of the uncertainty of each as to the actions of all do the traditional laws of the market rule; only by the appearance of freedom does economic necessity and automatism prevail; only by reason of the essential ignorance of each entrepreneur does the economist's power of forecasting the total situation emerge. As Engels once said, the economists' "natural law" was "based on the unconsciousness of the parties concerned". This rule of "natural law", based on "unconsciousness", was as far as classical Political Economy ventured to see—a rule of law later sanctified as the music of an immanent harmony. What Political Economy previously failed to see is that this very atomistic ignorance of each as to the intentions of others, through the influence it gives to expectations, holds at the same time the inevitability of economic fluctuations: fluctuations which generate an important modifying influence, as well as a potent motive force, shaping the future of the economic system.

CHAPTER VII

IMPERIALISM

IT was primarily as a critique of Mercantilism that classical Political Economy, and more particularly its theory of foreign trade, fired the minds of its contemporaries and won its place in history. To denounce Mercantilism as a system and to refute the fallacious reasoning of its apologists was a passion which dominated the writings alike of Adam Smith, of James Mill and of Ricardo. In view of the resemblance between Mercantilism and modern Imperialism, it is the more surprising that economists of our day should have had so little to say concerning the latter, and should even have treated it as a subject outside their scope. This resemblance between eighteenth-century colonialism and that of to-day, at least in superficial aspect, has often been observed (among the earliest, I believe, by Thorold Rogers in the 'eighties). The resemblance lies not merely in the fact that both are concerned with a colonial system, but in their employment of certain parallel monopolistic practices, and in a similar antithesis which their ideologies share to the doctrines of classical Political Economy.

The early economists had few illusions about Mercantilism; and their analysis disclosed very clearly the essential relations which underlay its elaborate superstructure of trade regulations and the ideologies created in its explanation and defence. They perceived that its essential character was a special form of monopolistic policy and that the gain which was sought from it was a monopoly-gain, and primarily the gain of a limited class. James Mill, who had described colonies as "a vast system of outdoor relief for the upper classes", wrote that: "The mother country, in compelling the colony to sell goods cheaper to her than she might sell them to other countries, merely imposes upon her a tribute; not direct, indeed, but not the less real because it is disguised"; [1] while Say, describing the system as "built upon compulsion, restriction and monopoly", declared that "the metropolis can compel the colony to purchase from her everything it may have occasion for; this monopoly, or this exclusive privilege, enables the producers of the metropolis to make the colonies pay more for the merchandise than it is worth".[2] Adam Smith, who had provided the classic discussion of the matter, denounced the system in these terms: "The monopoly of the colony trade, like all the other mean and malignant expedients of the mercantile system, depresses the industry of all other countries, but chiefly that of the colonies, without in the least increasing . . . that of the country in whose favour it is established. . . . The monopoly, indeed, raises the rate of mercantile profit, and thereby augments somewhat the gain of the merchants. . . . To promote the little interest of one little order of men in one country,

---

[1] *Elements of Pol. Economy*, Third Ed., p. 213.

[2] *Treatise on Pol. Econ.* (1821), Vol. I, p. 322 ; and *Catechism of Pol. Economy*, pp. 129-30. Cf. also Torrens, *Production of Wealth* (1821), p. 228 *et seq.* Torrens does not hesitate to refer in refreshingly strong terms to the "powerful junta of ship-owners and merchants, whose private interest is opposed to that of the public" as responsible for colonial regulations (p. 248).

it hurts the interest of all other orders of men in that country, and of all men in all other countries. . . . One great original source of revenue, the wages of labour, the monopoly must have rendered at all times less abundant than it otherwise would have been." [1]

Both Smith and Ricardo discussed the effect of foreign trade on the rate of profit. Both considered that it could exert an influence to raise the rate of profit in the home country, but for opposed reasons. Adam Smith had argued that colonial trade would do so by diverting capital into branches of trade in which it had a partial monopoly, and where, as a result, the profit that could be earned was higher. But this diversion of capital would also raise the rate of profit in all other trades as well (owing to the lessened competition of capital in them), and as a result would raise the price of commodities in the home country. This contention he used to show that the Mercantile System did damage alike to the home country and the colony.[2] This Ricardo denied. It might well be possible for "trade with a colony (to be) so regulated that it (should) at the same time be less beneficial to the colony, and more beneficial to the mother country than a perfectly free trade". At any rate, "any change from one foreign trade to another, or from home to foreign trade, cannot, in my opinion, affect the rate of profits. . . . There will be a worse distribution of the general capital and industry, and, therefore, less will be produced. . . . (But) if it even

---

[1] *Wealth of Nations* (Ed. 1826), pp. 571, 572. Cf. also the remarks of Sismondi on the colonial system under which "the metropolis reserved to itself all the profit of monopoly, but in a very restricted market"— so restricted as to mean that in the long run free trade would have been preferable for both metropolis and colony. (*Nouveaux Principes* (1819), I, p. 393.) [2] *Ibid.*, pp. 556-9.

had the effect of raising profits, it would not occasion the least alteration in prices; prices being regulated neither by wages nor profits."[1] The only way in which profit could be raised by foreign trade was through the effect of abundant and cheap food-imports on the price of labour; and this was most likely to be promoted by free trade and the widest possible extension of the market.

Marx includes foreign trade among the influences which counteract the tendency for the rate of profit to fall, and refers to the dispute between Smith and Ricardo. In this matter he seems to have sided with Smith against Ricardo (which was unusual for him). Foreign trade could raise the rate of profit, not only by cheapening subsistence, but also by "cheapening the elements of constant capital". In addition to this, capital invested in foreign trade, and *a fortiori* in regulated colonial trade, could earn a higher rate of profit; and there seemed "no reason why these higher rates of profit realized by capitals invested in certain lines and sent home by them should not enter as elements into the average rate of profit and tend to keep it up to that extent". "The favoured country recovers more labour in exchange for less labour, although this difference, this surplus, is pocketed by a certain class. . . . So far as the rate of profit is higher, because it is generally higher in the colonial country, it may go hand in hand with a low level of prices if the natural conditions are favourable. It is true that a compensation takes place, but it is not a compensation on [to?] the old level, as Ricardo thinks." This extra profit, which by competition of capitals eventually tends to enter into the *general* rate

[1] *Principles*, Third Ed., pp. 410 and 413.

of profit in the home country, he termed *super-profit*; remarking that this was something analogous to the gain of "a manufacturer who exploits a new invention before it has become general".[1]

It is not altogether clear whether Marx intended this to apply both to the case of simple exchange between two national economic units, either regulated or unregulated, and to the case where the relation between them includes the fact of an investment of capital in one by the other. Clearly these are two distinct cases; and it would seem as though, with regard to the former, Ricardo was substantially right: that the advantage derived from exchange by the country with the higher productivity of labour would not necessarily show itself in any rise in the rate of profit, which was a ratio of *values*; since the resulting attraction of gold into the monetary system of this country might have the effect of raising all prices equally and so of leaving *relative* prices unchanged. The gain from the trade would augment the rate of profit only if it showed itself in a cheapening of subsistence or of raw materials and instruments of production.[2] But what Marx doubtless had in mind was a relationship between home country and colony which included the fact of investment by the former in the latter; and here Adam Smith's view would appear to be justified: the rate of profit in the home country would in this case undoubtedly be raised, by reason of the fact that the field of investment for its capital had been extended.

[1] *Capital*, III, pp. 278-80.
[2] It might also have an effect on profit—which was not mentioned—if it led to a specialization by that country on lines of production which had different technical conditions, and hence a different "organic composition of capital" on the average from that which existed before.

No rigid line of demarcation can, of course, be drawn between these two cases: rather are they to be regarded as two types of relationship between countries, the effects of which shade into one another at the edges. It is unlikely that trade-relations between two countries will have no effect in cheapening foodstuffs and raw materials for the more developed country, particularly in the case of trade between an industrial and an agricultural area; and to this extent the investment-field for the capital of the former country can be said to be enlarged. On the other hand, if capital is actually invested outside the former country, the rate of profit in that country is likely to be raised quite apart from its incidental effects on relative prices. To define precisely the economic relationship which characterizes colonialism is, therefore, not easy. In such matters one cannot expect to find definitions which separate phenomena with the sharp lines of logic. Super-profit in Marx's sense can arise, it would seem, as much from free and unregulated exchange between countries of different productivity as from regulated exchange or from foreign investment; and hence is a product in some measure of most international trade. If we are to give a distinctive definition of this economic relationship, it must be in terms of something narrower than this; and the most convenient and satisfactory *economic definition* of *colony* and *colonialism* seems to consist in a relation between two countries or areas involving the creation of super-profit for the benefit of one of them, *either* by means of some form of monopolistically regulated trade between them, *or* by an investment of capital by one of them in the other at a higher rate of profit than that prevailing in the former. Each of these types of relationship represents a form of exploitation of one area by another (through trade or through investment) which is in important respects different from the trading relationship between two areas which takes place on the basis of free and unregulated trade.[1]

What characterized Mercantilism was a relationship of regulated trade between colony and metropolis, ordered in such a way as to turn the terms of trade in favour of the latter and against the former.[2] In this system investment in the colony, while it was found, seems to have played a subordinate rôle. Modern Imperialism repeats this feature of exploitation through trade; and, while in the early stages of Imperialism this feature may have been much less marked than it was in the colonial system of the seventeenth and eighteenth centuries, in the later stages it assumes a large and growing importance in the shape of the neo-Mercantilist policies of "autarky" of imperial units. But between Mercantilism and Im-

[1] The conception of foreign trade free of any monopolistic element is, of course, as abstract a conception as "free competition" in internal trade, and is as rarely found. We use the conception here primarily for analytical purposes.

[2] This had earlier parallels in the relationship which persisted between merchant capital and the peasantry and craftsmen at the close of the Middle Ages and in the period of "primitive accumulation". The various monopolistic provisions of the mercantile guilds, reinforced frequently by a policy on the part of the town governments, amounting to a sort of "colonialism" with regard to the surrounding countryside, gave rise to an exploitation-relation of this sort which seems to have constituted an important form of primitive accumulation. In the *Verlag*-system it reached a higher stage; finally reaching its mature and "pure" form in the exploitation of a proletariat by industrial capital and the creation of industrial surplus-value. (Cf. the present writer's *Capitalist Enterprise*, Chapters 14-16, 18-19.) It is of interest to note that this type of relationship formed the basis of the discussion in U.S.S.R. over the relationship between industry and peasant economy in 1925 and of Preobrajensky's theory of so-called "socialist primitive accumulation". (Cf. the writer's *Russian Econ. Development*, p. 160 *et seq.*)

perialism there lies, of course, the whole difference between a primitive stage in the growth of capitalism and the most advanced stage of large-scale industrial technique, of integration of finance with industry and of monopolistic organization and policies. Consequently, in the latter the export of capital comes to play a dominant rôle, and with it the export of capital goods and the hypertrophy of the industries producing the latter.[1] Indeed, among the contrasts which distinguish the old from the new colonial system, the fact of capital investment in the colonial area appears to be the chief. This investment takes a variety of forms; and to represent it as consisting exclusively, or even predominantly, in investment as *industrial* capital in the direct exploitation of a colonial proletariat is to give an over-simplified and mistaken picture of the actual process. Investment in the colony frequently takes the form of large-scale money-lending or of the exploitation of primitive forms of production, much as did merchant capital in Western Europe in the days of the *Verlag*-system.[2] Moreover, the keynote of colonial investment since its start has consisted in *privileged* investment: namely, investment

[1] Aggregate British capital-exports in 1913 were estimated to amount to £4000 million, of which one-half was invested in the British Empire, one-fifth in U.S.A., one-fifth in Central and South America, and only one-twentieth in Europe. The following percentages of the distribution of the combined exports of Germany, Britain and U.S.A. are instructive:

		Capital Goods.	*Consumption Goods.*
1800	. . .	26 per cent.	74 per cent.
1900	. . .	39 ,,	61 ,,
1913	. . .	46 ,,	54 ,,

(Inter. Chamber of Commerce, *Inter. Econ. Reconstruction*, pp. 30-2.)

[2] Examples of this appear to be furnished by the Niger Company or the Sudan Plantation Syndicate, or by much of French Equatorial Africa, where foreign capital exploits primitive economy through trade or money-lending, but shows little tendency to industrialize it.

in projects which carry with them some differential advantage, preference or actual monopoly, in the form of concession-rights or some grant of privileged status. Monopoly-rights and restrictive practices, not dissimilar to those in force in Stuart England, seem always to have constituted a large part of the attraction of colonial investment, and to Imperialism as a system of profit-extraction over wide areas to have furnished an essential ingredient.

Since investment in colonial areas represents a transfer of capital to areas where semi-monopolistic privileges are easy to procure, where labour is more plentiful and cheaper, and the "organic composition of capital" is lower, the process constitutes a very significant counter-acting influence to the tendency of the profit-rate in the home country to fall.[1] Moreover, it exerts this influence for a double reason. Not only does it mean that the capital exported to the colonial area is invested at a higher rate of profit than if it had been invested, instead, at home; but it also creates a tendency for the rate of profit at home (in the imperialist country) to be greater than it would otherwise have been. The latter occurs because the plethora of capital seeking investment in the metropolis is reduced by reason of the profitable colonial outlet, the pressure on the labour market is relieved and the capitalist is able to purchase labour-power at home at a lower price. Export of capital, in other words, figures as a means of recreating the in-dustrial reserve army at home by virtue of tapping fresh

---

[1] For instance, J. S. Mill, writing as early as the mid-nineteenth century, makes this striking statement concerning the export of capital: "I believe this to have been for many years one of the principal causes by which the decline of profits in England has been arrested." (*Principles*, Ed. Ashley, p. 738.)

fields of exploitation abroad. Capital thereby gains doubly: by the higher rate of profit it reaps abroad and by the higher "rate of surplus-value" it can maintain at home; and this double gain is the reason why, fundamentally, the interest of capital and of labour in this matter are opposed, and why a capitalist economy has a motive for imperialist policy which a socialist economy would not have.[1] Its significance can be seen if one supposes the process carried to an extreme: if one supposes unlimited proletarian strata in the colonies available to be tapped (and unlimited natural resources), and if one further supposes all obstacles to capital-export removed. The logical end of the process (if one cares to follow out a purely abstract hypothesis) would be to lower wage-rates (at least "efficiency-wages") in the older capitalist countries to the level prevailing in the colonial areas; and, so long as colonial areas remained to be tapped, to maintain the mass of the population throughout the world at this standard of life. For a number of concrete reasons, the process does not reach,

---

[1] With regard to the "compensation" of cheaper food imports resulting from colonial development, to which attention is frequently drawn, a well-informed writer has recently concluded as follows: "A latent divergence of interest between workers and capitalists was coming more and more to the front. Though capitalists had not been alone in gaining from the export of capital, the working class participated more by accident than design. It was only by a rare coincidence of interests that the most profitable risks happened to fructify in cheaper and cheaper foodstuffs and raw materials." He points out that building sultans' palaces, mining diamonds, constructing strategic railways, purchasing warships meant no such "compensation". Moreover, "the more new countries were opened up, the more apparent did the sectional conflict become. The likelihood that foreign investment would reduce the cost of British imports was less overwhelming, the fear that industries competing with our own would be fostered was more intense. . . . Foreign investment, it was apparent, might lower the standard of living instead of raising it." (A. K. Cairncross in *Review of Economic Studies*, Vol. III, No. 1.)

or even approach, this abstract limit (which on the face of it would seem to involve the "de-colonization" of the colony, as well as the partial de-industrialization of the imperial metropolis). But the tendency remains as a partial tendency even if it is countered by other factors.[1]

There is often an inclination to fasten attention upon this contrast between the Mercantile System and modern colonialism—namely, the fact of capital investment in the colony—even to the extent of denying that the particular type of exploitation which characterized the former can be said to exist to-day. Stress is consequently laid on the industrializing effect of Imperialism in backward countries, by contrast with the restrictive effect which the Mercantile System exercised on the economic development of its colonies; and a picture is created of a reproduction in the colonial areas of a fully fledged industrial capitalism of the normal type, leading to a

[1] This, of course, is not the whole of the matter. There may be incidental gains to the working class of the imperial metropolis, accruing to sections of it or even to the whole of it for a period. For instance, it may derive benefit from cheaper food imports which result from the opening up of undeveloped areas, or a particular group of workers may gain from the enlarged market for the products of that particular industry. Moreover, it may be possible for strongly organized workers to share some of the fruit of certain monopolistic practices, adjunct to Imperialism, which will be described below. Moreover, there is always the strictly relative sense in which a slave may benefit from the prosperity of his master: in the sense not of a comparison between his state as slave and as free, but his state as slave to a less prosperous and a more prosperous master. (Clearly this sense of "benefit" must always be subordinate to the more fundamental loss he suffers from his slave state.) So, if capitalism finds a partial escape in colonialism, it may avoid forms of pressure on the working class of the metropolis to which it would otherwise have had to resort. Compared with the latter alternative the metropolitan proletariat may be said to benefit from Imperialism. This is particularly relevant to an aspect of Fascism which will be mentioned below.

233

progressive de-colonization of the backward countries. This perspective emerges from a neglect of those features of resemblance between Imperialism and the old colonial system to which we have referred, and of the character-istics of colonial development which are associated with an age of monopolistic organization and policy. It is true that Imperialism exerts a revolutionary effect in the colonial area, more markedly than Mercantilism (which confined itself in the main to trade relations and the encouragement of agricultural plantations) ever did.[1] In so far as capital is to be invested as industrial capital, a proletariat must be created where this condition does not already exist; and this implies the disintegration of older forms of economy, tribal or semi-feudal, by a process of "primitive accumulation". As a condition of extending the investment field, Imperialism requires a partial revolution in the methods of transport: the harnessing of natural resources, and sometimes, though not in-variably, a measure of political as well as economic unification of the country. Yet this is subject to im-portant qualifications; and the positive rôle which the system plays, even in its early stages, in colonial areas seems to be considerably more limited, relatively to contemporary possibilities, than indigenous capitalism played in the original industrial countries. Frequently, for political reasons, it supports rather than supplants reactionary social and political forms (for instance, the

---

[1] It is to be noted that in speaking of colonies here we are referring to those which are properly colonies of the Imperialist epoch. Those parts of the British Empire which constitute the so-called Dominions are not properly colonies in this sense—they are the former colonies of the Mercantilist period, which have since achieved considerable in-dependence. (South Africa, on the other hand, with its large exploited native population is, again, in a special position.)

native States in India; the perpetuation of the political disintegration of China), especially when it needs to seek for allies against rivals within or without the colony. As at certain stages in the earlier history of capitalism merchant capital effected a compromise with feudal or semi-feudal interests or with the Court, in alliance against a *parvenu* industrial bourgeoisie (as in seventeenth-century England), so the imperialist interest may lie in alliance with the remnants of the old ruling class of the colonial country in opposition to the designs of a native bourgeoisie with its interest rooted in intensive industrialization. As we have said, capital investment in colonies is very largely privileged investment, with semi-monopolistic rights or restrictions attached; while in many cases it takes the form of the exploitation, and consequent perpetuation, of relatively primitive forms of production: a tendency which will be encouraged by the very poverty of the colony and the cheapness of its labour-supply. Again, it may run counter to the gain of the capitalist class of the imperialist country to encourage investment in types of colonial production which will compete with the exclusive advantage which that industry in the mother country has previously enjoyed. A monopolistic element, therefore, quickly enters in, discouraging certain types of colonial development which are rival to other imperial interests, and often limiting industrial development in the colony to types of production which are complementary and not rival to those of the metropolis.[1] Since an "infant" industry usually requires some differential

[1] To express it in abstract terms: it would be in the interest of the capitalist class of the metropolis as a whole to act as a discriminating monopolist in its investment, limiting investment in the colony so as to maintain a higher rate of profit there and so as not to compete with the products of home investment.

encouragement to launch it on its career, the mere absence of special encouragement to colonial industry may suffice to cramp industrialization within narrow limits.

That Imperialism will very soon bring monopoly-practices reminiscent of Mercantilism in its train is made probable by a special and distinctive feature of this system. While the mere export of capital does not depend upon an elaborate regulation of trade between colony and metropolis, as did Mercantilism, and can even thrive in company with a policy of the so-called "Open Door", it necessitates, as the colonial system of earlier centuries did not, a large measure of political control over the *internal* relations and structure of the colonial economy. This it requires, not merely to "protect property" and to ensure that the profit of the investment is not offset by political risks, but actually to create the essential conditions for the profitable investment of capital. Among these conditions is the existence of a proletariat sufficient to provide a plentiful and cheap labour-supply; and where this does not exist, suitable modifications of pre-existent social forms will need to be enforced (of which the reduction of tribal land-reserves and the introduction of differential taxation on natives living in the tribal reserve in East and South Africa are examples).[1] Here, in this closer control of the metropolis over the internal politics of the colony, seems to lie the basis of that political logic of Imperialism, which its history reveals, to graduate from "economic penetration" to "spheres of influence", from "spheres of influence"

[1] "In every tropical African possession the expropriation, exploitation and the virtual enslavement of the native inhabitants have been demanded by the white settlers and capitalists, and everywhere, except in British West Africa, it is being accomplished." (Leonard Woolf, *Econ. Imperialism*, p. 68.)

to protectorates or indirect control, and from protectorates *via* military occupation to annexation. As soon as political control arrives as handmaid to investment, the opportunity for monopolistic and preferential practices exists; and if this political control is used, it will presumably be used in the promotion of the particular interests it represents. The process of investment and the economic development of the colony will not operate in an idyllic environment of *laissez-faire*.

It would seem that these restrictive and monopolistic aspects of Imperialism become particularly prominent in the later stages of its development, and then come to constitute an essential element of the relationship between metropolis and colony. At first, when the field of investment is virgin and concession-hunting easy, attention is mainly directed to seizing such opportunities as lie to hand or to opening up new fields. This is the pioneering stage when there is still room for all. The Scramble for Africa of the 'eighties, with a whole continent before it, did not as yet imply acute rivalry. The Fashoda incident, it is true, followed very soon, before the scramble was complete, as portent of future storms. But there still remained sufficient room to permit the principle of "compensations" to be applied between the rivals, as it was applied, for instance, to mollify Franco-British rivalry in North Africa. The gangster-lust to "partition the globe" as exclusive "territories" still had virgin lands to feed on. The Morocco incident of 1911 was a more serious portent; and as soon as the hinterlands of British East and German East Africa were developed, the pressure of a latent rivalry in central Africa inevitably grew. Even so, it was probably in the Near East, along the road to Bagdad, to Teheran and to India, rather than in Africa, that the most dangerous gunpowder-train leading to August 1914 was laid.

Yet even in this early stage there is nothing like the free competition of classical doctrine in the bidding for investment-opportunities and concession-rights. Preferences of one type or another figure prominently in the game; and in establishing or maintaining these preferences political influence plays an outstanding rôle. The history of this development abounds in instances of political influence being decisive in determining to which of competing national groups a particular concession is assigned—the history of China, South America, of the Near East, of Egypt, Tripoli, Morocco.[1] Once attained, the special rights enjoyed by such bodies as the South Africa Company, the British and German East Africa Companies, the Niger Company, the Sudan Plantation Syndicate, the pre-war Bagdad Railway Company (to mention the more obvious examples) constituted them virtual monopolies over an extensive sphere. What is true of loans, constructional contracts and mining-concessions is true to a less extent of trade in commodities, and probably tends to become more characteristic of colonial trade as colonial development proceeds. As Professor Pigou has said: "There are openings for highly profitable investments in loans to weak governments whose officials can be bribed or cajoled, in building railways for such governments on favourable terms, in developing the natural resources of oil-fields, or in establishing rubber plantations on land taken from Africans and worked by the forced or 'stimulated'

[1] Cf. such works as: L. Woolf, *Empire and Commerce in Africa*; Earle, *Turkey, the Great Powers and the Bagdad Railway*; Brailsford, *War of Steel and Gold*; Nearing and Freeman, *Dollar Diplomacy*; T. W. Overlach, *Foreign Financial Control in China*.

labour of Africans at a very low wage. When the government of some civilized country has annexed, or is protecting, or has established a sphere of influence over any undeveloped region, these valuable concessions are apt to flow, even when they are not formally reserved, to financiers among its own nationals. These financiers are often rich and powerful. They have means of making their voices heard through newspapers, of influencing opinion, and of putting pressure on governments." [1]

The classical theory of foreign trade postulates that countries tend to specialize on producing those commodities in the production of which they have a comparative advantage, and that the gains of the trade are divided according to .the elasticities of the relevant national demands (expressed in terms of the commodities each exports to acquire the commodities it requires to import). It would hardly be incorrect to say that to-day the precise opposite is true: that each country attempts to create or to "earmark" for itself the demand for those things which it has the facilities to produce; and that economic hegemony consists in success in so doing. What is the economic significance of the spread of the culture, habits and customs of a particular nation to "backward areas" if it is not that the latter will tend to develop tastes for what the former has become fitted to produce, and hence historically has grown to appreciate and desire? This process is, of course, subject to important qualifications. A nation which has no coal can hardly train its colony to tastes which exclude coal altogether, or a nation which has no textiles to coerce its colony into going naked and buying jewellery instead. But a colony under British influence or domination is

[1] *Political Economy of War*, pp. 21-2.

239

likely for numerous reasons to prefer British engineers and British personnel for its industry, and enterprises staffed by British personnel are likely to have a bias towards using British patents and devices and placing construction-contracts with British firms. In a British colony the prevalent fashion (unless there is strong reason to the contrary) is likely to lie in the direction of British cloths and British styles; and in a German or a French or a Japanese colony in a different direction. The effect of such influence will, of course, be that the financiers, concession-hunters, contractors, trading companies, etc., will be able to enjoy a higher price of sale and a lower price of purchase than if these preferences had not existed and their transactions had taken place in a more perfectly competitive market. In other words, the "terms of trade" between metropolis and colony will be turned in favour of the former. The aphorism that "Trade follows the Flag" embodies the essential truth that a significant aspect of the rôle of colonies in international economics is that they constitute in large part "private markets" for the interests of the national group which controls them, even where the policy of the "Open Door" prevails. The number and extent of such privileged spheres which a national capitalism can enjoy will significantly determine the rate of profit which it can earn and the place it can hold in world economy. In this sense, the "search for markets", to which the under-consumptionists refer, will have an independent meaning: namely, the search for extended opportunities of deriving monopoly-profit by exploitation through trade, as distinct from the extraction of "normal" surplus-value.

But to-day even the nominal maintenance of "Open

Door" policies is becoming increasingly rare. Agreements as to spheres of influence run parallel to the territory-agreements between international cartels, which divide out the market into assigned "preserves". Political appeals are directly used to influence demands, and we see combines using political prejudices to exclude rival products (as, for example, in the notorious campaign against Russian oil a few years ago). So intimately are politics and economics entwined that the mere smell of an oil-concession has been known to throw at least one international conference of States into confusion. Current politics of "autarky" and economic nationalism, with their raising of tariff-walls round national or imperial units and their plethora of quota-arrangements, merely pursue the ideal of the restricted market and the monopolized preserve in a more perfected form; while the now-fashionable balanced-trade agreements and the revived gospel of export-surpluses are explicit recognition of that neo-Mercantilism which has always been latent in modern Imperialism. In this process monetary disturbances, on which the economist's attention has been mainly fastened, would seem to figure as effect rather than as cause: exchange-depreciation as one of the instruments of export-rivalry; and the opposition of rival currency systems, such as the gold-bloc, the sterling-bloc and the dollar-bloc, as an aspect of a manœuvre for position in the creation of protected and isolated economic areas. When a Hitler or a Mussolini preaches the need for colonial outlets, it is not abundance but restriction, not access to plenty for the people but monopolized preserves for big industry that he really desires.

The important question remains as to why this new colonialism should have appeared at the particular stage in history that it did. Lenin pointed out that Imperialism was the characteristic of capitalism in its monopoly-stage, particularly of the stage in which an integration of finance with industry took place, with its subordination of industrial decisions to large-scale financial strategy, which Hilferding had called "Finance-Capital".[1] Hence Imperialism implied not merely an export of capital to new areas where rejuvenated it could retrace its history, but an expansion of capitalism to new areas under specific conditions, with a consequent emergence of quite novel elements in the situation. Moreover, as recent events have shown (in Spain, for example), this lust of expansion is directed not only towards "backward" countries of Asia or Africa but towards neighbouring regions, the economic control over which can yield monopolistic advantages.[2] And for this association of Imperialism with the passing of capitalism in the metropolis into a monopoly-stage there is a strong evidence of fact as well as the presumption of abstract reasoning.

The simultaneity in the rise of modern Imperialism in the countries of western Europe is a notable fact which has been frequently mentioned. It was with surprising accord that in the 'seventies and early 'eighties of the last century the most advanced capitalist countries, Britain, Germany and France (with Britain ahead and somewhat more successful than the rest), showed a revived interest in colonies; and eager hands were

---

[1] Lenin, *Imperialism*; R. Hilferding, *Finanz-Kapital*.

[2] So much indeed has this desire for the fruits of monopolistic control over already developed spheres come to the forefront that it may well be that export of capital will in future play a much smaller rôle than in the pre-war epoch. Cf. the remark of Prof. B. Ohlin: "Conditions are so different from what they were in the nineteenth century that international capital movements will play a much smaller rôle than they did formerly." (In *International Econ. Reconstruction*, p. 75.)

stretched out in the notorious Scramble for Africa, by which within scarcely more than a decade a continent was carved out between a few great Powers.[1] Interest in China and the Far East was revived; and rivalry for "spheres of influence" here and in the Near East quickly imitated events in Africa. This conversion to new methods was sudden as well as simultaneous. It seemed to come unprepared by gradual steps in retreat from the previous policy, as represented by the Cobdenite ideal of international free trade. For thirty years the tide of British policy had been setting steadily in the direction of loosening the bonds between Britain and her older colonies of the Mercantile period; and the Scramble for Africa came close on the heels of Gladstone's most signal triumphs in crowning free trade and close on the heels of the Great Exhibition and of a series of commercial treaties which were acclaimed as marking the dawn of a free-trade world. Something more than the eloquence of a Disraeli seems necessary to explain this sudden turn of the tide. Within a few years there was revived protectionist talk under the slogan of "Fair Trade not Free Trade"; Joseph Chamberlain in due course was to lead his revolt from the Liberal Party; while in France and Germany, as in Britain, the value of colonies to the mother country was rediscovered in theory and in practice. Italy, for whom the industrial revolution came late in the century, showed a tardier

[1] "In the ten years 1880–1890 five million square miles of African territory, containing a population of over 60 millions, were seized by and subjected to European States. In Asia during the same ten years Britain annexed Burma and subjected to her control the Malay peninsula and Baluchistan; while France took the first steps towards subjecting or breaking up China by seizing Annam and Tonking. At the same time there took place a scramble for the islands of the Pacific between the three Great Powers." (L. Woolf, *Econ. Imperialism*, pp. 33-4.)

interest in northern Africa; and U.S.A., for special reasons of its own development, did not take the colonial road until the very end of the nineteenth century.[1] Last of all on the scene we see Japan, who made a transition to modern capitalism around the turn of the century with such phenomenal speed, to-day imitating and improving upon the policies of the European Powers and America a quarter to half a century before. The evidence of history suggests that Imperialism is associated with the maturing of capitalism in a country to a certain stage of its development, and that it blossoms rapidly when this stage is reached, but not before.

The two features of capitalist development with which it seems most reasonable to associate this new expansionist tendency are the following: on the one hand, the exhaustion or near-exhaustion, of the potentialities of what was termed in the previous chapter the "extensive" recruitment of the "industrial reserve army" within the old national boundaries; on the other hand, encouraged by the former, the raising of the technical level, or the organic composition of capital, to a point which requires a considerable development of the heavy constructional trades. These twin developments will probably be associated with a tendency to fairly sharp decline in the profitability of capital; while the technical development of the means of production will provide the basis for

[1] While in America industrialization of the Atlantic seaboard came relatively early in the century, complete and developed industrial capitalism did not come to the West and South till relatively late. There is evidence, I think, to suggest that for most of the nineteenth century U.S.A. capitalism was occupied with a form of "internal colonialism", in which the agricultural hinterland played the rôle of a colonial area to Big Capital entrenched in the East. At any rate, not until the turn of the century did U.S.A. cease to be on balance an *importer* of manufactured goods.

that concentration of capital out of which large monopolistic groupings are likely to grow. Capitalism becomes "over-ripe", in Lenin's phrase, in the sense that "capital lacks opportunities for profitable investment".[1] If it be true that these developments are marked by a sharp fall in the return on capital, this fact will provide a stimulus simultaneously to the adoption of monopolistic policies in home industry and to the search for new investment-fields abroad; while the growth of large monopolistic groupings, particularly if welded with finance, will provide the type of organization which alone is competent to undertake the strategy of large-scale economic conquest overseas. Moreover, there is a special reason why monopoly and colonialism are logically joined. While monopoly in a particular industry or group of industries may succeed in increasing the rate of profit, it is powerless so soon as it has become general to raise the rate of profit all round, unless it can cheapen the price of labour-power or squeeze some intermediate income-strata at home.[2] In pursuit of success, it is, therefore, relentlessly driven to extend the sphere of exploitation abroad.

As has been said above, it was far from the intention of Marx that his analysis of capitalist society should provide a few simple principles from which the whole future of that society could be mechanically deduced. The essence of his conception was that movement came from the conflict of opposed elements in that society, and from this interaction and movement new elements and new relationships emerged. The laws of the higher stage of organic development could not necessarily be

[1] *Imperialism* (Ed. 1933), p. 58.
[2] See above, p. 75.

deduced, at least *in toto*, from those of the lower stage, even though the former bore a definable relation to the latter. What gives to Lenin's analysis of this new stage of development so much of its importance is that he clearly enunciated the respects in which this new stage modified or transformed certain of the relationships which were characteristic of the earlier pre-imperialist stage—changes which have frequently been quoted as contradictions of the Marxian forecast. But while Imperialism undoubtedly introduced situations which were not and could not have been foreseen in the middle of the nineteenth century, these situations have features which ultimately seem to reinforce, rather than to nullify, the essentials of the forecast which Marx made.

First among these significant results of the new Imperialism was its effect on class relationships in the home country. The super-profit, and the new prosperity which the successful nation was able to acquire, created the possibility for the working class of the metropolis, or at least privileged sections of it, to share in some degree in the gains of this exploitation, if only in the form of a relaxation of the pressure on wages to which, thwarted of any such outlet, capital would probably have had to resort. Where labour organization was strong, it could exact concessions more easily than it could otherwise have done and secure for itself a certain privileged position. This to a large extent goes to explain the maintenance of what has often been called an "aristocracy of labour" in Britain and North America, and to a lesser extent in France and Germany: of a working class which stood in a preferential position relatively to the proletariat of the rest of the world. They were the "palace slaves" of the metropolis, who, contrasted with the "plantation slaves" on the periphery of Empire, felt a partial identity of interest with their masters and a reluctance to disturb the *status quo*: a fact apparently reflected in a whole epoch (the epoch of the Second International and of Social-Democracy) in the labour movement in those countries. In his Preface to the second edition (1892) of *The Condition of the Working Class in England*, Engels made his well-known statement about the British labour movement: "During the period of England's industrial monopoly, the English working class has to a certain extent shared in the benefits of the monopoly. These benefits were very unequally parcelled out; the privileged minority pocketed most, but even the great mass had at least a temporary share now and then. And that is the reason why since the dying out of Owenism there has been no Socialism in England. With the breakdown of that monopoly the English working class will lose that privileged position; it will find itself generally on a level with its fellow-workers abroad. And that is the reason why there will be Socialism again in England." Faced with the events of 1914, Lenin spoke mordantly of "the tendency of Imperialism (in England) to divide the workers, to reinforce opportunism among them, to engender a temporary gangrene in the workers' movement" as "manifest(ing) itself before the end of the nineteenth century", and referred to the leaders of Social Democracy at that time, the tribunes of the more pampered metropolitan "palace slaves", as "sergeant-majors of Capital in the ranks of Labour". At the same time there tended to develop in the imperialist countries both a large and overgrown so-called "middle class", whose livelihood depended directly or indirectly on the imperial connection, ranging from clerks in city offices to colonial administrators, and an inflated *rentier* element which thrived on the yield of foreign investments.

Secondly, the historical rôle of Imperialism in colonial areas has been to create a similar class structure to that which was found in the older capitalist countries. As pre-condition of industrial investment it required a rural and later an urban proletariat; and as industrialization proceeded a colonial bourgeoisie came to be created also, graduating from *compradores*, middlemen and usurers, land-speculators, organizers of domestic industry or well-to-do farmers, to become industrial entrepreneurs. It would seem to be as inevitable that this class, resenting the monopolistic privileges of foreign capital and the influence of absentee interests, should come into rivalry with imperialist interests, as that *parvenu* industrial capital in seventeenth-century England should have waged an anti-monopoly campaign which culminated in a civil war. Here, in the desire to dispossess foreign capital of its privileges and to pursue a course of State-encouraged development of native industry, lay the nucleus of a colonial nationalist movement—of a nationalism which should reproduce, in a different historical setting, the features of the bourgeois-democratic movements in Europe of 1789 and 1830 and 1848. As Mercantilism led to the revolt of the American colonies, so Imperialism leads to colonial revolt, to-day in Asia, perhaps to-morrow in Africa. Imperialism, as has been said, represents not a simple but a complex relation between metropolis and colony. It does not represent a reproduction in the colony of the "pure" type of industrial capitalism, carrying a simple relation between a colonial proletariat and industrial capital, whether native or foreign. (If it did, there would be no economic *raison d'être* for colonial nationalism, save as a purely proletarian and socialist movement.) It embraces also a relation of monopolistic exploitation through trade with the colonial economy as a whole. Hence large sections of the colonial *bourgeoisie* and *petite-bourgeoisie* have economic roots which bring them within the nationalist movement; and colonial nationalism, accordingly, represents a strongly mixed-class movement. The twentieth century, therefore, was destined to witness a new historical phenomenon in the shape of national-democratic revolts in the provinces of Empire, to join with the proletarian revolt at the metropolis of which Marx had spoken, to shake the pillars of Capital's rule. In this new epoch it might well happen that the centre of gravity even would be shifted, and the former, rather than the latter, set the pace of events.

A third consequence of Imperialism on the shape of events in world economy was an accentuated inequality of development between different countries and different areas. In the nineteenth century it seemed as though the march of industrialization exercised a "levelling" influence on different parts of the world. The growth of the world market, both for commodities and for capital, was generally considered as tending to lessen national differences and to bring different countries increasingly into conformity in their technical levels and even in their standards of life. It is probably true that there were always important qualifications to be made to this view. But with the rise of the new colonial system certain new types of inequality appeared which were significant in their influence alike on the internal class structure and the internal stability of various national

groups. Superficially viewed, monopoly might appear
to represent unification, co-ordination and a higher
degree of ordered planning. This may be in part
true of relations within the sphere of a particular
monopoly-control. But monopoly essentially spells
privilege, and economic privilege spells restriction and
exclusion. It necessarily means preference *over* someone else, exclusion *of* someone else; and here at once
the seeds of inequality and of rivalry lie embedded.
Those Powers which are most successful in a policy of
colonialism are able to acquire a new prosperity (for a
period at least) and enhanced internal stability. When
rivalry attains the stage of open conflict, and conflict
becomes war, the extension of territory by one group
will be purchasable only at the expense of another; as
in gang-wars "territory" is first enlarged by extension
into virgin tracts, but later can only be enlarged by
stealing territory from a rival gang. That this stage
was already reached by 1914, the Treaty of Versailles,
with its wholesale transfers of colonies from vanquished
to victors, seems ample witness. These new inequalities
and rivalries of the imperialist epoch Lenin in his theory
adduced to support two conclusions: first, the impossibility of what had been called "super-Imperialism"
(an internationalism of imperial Powers jointly and
peaceably to exploit the globe); secondly, the objective
possibility that the proletarian revolt against capitalism,
and the triumph of socialism, would come first, not in
the older capitalist countries which, being earliest and
most successful in the colonial race, had acquired a new
lease of prosperity, but in countries which, because they
were less developed industrially, constituted the "weakest
links" when a severe crisis, such as the Great War,

undermined the whole structure. In this latter conclusion he found both a justification for his own policy in Russia and the answer to what has so tirelessly been termed "the great paradox of Marxism", that the revolution which Marx had prophesied seventy years previously should have first come in Russia instead of in the countries of the West.

This conception of Imperialism, with its latent rivalry and its inner logic of expansion, offers an interesting parallel to the analysis of a slave economy which was made by Cairnes in his *Slave Power*. Cairnes here emphasized that in the Southern States of North America the only form of new investment and source of extended profit lay in the acquisition of more plantations and more slaves. Hence the uneasy economy of the Southern States was continually moved by an urge to expansion to acquire more slaves and to extend the plantation-system to the West. In the eventual limitations on this process lay the inevitability of its ultimate clash with the North. A similar lust for expansion clearly lies in the blood of capitalist economy; and it too is a lust which cannot be indefinitely sated. The very counterforce which it generates in the form of colonial nationalism places increasing barriers to any intensification of its monopoly-policy, and even serves to loosen the bonds of Empire. For capitalism as a whole colonialism can afford no more than transitional respite.

If the post-war economic crisis is set against this type of background, there emerges a different, as well as more illuminating, interpretation from that which we customarily meet. Some such background, indeed, seems essential if we are to make any sense of the bewildering nightmare of recent events—if we are concerned at all with searching for *causae causantes* and are not content with the superficial picture afforded by an analysis solely of "immediate causes". Viewed in this larger perspective the malady of our post-war world clearly goes deeper than "the dislocations of war-time production", "Government restrictions on trade and enterprise", "monetary disturbances" and similar factors which have figured so prominently in traditional treatments of the subject, and even for many economists appear to be the limit of their field of vision; and the clear shape of a "general crisis", lying deeper than the cyclical movement, begins to emerge. It was Marshall who said that "in economics, neither those effects of known causes,. nor those causes of known effects which are most patent, are generally the most important: 'that which is not seen' is often better worth studying than that 'which is seen'," particularly when one is concerned "not with some question of merely local or temporary interest", but with "the construction of a far-reaching policy for the public good".[1]

Speaking of the events of 1929-30 Professor Robbins has said (writing in 1934): "We live, not in the fourth, but in the nineteenth, year of the world crisis. . . . The depression (of 1929) has dwarfed all preceding movements of a similar nature both in magnitude and in intensity. . . . It has been calculated by the International Labour Office that in 1933, in the world at large, something like 30 million persons were out of work. There have been many depressions in modern economic history, but it is safe to say that there has never been anything to compare with this."[2] Even in 1927 Professor Cassel

---

[1] *Principles*, p. 778.
[2] *The Great Depression*, pp. 1 and 10-11.

had issued a warning that "the danger of unemployment being made a permanent feature of our society is much more imminent than seems to be generally recognized".[1] Several years after the worst, at least, of the war-created débris had been cleared from the economic field, the new crisis of 1929 came like a distorted echo to mock economists who had said that crises were destined to grow less acute; and it is probably more than coincidence that this depression should have raised so many parallels with that of the period when Imperialism was being born. If anything of what has been said above holds true, an interpretation of these events which is to be more than superficial must clearly start from a central fact. This central fact is that the field of profitable investment for capital is very much narrower than it was on the other side of that historical watershed of 1914–18. It is apparently narrower, less because the absolute limits of colonial exploitation have been approached than by reason of the limits which the very tensions created by Imperialism impose. During and after the war colonial nationalism became a powerful force; and in significant directions the bonds of Empire are looser, or at least are stretched much nearer to bursting point, than they were before. The remarkable expansion of productive forces in Asia and America was an outstanding feature of the gigantic world-investment-boom of the quinquennium, 1925–29. In U.S.A. between 1922–29 the output of capital goods rose by 70 per cent., and that of non-durable consumption goods by only 23 per cent.; the output per worker in manufacturing industry increasing by some 43 per cent. in the decade prior to 1929, while at the same time the

[1] In *Recent Monopolistic Tendencies*, League of Nations Surveys, 1927.

increase of employment failed to keep pace with the growth of population and the percentage of the national income paid in wages showed a decline.[1] In Asia, native colonial industries, fostered by protection, have risen to steal colonial markets from the industries of the metropolis and to undermine the supremacy of the latter; and a measure of tariff autonomy, for instance, has had to be conceded even to India. While the mineral wealth of Siberia has been withdrawn from the orbit of capitalist investment, China is increasingly being closed to the older Empires by a Japanese "Monroe Doctrine"; and the balance of the Near East has been drastically affected by the rise of a nationalist Turkey and a nationalist Persia, ready to seek alliance with Soviet Russia, and by the related instability of the Arab kingdoms. In the case of Britain, the attempt to place an isolating tariff-wall round the Empire seems to have been hampered as much by internal economic conflict within the Empire-unit as by the fact that it is so imperfectly composed to form a successful economic unit. In particular, the strength of the semi-emancipated colonies of the Mercantile period has sufficed to ensure that in the scheme of "imperial preference" it is probably they rather than British capitalism that have secured the economic gain.

Connected with this restriction of the frontiers of colonial super-profit is a further fact, that the very growth of monopolistic restrictions and barriers has had the effect of narrowing the field of further investment. The profit which restriction reaps in the first instance is purchased by excluding some capital which

[1] Cf. Hugh-Jones and Radice, *An American Experiment*, pp. 43-51; also League of Nations, *Course and Phases of the World Econ. Depression*, pp. 120-5: "the boom was rather a typical investment boom than a consumption boom".

would otherwise have entered the field; so that the cumulative effect of such restrictions is to overcrowd other fields and so to reduce the profit-yield elsewhere below what it would otherwise have been.[1] Hence as a "solution" for the fundamental trouble in one direction it operates by worsening the trouble somewhere else: it is a "beggar-my-neighbour" policy. Partly, of course, the brunt of this has been borne by "small business" as contrasted with "big business"—by the "small capital" which inhabits the non-monopolized or less restricted territories. At the same time it has probably not been without its effect on the larger units of finance-capital as well. Moreover, this very curtailment of the investment-field within the monopolistic areas sharpens the passion for capital-export to outside areas; since such export is both the only outlet for surplus capital and the necessary condition for maintaining the monopolistic regime.

In these circumstances it is hardly surprising, quite apart from the agricultural crisis (which seems to have had partly separate causes), that the great investment boom of 1925–29 should have broken against the sharp edge of fundamental factors such as these, which undermined the level of profit in expectation of which the boom had been built. What Marx termed "overproduction of capital" inevitably manifested itself in an acute form. The sudden cessation of investment, both international and domestic, started the galloping paralysis of 1930 and 1931. And once the slump had started the dominance of monopolistic restrictions seems to have accentuated and prolonged the result. In particular, it seems to have been responsible for vastly

[1] Cf. Robbins, *op. cit.*, pp. 65-8, 131-2.

increasing the purely material wastage of this depression and for throwing the burden of the depression with un-precedented heaviness on to the workers in the shape of unemployment and under-employment. This restrictive sabotage took place not only in the form of foreign trade restrictions, which caused so drastic a shrinkage of the export trades and which still remains to choke the limited recovery of the past four years, but in the form of cartel- and trust-control of prices,[1] designed to maintain the rate of profit on capital. To maintain price involved restricting output ; and this was responsible for transforming the crisis to such an abnormal extent into one of excess-capacity and unemployment, with its prodigious wastage of both man-power and machine-power.

If the extension of the investment-field through colonial exploitation is blocked, and unexpectedly blocked, the problem of the "industrial reserve army" at home emerges again in an acute form. The capital formerly devoted to foreign investment must either lie idle and redundant or be invested in partly occupied fields. It has been suggested above that there are only two ways by which monopoly-capital can successfully raise the *general* rate of profit by monopolistic action *per se*: either by cheapening labour-power and squeezing some intermediate strata at home or by extending or deepening the field of exploitation open to it abroad.

[1] For example, in Germany (where alone figures are available) the fall in price of cartellized goods (covering about a half of industrial raw materials and semi-manufactured goods) between January 1929 and January 1932 was only 19 per cent. and that of non-cartellized goods as much as 50 per cent. One effect of this seems to have been the peculiar feature of this crisis that the price of producers' goods has fallen less rapidly than the price of consumers' goods. (League of Nations, *World Economic Survey, 1931-32*, pp. 127-33.)

If checked along the latter route, it has no alternative but to revert to the former. Thwarted of its easy opportunities abroad, it is thrown back upon an intensified monopoly-policy at home: a policy of maintaining profit at the expense of small producers, small *rentier* and "middle class" elements who may be easily squeezed as income-receivers or as consumers, and by cheapening labour-power—as a recent writer has put it, "smash(ing) that last stronghold of rigidity, wage-rates".[1] It might seem that the latter presented no serious problem in view of the large army of unemployed which exists in all industrial countries. But the "reserve army" must not only exist, it must be capable of being made effective for the strategy for which it is intended. And here we are confronted with this significant difference between the position to-day and in the classic days of the early and mid-nineteenth century: namely, that in so far as labour has developed to-day strong defensive organizations capable of resistance, the old classic law of the "industrial reserve army" fails to operate unaided. This, indeed, is the crux of the complaint which has been on the lips of the majority of economists since 1920, when they have spoken of the need to reintroduce "flexibility" and "plasticity" into the limbs of the economic system, and in particular into the labour market. To-day recourse to this device requires extraordinary measures—extraordinary measures to break this resistance of which nineteenth-century liberalism scarcely

---

[1] Fraser, *Great Britain and the Gold Standard*, p. 115. The connection between thwarted colonialism and intensified "internal monopolization" is pointed out by P. Braun in *Fascism Make or Break*: "to make up for the lack of colonial monopolies, finance-capital tries to establish industrial monopolies in its own 'mother-country' . . . it demands all the more monopoly or extra profits at home" (pp. 9-10).

dreamed. Short of an unexpected burst of "autonomous" labour-saving invention or short of renewed prospects of colonial outlets, this is the alternative to which capitalism in an increasing number of countries is being driven.

When the early disciples of Adam Smith first began to lecture in the university on Political Economy, it is said that their reference to vulgar things like "corn" and "drawbacks" was regarded as a "profanation" of academic tradition, while the very title of Political Economy bred suspicion of "dangerous propositions".[1] Such is apt to be the reaction to-day when an economist makes explicit reference to current political events. Yet to-day more intimately even than in the days of Smith and Ricardo are economics and politics entwined, political events having patent economic causes and economic forecast waiting upon the orbits of political movements. To comprehend what it is possible to do as well as what is happening, fully and "in the round", the economist can exclude the political connection of economic events as little as the political strategist can ignore the converse. Particularly intimate does the connection appear to be between certain political movements of the last few years and the characteristics of the economic crisis as we have described them. Here we are in a field where much of the evidence is still unsifted, and where generalization rests on particular interpretations of political happenings, and this interpretation in turn upon one's vision of contemporary events. For the present this must remain a matter of judgment: to recite here the evidence for that judgment would be too tedious, and must be reserved for another place.

[1] Introduction to *Stewart's Biographies*, Ed. Hamilton, pp. li-lii.

The two movements of recent years which most clearly have their roots in the post-war maladies of capitalism are Fascism and the disintegration in the position of wide sections of the so-called "middle class". Between Fascism as an ideology of political and economic nationalism and Imperialism as a system characteristic of an epoch there is an evident connection. But the precise character of this connection, while it seems plain enough in its essentials and increasingly plain as events proceed, is not always even now appreciated. The events of the past few years afford abundant evidence to support the view that the historical rôle of Fascism is a double one. First, that of breaking and disbanding the independent organizations of the working class, and doing so not in the interest of the "middle class" or the "small man" but ultimately in the interest of Big Business. Secondly, that of organizing the nation both spiritually by intensive propaganda and practically by military preparations and authoritarian centralization for an ambitious campaign of territorial expansion. True, it employs for these purposes—particularly for the former—a unique demagogy of "radicalism", yoked to a highly modernized propaganda-machine, and seeks to build a social basis for itself in mass organizations created around these demagogic demands. This, indeed, constitutes a distinctive characteristic of it as an historical movement. But the "revolution" when it comes is at most a "palace revolution", and once the Fascist State is in being it is the masses, not Capital, which are regimented, and the radical programme, not surplus-value, that is jettisoned. If the Corporate State has economic significance, other than as a means of controlling labour-disputes, it would seem to be as machinery for giving State sanction and support to a

259

more complete and rigid monopolistic organization of industry.[1]

But the connection between Fascism and colonialism is not simply that the latter figures as an incidental product of the former. The connection appears to be fundamental, and concerned not merely with the results but with the origin and social roots of this movement. Fascism has been called a child of crisis. In a sense it is; but the aphorism is too simple. It is child of a special sort of crisis, and a complex product of special features of that crisis: namely, a crisis of monopoly-capitalism which derives its special gravity from the fact that the system finds the road blocked for it both to an extensive and a more intensive development of the field of exploitation.[2] To break through these limits, novel and exceptional measures—measures of political dictatorship —become the inevitable orders of the day. If one is to summarize shortly the historical pre-conditions of Fascism, one can speak, I think, of three factors as pre-eminent: a despair on the part of Capital of finding a normal solution for the impasse created by the limitation of the investment-field; considerable and depressed "middle class" or *déclassé* elements, ripe, in the absence of an alternative rallying-point, to be recruited to the Fascist creed; and a working class, privileged enough and strong enough to be resistant to normal pressure on its standard of life, but sufficiently disunited or non-class-conscious (at least, in its political leadership) to be *politically* weak in asserting its power or in resisting attack. The first of these conditions is most likely to

[1] Cf. such facts as are cited in R. Pascal, *Nazi Dictatorship*; H. Finer, *Mussolini's Italy*; Ernst Henri, *Hitler over Europe*; R. P. Dutt, *Fascism*; G. Salvemini, *Under the Axe of Fascism*; etc.

[2] Cf. above, pp. 126.

be characteristic of an imperialist country which is thwarted of the fruits of colonialism on which it previously relied. With regard to the second and third conditions: it will clearly be those middle strata, previously nourished directly or indirectly on the imperial connection, which will most acutely feel the pinch of such a situation; and it will be a nation whose economy has previously rested on colonialism which is most likely to have produced an "aristocracy of labour", with an ideology and a political movement corresponding thereto. It is clearly more than mere coincidence that the classic homes of Fascism should be in two countries which were so evidently thwarted of their colonial ambitions by the outcome of the Great War; as it may well be also that similar tendencies should first strike their roots in Britain, the original cradle both of parliamentary democracy and of trade unionism, simultaneously with the first serious appearance of "middle class unemployment"[1] and of portentous signs of a decline of Britain's position as a financial and exporting centre. This presumption is strengthened by the actual association of elements in the policies of Fascist States to which we have referred. While the first chapter of Fascist policy has been to disband the trade unions, the second chapter has consisted of revived military conquests and colonial acquisition. The political and economic nationalism which forms the pattern of Fascist ideology is a nationalism of Empire units and racial hegemony—a dream of reconstructed, not of liquidated, Imperialism, as some have maintained.

Indeed, the economic policy of Fascist States represents the essence of Imperialism as we have attempted

[1] Cf., for example, the *Report of the University Grants Committee for 1929–30 to 1934–35*, pp. 29-30.

261

to describe it in its most mature form. In the internal economy, at the same time as the working class is regimented and its exploitation intensified, the monopolistic organization of industry is carried to a high degree, is given the sanction of the State, and is even compulsorily imposed and maintained. External trade is dragooned on rigid mercantilist lines, so as to turn the terms of trade in favour of the country; and while tariffs and quota-restrictions raise the price-level at home, export is frequently subsidized in an open or concealed form. At the same time the Fascist State is fired by a lust for territorial expansion, not only in the direction of undeveloped countries, as formerly, but of neighbouring territory, the control over which could yield monopolistic advantages to the big industry of the metropolis. Moreover, in this colonial ambition the greed for easy monopolistic advantage takes pride of place, even exclusive place Thus Italy grasps at Africa, Japan at Manchuria and Mongolia, and Germany at the mineral resources of Morocco and Spain, while at the same time turning her eyes towards the Ukraine, the Baltic States, Austria and the Balkans. Close on the heels of territorial ambition stalks rearmament, and with rearmament the organization of the national economy on a virtual war-basis, with war-time controls and war-time inflationary finance.[1] The stage

---

[1] A year ago the *Economist* quoted from the *Frankfurter Zeitung* the following changes in economic indices in Germany between 1932 and the end of 1935: an increase in the output of producers' goods (mainly under the stimulus of rearmament orders) of 113 per cent., as against an increased output of consumers' goods of only 14 per cent.; a decline in average hourly wage-rates for male workers of 5 per cent., and an increase in the total wage- and salary-bill of 21 per cent., against an increase in production (in values) of 53 per cent. (*Economist*, April 18, 1936.) While money wages have shown a tendency to decline, the cost of living appears to have increased between 1933 and 1936 by 15 to

is more clearly set than ever before—the curtain is even already raised—for a gangster-war to repartition the globe.

But there are characteristics of this latter-day development which are already exerting an influence on the social structure in the home countries of so radical a kind as to constitute a political landmark of no small importance. I refer to the disintegrating effect of recent economic events on the various middle strata of the metropolitan economy. The economic position of these strata has many links, direct and indirect, with the colonial system; and with any shrinkage of colonial super-profit this position, which was previously one of considerable privilege, becomes immediately insecure. But it is also to a large extent these strata who are adversely affected by the new stage of intensified monopolistic development in the home country, in particular by the increasing emphasis on the purely restrictive aspect of this development, such as economic nationalism and the paralysis of foreign trade, price-control by cartels and restriction-schemes, which are apt to bear with special heaviness on the small producer as well as on the consumer. That the increasing radicalization of large sections of this so-called "middle class", which we are witnessing to-day, and their willingness to align themselves (for the first time since 1848) with the proletariat in an organized "people's front" of "the left" is connected with a fundamental modification of their economic position in

20 per cent. (Cf. *Dept. of Overseas Trade Report on Germany*, 1936, pp. 229-31; also *Economist*, January 26 and July 13, 1935.) The intensive rearmament activity accounts for some two-thirds of the output of the producers' goods industries (as compared with one-fifth in 1928) and has apparently only been made possible by rationing of metals and by the prohibition of new investment and construction in a whole range of trades such as textiles, paper, steel tubes, lead, cellulose, radio. (*D.O.T. Report*, pp. 83, 84, 121.)

contemporary society, is a suggestion to which too little attention seems to have been paid. This tendency of previously privileged strata to pass over into a relationship of actual antagonism to capitalism, forming the basis for a new and wide popular unity in opposition to monopoly, is strengthened by the fact that to-day the mechanism of capitalist society is increasingly evident as what it really is. As the kid-glove in politics is shed, so economic reality breaks through the illusionist's veil. This is no accident easily to be repaired. It is because the system operates in such a way as to have plainly written on its face what its motive is. The very remedies to which it has recourse increasingly betray its character —betray it as a system "built upon compulsion, restriction and monopoly" and levying tribute on the peoples of the world; as a "mean and malignant" system which jettisons industrial and social progress in "the little interest of one little order of men".

One is hardly surprised to find that, contrasted with the overwhelming evidence of fact as to the true nature of Imperialism, the ideology of Imperialism should represent reality in an inverted form. In the past the economic basis of the system has been concealed by a political idealism which has represented the aims of colonialism purely in terms of the passion for political or racial hegemony. But with increasing frequency in recent years another aspect of colonialism has been stressed. A nation requires colonies, it is said, because of over-population at home, to enable its people to have access to land and to natural resources of which they are starved. This is a plea which has been made for the colonial ambitions of each of the three outstanding expansionist nations of to-day, Japan, Italy and Germany.

Not monopoly-rights and privileged spheres of investment, not "the little interest of one little order of men",
but the interest of the whole people is represented as the
raison d'être of this lust for conquest. To judge by its
ready acceptance, this explanation is plausible; but it
does not appear to be capable of withstanding anything
more than the most superficial scrutiny of the facts.
The plea that a nation needs colonies to give it access
to natural resources would be more convincing if it were
true that countries were accustomed (apart from war-
time) to refuse to sell to other nationals the produce of
their colonies, or even to discriminate markedly in the
price at which they sell them. Of this there is little or
no evidence. It is not export-duties, but import-duties
which imperial units are wont to impose. It is markets,
concession-rights and investment opportunities, not the
sale of its colonial products, that an imperialist country
seeks to reserve for itself. If it were true that the desire
for colonies is to be explained by pressure of population
at home, then we should expect that the only areas which
States struggled to acquire would be those whose soil
and climate made them suitable for settlement by the
inhabitants of the mother country. On the contrary,
the most coveted colonial areas are frequently the least
suitable for such settlement; [1] and mining-concessions,
to be worked by native labour, are more often the pre-

---

[1] To take the case of Africa, as Mr. Woolf has written: "Algeria
and South Africa have been in the hands of European States for a
century or more; they are pre-eminently 'white men's countries'; yet
in both places Europeans form only a small minority of the population.
The complete failure of Europeans to colonize Africa is shown still
more plainly in the case of the tropical African possessions of European
States. In 1914 the four African colonies of Germany had an area of
930,000 square miles and a population of nearly 12 million; the total
white population was only 20,000. If we take the four British possessions

occupation of the imperialist pioneer than homes and holdings for the unemployed of the home country. Such an explanation clearly has the matter standing on its head. Not surplus of labour relative to capital, but surplus of capital relative to labour-power is the driving-force behind colonial acquisition.

There is another and different interpretation of Imperialism to which a reference should, perhaps, be made in conclusion, both because it has gained a certain currency among critics of Imperialism and because it bears a certain resemblance to the interpretation which has been outlined above. This is the interpretation of the expansionist tendencies of capitalism in terms of under-consumption in the home market. Mr. J. A. Hobson, the principal exponent of this view, has attributed the desire for colonial expansion to the fact that "the business interests of the nation as a whole are subordinated to those of certain sectional interests that usurp control of the natural resources and use them for their private gain". But the emphasis of his theory is to show that this private gain consists in access to markets abroad, because of the lack of markets that is caused by the limited consumption of the mass of the population at home. "Whatever is produced in England," he else-

of East Africa, Nyassaland, Nigeria and the Gold Coast, we find that the area is roughly 700,000 square miles, and the total population about 22 million; the European population is 11,000." (L. Woolf, *Econ. Imperialism*, pp. 54-5.) Sir Norman Angell has pointed out that Japan's sparsely populated colonies of Korea and Formosa have in forty years taken "a total of less than one year's increase of the Japanese population"; that in 1914 there were "more Germans earning their livelihood in the city of Paris than in all the German colonies in the whole world combined"; while in Italian Eritrea "after fifty years of ownership there were at the last census, in the 2000 square miles of territory in Eritrea most suitable for European residence, just about 400 Italians". (*This Have and Have-not Business*, pp. 115-17.)

266

where writes, "can be consumed in England provided that the income or power to demand commodities is properly distributed. An intelligent progressive community . . . can find full employment for an unlimited quantity of capital and labour within the limits of the country which it occupies."[1] The implication of this view is that the pursuance of a policy of social reform and of high wages in the home country would be an alternative solution for the system, which would remove the necessity for expansion to find new markets abroad. More recently Mr. G. D. H. Cole has enunciated a somewhat similar view, and, applying it to an interpretation of Fascism as primarily a middle-class movement, promoting essentially middle-class interests and seeking to reconcile Capital and Labour, he has written as follows: "Are the capitalist autocrats able so to overcome their instinctive opposition to working-class claims as to persist in handing over to the defeated workers [*i.e.* in a Fascist State] the higher and higher incomes required to afford an adequate outlet for the expanding production of industry? If they do not, the old capitalist contradiction will recur." The implication of this passage presumably is that, if capitalism were to do as Mr. Cole suggests, it would be rid of both the cause of economic crises and the need for colonial adventures.

Such an interpretation clearly depends for most of its strength on the analysis of economic crises in terms of under-consumption which has been discussed in an earlier chapter. If its validity as an explanation of crises is impugned, there is little to recommend its application in this particular case. But apart from its logical coherence as a theory, the decisive test must be its ability to generalize essential fact; and of the evidence of available

[1] *Imperialism*, pp. 76-8 *et seq.*

facts which are relevant to its validity there is very little to afford a presumption in favour of this hypothesis and its corollaries and a good deal to afford a presumption against it. In the recent history of the Corporate or the Totalitarian State there is hardly an atom of evidence to favour Mr. Cole's interpretation (which he would probably amend to-day) and much to contradict it. It does not seem to be in the lowest-wage countries that the lust for colonies is greatest or first born; and there seems to be no known case of any important section of the capitalist class (other than those who manufacture things of working-class consumption) or any capitalist State seriously treating a policy of raising wages at home as an alternative to the sweets of Empire. On the contrary, with increasing and surprising unanimity the propertied class of all countries, however various their attitudes on other matters, seem to unite spontaneously, as though prompted by animal-instinct, alike to suppress any serious threat to their colonial dominion and to resist any movement which shows signs of substantially strengthening the political and economic position of their workers. It may be said that this is because the instinct of property is persistently blind to its own best interest, even when this has been repeatedly indicated to them by under-consumptionists. But one would need much more evidence than any that has been offered to convince one that so universal and persistent a contradiction between action and interest can be true. The truth rather seems to be that while a particular capitalist may profit if other people pay his customers a handsome income, he will hardly profit by giving people the money with which to purchase his own goods. While, again, within certain limits, Lord Brassey's principle of "the economy of high wages" may apply and it will not profit even the strongest monopolist to exhaust the source on which he feeds, the essential truth remains that the rule of monopoly-profit is to give the least possible to acquire the most. To invest and to produce in order to raise the standard of life at home would certainly be, in a socialist economy, an alternative to colonial acquisition. For an economy motivated by social ends foreign investment might well appear a hindrance rather than an aid, in that it diverted capital resources from urgent development work at home. But only confusion is likely to result from transferring this analogy to a capitalist economy, which is in fact motivated not by social ends but by the profit of a limited section of society. "As long as capitalism remains capitalism, surplus capital will not be used for the purpose of raising the standard of living of the masses, since this would mean a decrease in profits for the capitalists: instead, it will be used to increase profits by exporting the capital abroad to backward countries." [1]

[1] Lenin, *Imperialism* (Ed. 1933), p. 58.

Chapter VIII

THE QUESTION OF ECONOMIC LAW IN A SOCIALIST ECONOMY

THE concept of a socialist economy has from time to time been employed by economists as an abstract term of comparison by which to throw into relief the specific features of an individualist economy, or else (as has been more frequent) to illustrate the alleged universality of economic laws. Such comparisons in the pre-war era were invariably of a very abstract kind, resting on a definition of socialism and of capitalism in terms of some single aspect of the difference between them separated from all the rest. But for such treatment to-day there is little excuse. The growth of Soviet economy in recent years, moreover its capacity for maintaining a steady "boom" rate of expansion over a decade, the large-scale constructional efforts which it has achieved, and its substitution of a state of scarcity for surplus in the labour market, have not only quickened interest, study and controversy, but have provided a concrete basis of comparison which before was lacking. Any examination of a socialist economy, if it is to be concrete, must clearly start from this essential fact: that the fundamental character of socialism consists in its abolition of the class relation which forms the basis of capitalist production through the expropriation of the propertied class and the socialization of land and capital.

From this transformation of the property basis it derives its specifically social character as a form of production, in the shape of a co-ordination of the constituent parts of the system by methods more direct than the influence of the market. This co-ordination a society rooted in what Engels termed the "individual appropriation of the means of production" may strive to imitate, but can never attain, by reason of the atomistic property-rights on which the system rests. As Professor Robbins has said, "planning involves central control; and central control excludes the right of individual disposal".[1] So far as what may be termed the mechanics of each system are concerned (with which the present chapter will mainly deal), the essential contrast is between an economy where the multifarious decisions which rule production are taken each in ignorance of all the rest and an economy where such decisions are co-ordinated and unified.

In face of the revolutionary threat to the capitalist order in the post-war years, a theoretical counter-attack on socialism developed from an influential quarter. This had some influence on the Continent, and more recently has exercised a limited influence and stimulated a considerable body of discussion in this country. The attack was uncompromising enough. Gathering implications and hints from earlier writings, Professor von Mises, of Vienna, declared it possible, as a direct corollary of economic theory, to demonstrate the *a priori* impossibility of socialism, on the ground that in the absence of the valuations of the individualist market, economic calculation and the reign of economic rationality must disappear. For all its parade of superior rationality, socialism must

---

[1] *The Great Depression*, p. 146; cf. also Barbara Wootton, *Plan or No Plan*, pp. 318-21.

result in chaos and in the rule of unguided bureaucratic whim. "In place of the economy of the 'anarchic' method of production, recourse will be had to the senseless output of an absurd apparatus. The wheels will turn, but will run to no effect. . . . There is only groping in the dark." [1] Similar, if more guarded, views were being expressed simultaneously by Brutzkus in Petrograd in 1920; and in less dogmatic form the doctrine has been reproduced in this country by Professor Hayek and Professor Robbins.[2]

Whether traditional economic theory can be held to imply any such corollary has been a subject of considerable dispute; and there seems little valid ground for supposing that the subjective theory of value even in its most uncompromising form can sustain any such conclusion. But there is a more subtle implication of traditional economic doctrine which has gained much wider acceptance, and has even been adopted apparently without question by most of those who have taken up the challenge which Professor Mises threw down. It is the implication that in essentials the same economic laws must rule in a socialist economy as rule in a capitalist economy, so that the economic problem must have the same general shape and be handled by similar mechanisms in the two systems. A difference in the distribution of income, it is said, merely represents a change of data, which has precisely the same significance as any change

---

[1] Mises in *Collectivist Econ. Planning*, Ed. Hayek, pp. 106 and 110.

[2] L. Mises, *Die Gemeinwirtschaft*, trans. in Eng. as *Socialism*; *Collectivist Econ. Planning*, Ed. Hayek; B. Brutzkus, *Econ. Planning in Sov. Russia*; L. Robbins, *The Great Depression*, p. 145 *et seq.* For the subsequent discussion cf. H. D. Dickinson in *Econ. Journal*, June 1933; A. P. Lerner in *Review of Econ. Studies*, October 1934; O. Lange, *ibid.*, October 1936; E. F. M. Durbin in *Econ. Journal*, December 1936; etc.

in tastes and in demand. The difference in this respect between socialism and capitalism is no difference of kind but only a difference of degree from the changes in distribution of income which are occurring every day. Such a change in data will leave the equations themselves, and the nature of the determining conditions unchanged. As for the disequilibrating effects of uncertainty: the essence of these will be the same so long as acts of God and the incalculable incidence of technical discovery are with us and consumers' choice with its vagaries remains unregimented. In this way the "problem of production" is abstractly separated from the "problem of distribution", and socialism declared (as J. S. Mill originally declared it) to be predominantly concerned with the latter. As a system of production and exchange a socialist economy must not seek to behave in too dissimilar a manner from a capitalist economy, even if, in the former, organizational forms and property-rights, and with them the distribution of the product and the social ends which production serves, are radically transformed. Consistently with this view, most of the socialist critics of Professor Mises have argued, in one key or another, that a socialist economy can escape the irrationality which is predicted of it if, but only if, it closely imitates the mechanism of the competitive market and consents to be ruled by the values which this market affirms. What this view seems to overlook is the full significance of the difference between socialism and capitalism, and in particular to fail to appreciate the crucial significance of a planned economy as consisting in the unification of all the major decisions which rule investment and production, by contrast with their atomistic diffusion. The difference is a difference of calculability of events in the one which are incalculable in the other, with a consequent difference in the shape which events tend to assume.

A changing world in which there is perfect certainty as to the future must, of course, remain a figment of the imagination, even if it is an ideal norm which rationality is always striving to attain. Events which the most expert and far-sighted must fail to foresee will always occur to deflect the path and introduce temporary disequilibrium until a readjustment can be made. Formally considered, such unforeseen changes belong to what one may call the theory of displacements and introduce no novel element into the statement of economic laws. If such displacements occur at a faster rate than readjustments can operate, then the system can get progressively further away from its "normal" path as time proceeds, as the writing of Tristram Shandy's autobiography got further from its conclusion ·as his life progressed. Even so, if these displacements show any regularity of incidence, they are likely to be discounted ahead, and so to pass over from the unknown and unforeseen to the probable and partly anticipated. But while such unforeseen displacements of data will cause maladjustment when they occur, they need not give rise to an oscillation or fluctuation.

Whenever there is an unforeseen element, the expectation as to what is likely to occur will, of course, be a factor shaping what occurs before the displacement and helping to shape what happens after it. But, as was suggested at the close of Chapter VI, it is in an individualist economy that what may be called the theory of profit-expectations acquires its unique importance, by reason of the peculiar type of uncertainty which is so essential a part of the mechanism of such an economy; just as the theory of frictions assumes the special form which was discussed in the same chapter because of the characteristics of an individualist system. The "automatic adjustment" and "rule of rationality" which is held to be the special virtue of a competitive market can only operate through the influence of price-changes *after the event*. Each set of events occurs as a result of decisions taken in blindness to other decisions and hence on the basis of guesses as to what their joint outcome will be. Only after these decisions have been embodied in action will the resulting price-movements afford evidence as to the facts of the total situation and so furnish an automatic corrective.[1] But where decisions have to be made some distance ahead of the market-events into which they mature, as is particularly true and probably increasingly true of all acts of investment, this corrective of resulting price-movements may not occur for some time, perhaps for a period of many years. In the meantime, guesses have to serve for knowledge, and mistaken decisions continue to be made and embodied in action. Moreover, once a decision is made and embodied in a durable act of investment, a revision of the decision may not be quickly possible and the legacy of the mistake may persist in the resulting maladjustment for years and decades—as, for instance, railway construction, mine-sinkings, town-planning (or the absence of it) bear witness. Such time-lags will give opportunity for the original guess to be magnified in its result, and for extensive and devastating

[1] Cf. E. F. M. Durbin in *Econ. Journal*, December 1935. Under competition the entrepreneur "is unaware of the reaction of his competitors' supply to the change of price which is common to him and them, and also of the effect on market-price of their combined change of output. In these conditions it is impossible for industries to make the correct long-period adjustments" (p. 704).

fluctuations to arise. Competition necessarily implies not only diffusion but also autonomy of separate decisions; and it is the separate autonomy of individual decisions which produces these results. If it were possible as some desire for a socialist economy to imitate such competition and its "automatic" adjustments, this system must necessarily inherit also the tendencies to disequilibrium and fluctuation which are the product of economic anarchy; just as, conversely, an attempt to graft elements of planning on to a capitalist system cannot subdue the fundamental anarchy which is the sinew of the system, precisely because such "planning" must respect the autonomy of individual property-rights—even become handmaid to existing monopoly-interests as current experience seems to show. Either planning means overriding the autonomy of separate decisions or it apparently means nothing at all. Those who dream of marrying collectivism to economic anarchy must, at any rate, not pretend that the progeny of this strange match will inherit only the virtues of its ill-mated parents.

We have said that by an economic law one must mean a generalized description of how things actually behave in the real world. If this is our meaning, then it should be immediately clear that the alleged identity of the economic laws which rule a capitalist and a socialist economy is based on an abstract analogy which starts from the assumption of a *laissez-faire* world of perfect certainty (save for certain objective "displacements") where neither frictions nor expectations can exert any appreciable influence. The assertion is not dissimilar to the statement that a railway system which worked without time-tables, each engine-driver being autonomous, would operate in a similar manner to a planned railway system as we know it. In the former, it is true, some form of traffic-equilibrium would tend spontaneously to emerge. But it would do so only *after* the occurrence of accidents and congesting delays had exerted their influence, and *after* the various shifts and oscillations incidental to eventual adjustment had worked out their full effects. After a series of accidents and congestions at crowded bottle-necks at times of competition for the larger midday traffic, a series of fluctuations might well develop, there being for a time an alternate rush of drivers to midnight and back again to midday-times in the alternate belief that one or other was the less crowded part of the day, or similar fluctuations between competing for the Scottish traffic or the Dover boat-train traffic, and so forth. To make the analogy closer one needs to suppose that a driver cannot alter his time and course at a moment's notice; but, like motor-coaches on the roads, must announce a programme of running for a year and sometimes years ahead. Eventually, no doubt, some sort of stable distribution of traffic would result—a sort of spontaneous time-table forged from experience and embodied in custom and tacit understandings. Yet any such equilibrium that was reached would be essentially an unstable one; since any shift of demand, or the opening of new lines and the closing of old ones, or a change in the power and speed of locomotives would reintroduce the influence of uncertainty and the fluctuating effect of expectation.[1]

[1] It is sometimes asserted that the aggregate "mistake" in an individualist world will tend to be small because individual expectations will have a random distribution and so tend largely to cancel out in their effects. But it is a familiar fact that actually, for a variety of reasons, mistaken expectations of a mass of individuals not only tend to have a pronounced bias in a particular direction at a particular time but also to some extent a reinforcing influence on one another. Apart from this, however, where uncertainty prevails, while there is a

Every decision by an entrepreneur with regard to production is in one sense of the word an act of investment. But when one speaks of acts of investment as of predominant importance in determining, on the one hand, the nature and extent of fluctuations, and on the other hand the long-period path of development, one refers to investment in fixed capital—to construction of durable plant and equipment. In the theory of profit-expectations this is of major importance, both by reason of the longer "period of gestation" of such acts (to use Mr. D. H. Robertson's phrase) and the durability of the result. In addition to such factors as demand and the future course of technical invention, such decisions will depend for their "correctness" on four main types of fact, with regard to each of which, in an individualist economy, the individual or individuals who make the investment decision are partly or wholly ignorant: first, parallel and rival acts of investment which are being made simultaneously, or will soon be made, in the same line of production or in competing processes; secondly, acts of investment which are being made or will be made in complementary processes (*e.g.* in subsidiary or by-product industries, transport or power facilities, etc.); thirdly, the amount of saving and investment which is being currently undertaken throughout the economic system as a whole; fourthly, the future course of capital accumulation (and hence of the rate of interest) over the period of economic life of the fixed capital in question.

The results of ignorance of the first set of facts is

greater probability that the average expectation will arrive at the "correct" position than at *any single one* of the other n possible positions, there will be a very much smaller probability of its arriving at this position than at *some one* of the n possible positions—absence of mistake will be a coincidence and a rarity.

278

fairly familiar, in the shape of the competitive tendency to over-investment in certain industries during the optimism of a boom. The tendency in the case of a fluctuating demand for investment to respond to the "peak" demand, so that the industry is loaded with plant and equipment which is partly derelict most of the time, has frequently been emphasized. Examples consist in the chaotic duplication of railway facilities, the frequent overlapping of public utility services, the mushroom growth of shopping and entertainment facilities in new urban districts where (in respect to shops at least) the rate of mortality of businesses seems to be extraordinarily high. But another aspect of this—its effect in leading to *under-investment*—which is also an effect of the second type of ignorance seems to have received less notice and its significance to have been under-estimated. The fear lest rivals may cut in and seize the fruit of an investment may exercise an important deterrent effect, particularly where costly minimum units of investment in durable plant are involved. In the case of new inventions the danger of this deterrent is met by conferring a temporary monopoly under the patent laws. But the same danger may exist in the case of any large-scale investment; and examples of it are doubtless more important than we are generally aware since they are not brought to our notice as are the results of over-investment, which force our attention. Here again, transport and power facilities seem to provide the most evident examples. A particular case is the unwillingness railway companies have shown to electrify suburban railway services round London on the ground of the risk which existed of the investment being reduced in value by the construction of rival facilities by some other authority, such as tramways or tubes.[1] An example of the effects of the second type of case is probably to be found in the primitive development in this country of the complex of processes for coal-utilization, many of which depend intimately on other complementary developments; or again the failure of an industry to shift to a new and more economic location, because each firm in the industry is reluctant to move and suffer the loss of nearness to subsidiary industries or processes, while the latter in turn hesitate to incur the risk of moving until the rest of the industry has already moved. Each waiting upon the other results in nothing at all being done.

But it is ignorance of more general facts of our third and fourth type which clearly has major importance, and the significance of which is the least understood. The difference between these two cases is merely as to the time to which they refer: they have been separated here merely because, while both are relevant to the distribution of investment in the immediate present, the second of them relates especially to the pattern of investment through time. In both cases, knowledge about the total situation is vital to the individual decision because it is on the total of present and future investment decisions and their nature that both the level of costs and the level of demand appropriate to each individual case depends. To illustrate this connection let us suppose that certain investment decisions in an industry have been made on the basis of the expectation that the aggregate volume of new investment and its approximate distribution would be the same during the current and the ensuing years as it had been over the immediately preceding period. Let us suppose that its total volume

[1] Cf. G. J. Ponsonby, *London Passenger Transport Problem*, pp. 47-8.

actually increases in the current and ensuing years, both because the total national income is larger and because there is a general tendency to consume a smaller proportion of income. Then four principal changes will occur in the data on which the original investment-decisions in the industry in question were based, decisions which are now irrevocable (in the main): first, owing to the changed level of consumption which probably makes the demand for their products smaller than was expected; secondly, owing to the increased investment and later an increased and cheapened output of goods in other industries, which again will tend to modify the demand (perhaps increasing it, perhaps decreasing it) for their particular products; third, owing to the effect of increased investment and construction on the level of costs in general, which will probably make the costs of production in this particular industry higher than had been anticipated; finally, there is likely to be some change in the demand for the products of this and other industries owing to a changed distribution of income as a net result of these changes. Indeed, if one approaches the matter from this angle, it would seem to become increasingly clear that a very considerable part of the demand-fluctuations which figure in so many discussions as an unavoidable accompaniment of free consumers' choice are actually the result of altered distribution of income produced either by fluctuations or by changes of this type which are uncertain in an individualist system.

A particular example of this, of considerable significance, is the demand for all products of the constructional trades. This demand depends directly on the total volume of investment. It is a demand which is peculiarly fluctuating, since the rhythm of this fluctuation is derived in an exaggerated form from the rhythm of activity of industry as a whole. Uncertainty as to what this demand will be, combined with the fact of fluctuation, imposes a heavy cost on these industries in view of the inability to adapt productive equipment to demand, which takes the shape of a recurrent excess-capacity.[1] It has recently been suggested that this is a powerful reason rendering the "financial optimum" (when uncertainty is allowed for) much smaller than the "technical optimum" in the steel industry, and preventing steel plants from being constructed on the most efficient scale.[2] An investment-programme which was constant and knowable in advance could remove both this fluctuation in demand and the uncertainty.

It might at first sight seem that facts of our fourth type—changes occurring in the future—are not relevant to the correctness or incorrectness of a previous investment from a *social* point of view—from the standpoint of "social production" or the collective interest—but relevant only to the profit which the capitalist can eventually obtain. But this is not so. And it is because this is not so that the investment problem of a socialist

---

[1] Cf. "A change from 3 to 6 per cent. in the output of the commodity might cause as much as a 40 or 50 per cent. increase in the smaller figure representing the requirements for production of capital equipment." (J. M. Clark, *Strategic Factors in Business Cycles*, p. 42.) Prof. Ragnar Frisch has pointed out that an expansion in the demand for constructional goods need not result in over-production in the constructional trades. (*Journal of Pol. Econ.*, 1931, p. 646. Cf. also Fowler, *Depreciation of Capital*, pp. 50-2.) But this qualification only holds if the rate of incrementation of investment is controlled so as to slacken off only in the degree to which the replacement-demand for equipment is increased by the new construction—a not impossible, but an unlikely, balance.

[2] Cf. *Britain without Capitalists*, pp. 382 and 390. With a planned investment-programme it becomes economic to build plants of the size of Magnitostroi and Kusnetskstroi.

economy would conform to a different principle from that which rules in a capitalist economy   A socialist economy would clearly be ruled by the aim of augmenting its capital construction at a more or less rapid rate until the "saturation point" of capital-equipment was reached—that is, until no further gain in productivity would result from using labour to embody itself as "stored-up labour"; where only the use and maintenance or replacement of existing plant and equipment took place; and where the whole current net output of labour could accrue to labour as current consumption.[1]   If perfect foresight were possible, the interest of the socialist State would lie in planning its investment programme so as to make the progress of construction and technical innovation follow a smooth path of ordered development into the future until this ideal goal of capital saturation was reached.   Actually, perfect foresight would not and could not exist, and any construction-programme sketched over the future would be subject to various displacements as unforeseen events occurred.   But to the extent that it was able to sketch an investment-programme over a period of years into the future, it would to that extent substantially alter the "investment-pattern" in each year as compared to what this would be in a capitalist society where no such degree of certainty with regard to the future was possible.

To make this difference of investment-pattern clear,

---

[1] Of course, so long as technical discovery continued, this point would probably never actually be reached; but it would continually be a goal which would be approached.   The point can be more precisely defined as that where the additional product resulting from an additional application of labour as "stored-up labour" is equal to that resulting from an additional application of labour as "current labour". Cf. NOTE to this chapter.

one must realize that from the standpoint of a socialist economy what figures in a capitalist economy as a problem of saving and investment is presented directly and consciously as a problem of distributing labour between various types of production having each a relation to different points of time. By relation to a particular point of time is meant the point of time at which the labour in question yields its final fruit in finished consumption goods. Broadly speaking, this means the manner in which labour is distributed between what Marx termed industries producing means of consumption and industries producing means of production. But inside the latter there will be gradations according to the time-destination of the means of production which are being constructed—whether new automatic looms which can be completed and installed next year or in building a blast-furnace to turn out constructional materials for a new power-scheme which will not be fully completed and in use until ten years hence.

Since industries have different technical "levels" (the "organic composition of capital" is different), this at the same time implies a certain distribution of labour between different industries at any given moment and between industries which make machinery and equipment for the former. The whole decision is a complex one, which must necessarily be a unified decision if the various elements in it are to be consistent with one another—unified in the sense of being made simultaneously and (in its final form) by some single authority, since only in this way can the separate decisions be made in full knowledge of all the other relevant decisions which are concurrently being made. If such separate decisions are made independently, they will necessarily be made in partial ignorance of all the rest, and hence at any one time will be inconsistent with one another (save by very rare coincidence)—inconsistencies which can only be subsequently corrected by jerks in development, and probably by jerks productive of fluctuations. In other words, the proportion of the national income which is saved, the proportions in which consumption goods and constructional goods are produced,[1] the balance between industries of different technical levels, and the distribution of constructional work between projects of different types in respect to their relation to the future are all intimately dependent on one another—logically they are separate facets of a single decision concerning the distribution of labour in production. The present output of consumption goods, and hence the level of real wages, cannot be decided independently of knowledge as to the productivity of additional "stored-up labour" devoted to increasing output two, three, four or five years hence; and whether to start constructional work designed to mature into final output in three years' time—or five years' or ten years'—cannot be properly decided without knowledge as to what the total output of consumers' goods will be in those future years and how many other projects designed to mature in those years are likely to be launched next year and the year after, and so forth. These things can no more be decided separately than a housewife on going into the market can decide how much of her housekeeping money to spend to-day and how much to spend instead to-morrow

[1] These proportions and the proportions of the national income spent and saved are not, of course, identical, unless investment (and saving) is used to mean *gross* investment, including repair and replacement. Actually, no such identity is implied here—merely that the two sets of decisions are dependent on one another in a major degree.

or next week until she has seen what prices rule in the market and what range of alternatives confront her.[1]

In a capitalist economy there would seem to exist a prevailing tendency to under-estimate the effect of capital accumulation in the future in lowering the rate of interest. To the extent that this is so, there will be a constant tendency to *over*-invest in projects of a type which yield the prevailing rate of interest, and hence are appropriate to the situation of the immediate moment, but will be inappropriate in the near future and partly obsolete, owing to the fact that the future, being richer in capital, will be in a position to utilize equipment of a more "advanced" type.[2] This tendency is probably strength-

---

[1] It is essentially for this reason that the essence of socialist production cannot be attained so long as the two aspects of "saving" (decisions governing the level of consumption) and "investment" (decisions relating to actual constructional work) are separated, and each made autonomously; *e.g.* connected by a loan-rate of interest, as some have suggested could persist under socialism. True, such a loan-rate, if continually adjusted, might eventually bring about some sort of temporary equilibrium between the two sets of decisions, but only tardily and as *post facto* corrections of mistakes and fluctuations. For example, if each industrial manager were left to compete for as much capital as he thought he could productively employ at a given loan-rate, he might embark on constructional projects in ignorance of what was happening elsewhere, and only later, after his and others' actions had reacted on the loan-rate, would he discover his mistake. Moreover, if a socialist economy were to adopt the pricing-system and the decentralization of decisions characteristic of capitalism, there is no reason why it should not be subject to the same sort of instability as was discussed at the end of Chapter VI: instability due, especially to the fact that profits (and hence demand for capital) will be cumulatively dependent on the rate of investment, itself The reasons for thinking so are more fully discussed in an article by the present writer in *The Economic Journal* for December 1939.

[2] Or what the Austrians term "longer" or "more roundabout" methods of production. I am speaking here only of the effect of increasing capital accumulation in a *constant* state of technical knowledge, and of obsolescence of older methods due to this. Obsolescence arising from new technical discoveries is another matter. (Incidentally, new inventions will tend initially towards a reversion to "shorter" methods

ened by the wish being father to the thought: the desire that the return on capital shall not fall refusing to admit such a fall to the extent of refraining from investing in projects which, according to available signs, promise a higher interest-yield. Moreover, the same reason enters here which in a boom will cause an industrialist to expand his production even if he realizes that the market is being overstocked and that prices will eventually fall: namely, uncertainty as to the exact time-incidence of the fall, creating the possibility that he may get into the market first, combined with the knowledge that any action of his own will exert a negligible influence in determining what occurs.

The result of this will be a tendency to continue investment in a particular type of capital too long and too late, beyond the point where the actual situation (in particular, the volume of capital maturing or in process of inauguration and the future movement of real income) requires that a transition should be made to investment in a different type with a lower interest-yield. As capital accumulation proceeds and traces a path through successive types of investment, there will be a continual tendency to over-invest in each type through blindness to the total situation and to future movements in real income and in interest-rates. The result will be a more rapid rate of obsolescence and wastage of plant and equipment than would otherwise be the case, most

rather than to "longer" methods. Cf. Armstrong, *Saving and Investment*, pp.164-6.) But even in the case of new technical discoveries, a socialist economy, with planned industrial research, abolition of secret research and processes, etc., would doubtless be in a better position to forecast them and hence to discount their effects in advance; even if to a considerable extent they must always represent an unforeseeable factor in development.

287

markedly at points of time when technical transitions from one investment-type to another occur, leading to jerks in development—jerks tending to give rise to exaggerated fluctuations owing to the relative over-investment in the more obsolete types, due to yield output at a certain point in the future, and corresponding under-investment in the newer and lower interest-yielding types, particularly in those which are due to yield output at a somewhat later point of time in the future.[1] As a consequence, the rate of development will be continually retarded through time. But even if it is not true that a capitalist economy will have a persistent bias towards *under*-estimating the future decline in interest-rates (and it is true that even if it does, this fact may be partly counterbalanced by the effect of under-estimating new technical discoveries), it will remain true that, being largely blind to future movements of investment and saving, such an economy will tend continually to make mistaken investment-decisions in one direction or another—mistakes which necessarily introduce discontinuities and oscillations. At any rate, it is clear that a socialist economy, to the extent that *ex natura* it can be more far-seeing, will distribute its investments between different types of new construction according to a different pattern over time. This does not necessarily mean that it will invest in a

---

[1] It might seem at first sight that while this would cause a continual retardation in the transition to newer types, it would not change the rate of obsolescence of older equipment, which would continue in use until there was sufficient new equipment to take its place. But this is not so, since the investment in the old equipment was undertaken on the basis of an *over*-estimate of the price of finished products in the future. When subsequently the unanticipated volume of investment shows itself in a higher wage-level and or lower prices of products than was anticipated, much of the old plant will fall out of profitable use.

wide variety of types of construction in any one technically homogeneous line of production (a "type" being
defined by its reference to a point of time in the future,
and hence by its productivity in relation to its period of
maturing into final output); but it means that it may
maintain currently in use, and *a fortiori* in use and in
construction, a considerable variety of types even in one
homogeneous line of production, and that it will pass
earlier and more evenly from the construction and use
of one type to the next.[1]

The important question here arises as to whether it
would be rational for a socialist economy to invest
simultaneously in projects of a wide variety of types,
or to invest at any one time in a particular type of
constructional project appropriate to the conditions prevailing at that time, passing on to newer and more
complicated projects gradually and *successively*. Would
it be proper to spread investment between types of
project appropriate to the situation in the immediate
future and to the different situation (different in that
productivity and income would be greater) of five years,
ten years, twenty years or even fifty years hence?[2] For

[1] Mr. Lerner has pointed out that *if* an individualist economy had
the same degree of foreknowledge, the same distribution of investment
could be brought about by appropriate movements of long- and short-
term rates of interest. (*Review of Econ. Studies*, Vol. 2, No. 1.) This is,
of course, true, provided differences of rates were sufficiently graded
according to the investment-period. But such a hypothesis implies
a contradiction, since it is the nature of an individualist economy that
it cannot have this degree of foresight. Mr. Lerner is postulating a
state of affairs where expectations could have no influence and fluctuations
could not arise to explain the effect of expectations and the causes of
fluctuations.

[2] In an article in *The Economic Journal* for December 1933, I stated
that the principle on which a socialist economy would distribute its
investment would be that of simultaneous construction of capital equipment of varying interest-yields (as contrasted with the principle of

example, "during the First Five-Year Plan (in U.S.S.R.) the principal type of freight locomotive became the type 'E' engine, the tractive power of which is 75 per cent. greater than that of the most widely used engine in pre-war Russia. Under the Second Five-Year Plan the output of type 'E' locomotives . . . is being supplemented by the manufacture of type 'F.D.' locomotives, whose tractive power exceeds that of the type 'E' locomotive by 30 per cent." [1] Is there any general principle by which to determine the rate at which it will be economic to supplant the pre-war type by E and to supplant E type by F.D.; and whether E will first be invested in until it has supplanted the pre-war type and type F.D. will only later be constructed; or whether, on the contrary, F.D. locomotives will be constructed from the outset, at the same time as type E and even some of the pre-war type are still being made? No general answer to this question seems possible; since the answer will depend not only on policy with regard to the income of the immediate future and of the more distant future, but on the technical situation which confronts the economy. If the loss involved in restricted consumption over the immediate future is more than balanced by the gain of productivity in later years, then a policy of so revolutionizing technique as to attain to maximum productivity in the shortest possible time will be the appropriate one; and in certain technical situations this end will be served (for reasons which are discussed in a NOTE to this chapter) by simultaneous investment

uniform interest-yield at any one point of time). I am now convinced that this would not necessarily be the case. Nevertheless it would remain true, I believe, in certain situations which are by no means unimportant or unlikely to occur.

[1] *The Second Five-Year Plan*, Ed. Gosplan, xxxvii.

in projects of a wide variety of types even in a single homogeneous industry. But where a more gradual progress of productivity is required, investment policy would tread the more familiar course of a chronological order in its choice of investment-types, passing successively from one to the next as the total situation developed. The pattern of investment in these various types, however, sketched through time, would be substantially different from that in a capitalist economy. The nature of this pattern can only, I think, be shortly defined as one which would enable transitions to newer methods to take place gradually and continuously by substituting the new type of equipment for the old as the latter in each case reached the end of its natural life; instead of in "waves" of obsolescence attaching to old equipment which was still in good physical condition—obsolescence due to the fact that this type of equipment has been created to excess. It is to be noted that in so far as in this latter case the depreciation of old equipment is due to *delay* in the transition to investment in new types, and not to too hasty transition, it will be associated with a general lagging-behind of technical development, not with its acceleration.

To use a simple analogy: let us suppose that a man were destined to inherit a fortune in five years' time. If he were ignorant of this fact, he might start to-day to build a house for himself, which, when his riches came, would prove superfluous, because he would then be rich enough to live in a mansion. But if he could calculate in advance that the fortune was due to arrive, then, clearly, he would not undertake the building of the house: instead, he would probably use the money to build himself a cheaper and temporary bungalow for the five years, while at the same time beginning to lay the foundations of the mansion so that he might move into it the sooner when his legacy arrived.[1]

I have elsewhere used the analogy of the so-called pursuit-curve to illustrate the difference between the two paths of development appropriate to the two types of economy. It can be used as a general illustration of adaptation to a moving situation through the medium of automatic responses at each moment of time, as contrasted with adaptation to the same situation as a result of foresight and rational calculation. A dog is situated at some distance from a path along which his master is riding. He runs towards his master, and acting on the basis of automatic responses he runs always towards the point at which he sees his master at the moment. His path towards his master accordingly is a curve, the precise shape of which is a function of his own speed and that of his master and of the angle and distance from the path at which he starts. If, however, the dog could have acted on foresight and calculation, in knowledge both of his own speed and that of his master, he would have taken a straight line to the point along the path which his master would subsequently reach, thereby reaching him the sooner and saving effort in so doing. This analogy, of course, must not be taken too literally. In

[1] Here he would almost certainly complete the bungalow *before* starting the foundations of the mansion; and on bungalow- and mansion-building combined he would probably in those five years spend less than he would have spent on the house. The resultant shifts of investment are a double result of the expectation of higher future income: of the knowledge that he will in all other respects be more comfortable at the end of five years and hence have less urgent need of money than he now has, and of the knowledge that for this reason it will be practicable to build a mansion. Hence, he reverts to the cheaper and less comfortable bungalow for the immediate present, but in other respects stints himself less than he otherwise would have done.

certain circumstances, as we have said, the aim of a socialist economy might be to reach the point of capital-saturation at the earliest point of time, irrespective of a restriction of the standard of consumption in the intervening years; and at certain periods of technical or of social transition this might well be the appropriate policy to pursue for a period. As a long-term policy, however, it is possible and even probable that a socialist economy would aim to effect a slower but steady increase in the output of consumption goods year by year at the maximum possible rate consistent with maintaining a balance between present and future needs. If we were to plot a curve of actual capital construction, measuring time along one axis and aggregate capital in terms of its productivity, or some similar quantity, along the other axis, then the path of development appropriate to a socialist economy would still be a curve, but a continuous curve, by contrast with a discontinuous curve, subject to wave-like movements, in a capitalist economy. In actuality, of course, no socialist economy would attain to this ideal continuous curve, partly owing to imperfect planning, partly on account of displacements due to unforeseeable events. But it would have a tendency to approximate to such a curve which an individualist economy lacks. A motor may not attain the speed it would have according to some ideal "norm" of efficiency. Under certain circumstances it may even be more sluggish than a tricycle. Yet there can be no doubt as to its different potentiality as an instrument of motion.

What has so far been said is independent of the *rate* of capital accumulation: in other words, no assumption has been made as to the principle determining this in a socialist economy—whether it will be greater than, equal to or less than what would prevail in a capitalist economy. Clearly, this is of fundamental importance, since, if it is different, then the balance between different industries and the distribution of labour between them as well as the inclination of the curve of constructional development towards the capital-saturation point will be further modified. Here again the uncritical attempt to apply the economic categories of a capitalist economy to a socialist economy seems to have led to confusion of thought. It has frequently been asserted that since there would be no free loan market in a socialist economy, there would be no means of "discovering" the "natural rate of interest", and hence no criterion as to the proper proportion of the national income to be invested in constructional work and no means of ensuring that investment policy corresponded to the "real savings" of the community.

In a capitalist economy the rate of capital accumulation is determined by two main factors: by the distribution of income, which determines the size of the income of the investing class, and by the accustomed standards of consumption of this class. On these factors what has been termed the "time-preference", or the rate of discounting the future as compared with the present, of the community principally depends. Any increase in capitalists' income tends to lower this time-preference, or discount of the future, and so to increase the rate of capital accumulation; while conversely any increase in their accustomed standards of consumption (by intensifying the desire for the immediate fruits of income) tends to raise this time-preference. Even more directly, therefore, than in other spheres, does the "spontaneous verdict" of the market here reflect the influence of "arbitrary" historical and institutional factors. While capital accumulation, as it proceeds, by augmenting the mass of surplus-value tends to produce a continual increase of new investment, this tendency is continually held in check by the rising standards of expenditure of the rich which seem to follow fairly closely behind increased income. Hence the fact of private ownership and private accumulation of capital, which in earlier days appeared as an instrument of rapid accumulation, subsequently becomes with increasing clearness a brake on the rate of capital-development. Moreover, as we have seen in connection with crises and imperialism, a capitalist system is naturally productive of various resistances to any sharp fall in the profit-rate, whether these resistances take the form of direct pressure on wages, monopolistic policies or colonial expansion. At any rate, definite braking influences clearly operate against any tendency to approach towards what we have termed the point of capital-saturation. An approach to such a point (involving as it would a fall of interest-rates to zero) would seem a clear *reductio ad absurdum* of a capitalist society.

If, by contrast to this, one is to define any principle which would rule the rate of capital accumulation in a socialist economy, it seems evident that this must consist in an attitude of *equal* regard for present and future, *ceteris paribus*—in other words, an absence of the time-preference which is a characteristic of a capitalist economy. This, at least, is the only principle which would not involve inconsistency or contradiction. This would imply a greater rate of capital accumulation than prevails in a capitalist economy and (particularly in the more advanced stages of development) a path of development tending much more rapidly to approach towards the point of capital-saturation. But, as we have said, this would not necessarily imply a rate of capital-construction designed so as to reach this point at the *earliest* possible date; since this, logically applied, would involve the absurd situation of investing 100 per cent. of the national income in capital construction—devoting the *whole* of the labour-force of society to the immediate construction of the most advanced (in the sense of absolutely most productive) mechanical devices and equipment that were known. This (or anything approaching it) would be actually to give the future *greater* weight than the present—to discount the present in favour of the future goal. But it may well imply the attainment of maximum productivity at the earliest possible date consistent with the provision of a certain minimum level of income in the intervening years. At any rate, it clearly implies a much greater regard for the future and a more rapid progress than that to which we are accustomed in individualist societies.[1]

Circumstances, of course, might well arise which would lead to qualifications of this principle. On the one hand, a slower path of development might be exacted by the need for various reasons (in particular the previous neglect of human needs in a class society) to raise the standard of life more quickly in the immediate future, instead of investing in material equipment, even at the expense of a less rapid rate of increase at a more distant future. On the other hand, circumstances might demand some compromise between this principle and that of attaining a point of higher development of the productive

[1] Cf. Armstrong, *op. cit.*, p. 21 *et seq.*; and F. P. Ramsey in *Econ. Journal*, December 1928; and NOTE to this chapter.

forces in the shortest space of time. For instance, this might well be so for a transitional period in an economy of low industrialization, since a certain level of industrialization was a pre-condition for the successful operation of a socialist economy and for the liquidation of private enterprise and the private capitalist (as with the U.S.S.R. under the First Five-Year Plan) or for the duration of some complex and large-scale industrial transition. In this case the path of development would be more direct and rapid, and a "spread" of current investment would take place between a variety of types of construction. The analogy to the straight line of the rational dog towards the future position of his master would then be a precise one.

The distribution of resources appropriate to this scheme of development would not be something which had to be calculated on the basis of an interest-rate which in turn needed to be determined from market data. The decision as to how much of the social labour-force to invest in constructional work of a particular type, the resulting balance between various lines of production, and the level of real wages would all be aspects of a single decision which itself constituted the attitude of the socialist economy to present income and future income—they would be different facets of the distribution of labour between production for the present and for the future. There would need, of course, to be an internal consistency between the various aspects of this decision. But the data required for giving concrete shape to the decision would consist in the main of some quantitative scale of wants and of their extended satisfaction, the productivity of various types of equipment, the cost and period of time involved in their construction, and the available resources. For none of these would it be necessary to rely on values registered by a "capital market" to supply.[1]

It is the contention of Professor Mises and his school, as we have seen, that a socialist economy, lacking the values registered on a competitive market, would be powerless to make any but quite arbitrary calculations as a basis for distributing productive resources between their various uses. Lacking any assessment of values, it would also lack any measurement of costs. The vaunted "measurement and calculation" of Mr. and Mrs. Webb, the strict "economic accountancy" demanded by Lenin, would have no quantitative basis. Hence of two rival methods of production it would be impossible to say which was the more economic, because any comparison of costs against their value-productivity would be impossible. In view of the extreme arbitrariness which attaches to the values of the free market of *laissez-faire*, this claim, if it were true, would have little force

---

[1] For example, Mr. L. E. Hubbard, speaking of the U.S.S.R. during the First Five-Year Plan, states that "the Government was unable to tell with scientific exactness whether a ton of wheat . . . was more advantageously consumed internally or sold abroad to buy foreign goods". (*Soviet Money and Finance*, p. 289.) But no free market could have provided any "scientific" answer to this question. The State was exporting wheat to buy, *e.g.*, tractors to produce more wheat next year. It would clearly need to know whether the future wheat produced by the tractor was greater than the wheat-price of a tractor. But whether the transaction was advantageous or not depended entirely on the State's own valuation of present loss against future gain; of which the decision to conduct the transaction was presumably (unless it was entirely irrational) itself the expression. True, if the choice were between wheat exports and tea imports, the relative market-prices of wheat and tea (the *internal* prices would suffice) would be some indication of their relative importance; but by no means necessarily a final or "scientific" criterion.

in condemning a socialist economy as less rational than a capitalist economy. But the claim would seem to thrive only by virtue of misapprehension. It is true, of course, that in order to make any comparison of economic quantities, differences between qualitatively diverse goods must be reducible to quantitative terms. In other words, to compare boots against bread, or silk against saxophones, these must have some magnitude assigned to them and their relative importance expressed quantitatively. But, in the first place, for this to be done, *any* scale of priorities, however determined, would suffice—suffice, that is, to render quantitative calculation possible. Such a scale of priorities might be constructed in a number of ways, several of which might yield results less arbitrary than the "spontaneous" construction of a scale of market-values in a *laissez-faire* world. It might be constructed in an authoritarian manner, as a doctor prescribes a diet for a patient, or on the basis of sampling opinion by means of questionnaires,[1] or on the basis of information supplied by co-operative societies, or by a combination of these methods. This might be so arranged as to give ample expression to popular choice, so far as it was vocal; though it is true that there exists the strong danger of determination in a too bureaucratic manner if these methods were exclusively relied on, and it is true that the method of questionnaires is unlikely to yield results possessing a high degree of precision or of subtlety. But, in the second place, there is no reason to suppose that a free consumers' market, registering consumers' preferences, would not exist in a socialist economy, save

---

[1] One method employed by trusts in the clothing and furniture industries in U.S.S.R., particularly with respect to new designs, is to hold exhibitions of models and ask the visiting public to record their vote as to their order of preference between various exhibits.

for exceptional periods of transition or of acute shortage. Marx, it is true, referred to a "higher stage of socialism", or communism, where income should be distributed "to each according to his needs" without the intervention of a pricing-system. But this stage, he was careful to add, would not arrive as an invocation from heaven, but would develop in the degree that "the mastery of the productive forces" enabled the problem of scarcity to be surmounted. "Justice can never rise superior to the economic conditions of society and the cultural development conditioned by them." But in what he termed "the first or lower stage of socialism" different money wages would be paid in proportion to different qualities and quantities of work performed, and as a logical corollary of this there would naturally be a free consumers' market where such money incomes could be spent.[1]

It is claimed, however, that a consumers' market on which consumers' goods were priced would not alone be sufficient. Without a market for intermediate goods and factors of production, the latter could not be valued, and there would be no basis for the representation of costs.[2] But this contention again would seem to rest upon a misunderstanding of the nature of the problem in a socialist economy. In an individualist economy the law of the market forces each autonomous entrepreneur to conform to the requirements of the total situation by the pressure on him of price-movements, including movements in the prices of the factors of production and intermediate goods which he buys. Were the latter

[1] Cf. Marx, *Critique of the Gotha Programme.*
[2] Cf. Prof. G. Halm in *Collectivist Economic Planning*, pp. 150-1; Mises, *op. cit.*, p. 119.

not subject to the process of competitive pricing, there would be no instrument by which the entrepreneur was made to "toe the line" and the "principle of cost" enabled to prevail. But the movement of costs is here no more than a mediating instrument appropriate to a situation where productive decisions are made atomistically. It is the vehicle by which the more fundamental problem of the allocation of resources is solved. To the entrepreneur in an individualist economy it figures necessarily as a problem of cost. To one surveying the situation as a whole it figures as a problem of allocation, and hence of relative productivities in various uses. And in a planned economy this is essentially what the problem becomes. To solve this problem, given the quantity of available resources and the relative values of finished products, what needs to be known is the actual productivity of these resources when applied in various uses; and this is a piece of concrete information of a technical character which does not require the intervention of a market either to discover or to reflect. It is not a case of having first to discover what costs are, and *then* by comparing them with relative productivities to solve the problem of allocation. Only on the basis of these data concerning relative productivities can "costs" be properly determined; and when these data are given, the problem of allocation is *ipso facto* solved. True, in an individualist economy, a market for, say, capital serves to *generalize* such data in the form of a price, and through the medium of this price procures the distribution of resources "automatically" between entrepreneurs. But this is the only instrument which exists in such an economy for handling the matter. That in a socialist economy it should be thought necessary for the managers of various plants, having ascertained the necessary data about productivities, to use these data to play an elaborate game of bidding for capital on a market, instead of transmitting the information direct to some planning authority, is a "Heath Robinson" kind of suggestion which it is hard to take seriously. Moreover, it has the positive disadvantage that in playing such a game the managers of socialist enterprises would be as much "in blinkers" as to the concurrent decisions being made elsewhere as are private entrepreneurs to-day, and thus would be subject to a similar degree of competitive uncertainty.

Nor need the decision of a planning authority about such an allocation be abnormally complex, so long as data about relative productivities can be generalized, and detailed application of any general decision can be decentralized. For instance, data would be present before a planning authority in some form such as this: an allocation of an additional £x of capital to the textile industry would enable it to increase its output-programme by y yards of cloth, while an allocation of £x of capital to the boot industry would enable it to increase its output-programme by z pairs of boots; and so forth. Perhaps the data requisite for a final decision would need to be somewhat more complex than this, e.g. of the kind that £x in the textile industry would yield y yards of cloth if at the same time it could procure additional labour of an amount z, but would yield only $y-n$ yards of cloth if additional labour could not be procured; or it might be a question of choosing between several alternative types of construction in the industry, one involving the allocation of x_1 tons of material A, another of x_2 tons of material B, and another of x_3 tons of material C. But if

the relative productivities of the rival construction
methods can be estimated, it should not be an impractic-
able task for the planning authority to compare these
estimates with data as to the alternative uses for materials
A and B and C, and thereby make a choice between
them on the principle of giving priority in the assignment
of each material to the use in which its net productivity
is greatest. As regards the detailed information relating
to each factory inside the industry: this would presumably be for the textile industry to know; and how best
to distribute resources allocated to it between different
plants or sections of the trade for the industry itself to
determine. Presumably it would be on such detailed
data that the original generalized statement about capital
productivity in the industry would be based; but these
constituent details need not trouble the higher planning
authority. Large-scale allocations, in other words,
need alone be made by the central authorities; the
detailed assignment of these larger allocations being
decentralized to subordinate authorities possessing more
detailed information. It is to be noted that there would
be no necessity for the higher planning authority to have
before it data as to relative productivities in every
imaginable combination of possible situations—"the
millions of equations" of which Professors Hayek and
Robbins speak with so much scorn. In practice the
question would always at any one time arise in the form
of a movement *from* a pre-existing situation, and the
relative productivity of changes in the neighbourhood
of this initial situation is all that would be required, and
probably all that in any system could be known. Planning authorities would no more need to know the
productivity of every conceivable combination of re-

sources than the private entrepreneur needs to know it to-day in order to decide whether to shift resources from one use to another.

In an economy where every detail in the allocation of resources including labour-power was planned, the way in which costs were calculated for purposes of accounting would, therefore, seem to be of no importance. To decide whether resources could be better employed elsewhere than in the place in question, one would need to know the relative productivities of such resources there and elsewhere. To compare the inefficient management with the efficient one would need simply to know the amount of product and the amount of resources allocated and to compare the result with some similar factory, or to compare the product with past experience or with what had been estimated. To facilitate such comparisons, the ratios would doubtless be expressed in a money form; but provided that the system of translation of things into money was uniform, any system of translation would presumably suffice to compare like things with like. Actually, of course, it would be cumbrous and unnecessary to allocate every detail of resources according to a uniform plan. What would doubtless be essential for a socialist economy would be to allocate capital equipment and basic raw materials and power-resources in this way; but decisions as to the purchase and use of minor requisites could be left to the discretion of industrial managers themselves. Probably the employment of labour would also (subject to certain limiting conditions) come within this latter category. To the extent that such things were obtained by enterprises in decentralized fashion "outside the plan" (*e.g.* a factory contracting direct with a farm or with another factory on its own initiative), the question of the "pricing" of these goods would again emerge as a decisive factor determining their utilization, as it would also as a basis for subsequently calculating the efficiency or inefficiency of such operations. But so also in such cases, where the practice was at all general, would some form of competitive market for such goods *ipso facto* exist.

In practice, therefore, the calculation of the money-cost of goods on the basis of the wages paid out in the course of their production (including the wage-cost of repairing any wear and tear of equipment) would doubtless play an important part in socialist accounting. It is frequently supposed that this would be seriously incomplete if it included no item for rent or interest on account of scarce and durable factors of production. But according to a familiar economic principle, once such durable instruments (*e.g.* buildings or equipment) have been allocated and fixed—as we have assumed they would be through planned decisions based on an estimate of comparative productivities, and not through "ordeal by the rate of interest"—a calculation of "overhead costs" on account of them has no relevance to their current use; and maximum productivity is satisfied if, and only if, output is carried to the point where the price of the output is equal to its marginal cost. Even with mobile productive resources, such as raw materials, whose allocation was determined by some form of market relationship and was not covered by the plan, maximum productivity would be sufficiently satisfied if these were priced at the equivalent of their marginal labour cost at all stages of their production. Indeed, to attempt to budget for such an item as "overhead cost" will frequently prevent the most economic employment of plant and equipment by limiting their intensive utilization: a form of wasteful restriction which undoubtedly occurs on a not inconsiderable scale to-day.[1]

The fact that the existence of a consumers' market afforded scope for free consumers' choice and a means by which this choice could influence production would not mean that a socialist economy necessarily acknowledged its unqualified sovereignty. While a consumers' market would probably provide the most important basis for valuing goods relatively to one another—establishing

[1] Cf. the present writer's *Russian Econ. Development*, pp. 176-80. For an illuminating description of the system of "planned costs" and "accounting prices" in Soviet economy, cf. W. B. Reddaway, *Russian Financial System.*

"Overhead cost" has here necessarily been used rather loosely. The principle referred to would require that in any short-period situation many other items than mere interest and rent should be neglected, *e.g.* in the case of taking extra passengers in a half-empty train, when even the wages of the driver and fireman would not be included in the fare charged; or in the case of a hotel with empty bedrooms, where only the mere cost of washing bed-linen should be charged to visitors arriving late in the day. The full and logical application of the principle, therefore, is hardly consistent with a price-system at all, at least with any system of uniform and stable prices. In the example quoted, however, it would not follow that the train should *continue* to be run throughout the year if passengers could only be wooed into travelling on it by fares so low as not to cover even the driver's and fireman's wages. In a factory an analogous case would be the salaries of the office staff and the wages of auxiliary workers: to any particular run of output these would presumably figure as an "overhead". Any dividing line that is drawn must, therefore, be an arbitrary one; and if any general rule is to be laid down, the most satisfactory compromise would seem to be that suggested above, which includes wages and salaries in the estimate of cost, but not rents and interest.

Mr. Durbin has raised the problem of repair and maintenance of plant and equipment. (*Econ. Journal*, December 1936.) This, it is true, has special accounting difficulties attaching to it. But I am unconvinced that it constitutes the crucial problem that he represents it to be. The problem as he puts it is that maintenance cannot be separated from prime costs of current output. If it cannot, then the proper course would seem to be to include an allowance for it, with other semi-over-a scale of their relative social importance in satisfying wants—this is not to say that it would not be modified by other criteria, and even frequently overridden.[1] In the case of new wants, and the development of new types and qualities of goods, the market could provide no direct guidance, except after their creation; and authoritarianism here necessarily reigns. Consumers' choice as expressed through the market is necessarily and always limited to choice between the range of available alternatives; and the initiative will necessarily come in the

heads like auxiliary workers, in estimating marginal costs, separating depreciation from interest charges. If output was being sold at a price which covered these maintenance costs, then this would be a presumption that the equipment in question was worth maintaining. The cases where this might hinder a change-over to a smaller and less costly plant, and result in too small an output being produced by too large a plant, do not strike me as likely to be very considerable; since any large-scale and long-lasting reconstructions of equipment *would* be distinguishable from current prime costs, and decisions about them be made in the same way as any decisions concerning new investment. At any rate, such incidental waste is likely to be much smaller than what occurs to-day from the restriction of firms in an imperfect market seeking to maximize the return on capital. This I think Mr. Durbin fully admits. But I think it might also prove to be less than the waste involved from undue restriction of utilization from an attempt to fix a price to include Mr. Durbin's "normal profit".

It is to be noted that this problem of calculating only *marginal* costs in deciding on the intensiveness of use of plant and equipment applies, not only to cases of a single-plant line of production (as, for instance, Mr. R. L. Hall, in *The Economic System in a Socialist State*, seems to imply), but to any case where the supply of such equipment is not "perfectly" adjusted to current demand, which will tend to be the rule and not the exception in a world of changing and fluctuating demand.

[1] Prof. Hayek has interpreted the present writer as desiring to banish consumers' choice completely and to substitute "barrack-room" regimentation of consumption (*Collectivist Econ. Planning*, p. 215), because I attempted to argue (*a*) that consumers' choice is not free under capitalism, (*b*) that the dictates of individual money-demand, as expressed on a retail market, would not invariably be the best guide, and need not be the exclusive guide to production under socialism. Prof. Hayek's interpretation seems hardly reasonable, and is at any rate not a correct one.

first instance from the producer, unless special means are developed outside the market system to enable the consumer to express some initiative in the matter—means which are virtually non-existent to-day.[1]   Nor is the subsequent judgment of the market decisive in this matter; and the fact that it is not raises a broader issue —namely, that of non-available alternatives. The fact that a commodity introduced on to the market is bought by consumers and succeeds in covering its expenses of production is no evidence that this is the commodity which consumers would have preferred that the resources of the community should be expended in producing. They may buy it, as consumers buy poor quality milk or indifferently cooked meals or jerry-built houses, simply *faute de mieux*. Of three alternative commodities, A, B and C, which might have been introduced on to the market, the consumers, if put to the test, might greatly have preferred C. But since producers, with whom the initiative lies, offer only A, consumers spend their money upon it and thereby enable it to register its commercial success, because they have no means of expressing their superior preference for C. It may well be the case that the majority of the choices registered on the market are in fact second-best preferences as compared with the choices consumers would have made if the requisite alternatives had been available.

But, apart from the matter of new wants, there are two important respects in which consumers' choice expressed individualistically through the market could not be trusted as an adequate criterion of social utility. In

---

[1] Cf. R. G. Hawtrey (*The Economic Problem*, p. 203): "their choice is as a rule absolutely limited to things on sale, and among the things on sale to those of which they can obtain information through the market."

the first place, there clearly exists an inevitable short-sightedness in the individual's choice, owing to the limited perspective both in space and time from which the individual, *qua* isolated individual, necessarily views the range of available alternatives. This limitation with regard to time is familiar enough, and has been referred to as the deficiency of the "telescopic faculty" of the individual with regard to the future—a deficiency which the ideally rational individual presumably would not have.[1] But this deficiency of vision seems to apply equally to opportunities which are distant in space as to those which are distant in time; and since the individual consumer never has more than a very restricted range of alternatives near at hand on which to exercise his choice—near to the eye and exciting the senses, or at least conveying a certainty by their presence which the imagination of distant alternatives can seldom have—individual preference will tend to be vitiated by some degree of short-sightedness and irrationality. It is this fact, indeed, of which the salesman makes such ready use in creating preferences for objects which he forces upon the consumers' gaze. It is this fact which gives an opportunity for expert or collective buying to make a choice which the individual will subsequently admit is superior to what he would himself have made—for instance, can make the menus provided by a club or an hotel give more satisfaction than the meals which the average individual, if left to his own initiative, would have chosen. To this extent there is clearly room for collective choice in some form to modify individual expression of choice by consumers.

Secondly, there is the whole class of things where the

---

[1] Cf. Pigou, *Econs. of Welfare*, pp. 24-67.

individual interest in acquiring them, as registered atomistically on a market, conflicts with (or at least diverges from) the social or collective interest of consumers in general. This includes all those cases where a benefit cannot be conferred on one individual without simultaneously benefiting [1] others, so that the benefit conferred cannot be separately assessed for each individual. The most evident examples of this type are continuous services, rather than separate commodities, many of which are generally recognized, even in an individualist economy, as being the province of collective supply on principles other than those of the market: for instance, health, education, research, upkeep and lighting of streets, protection against fire or against crime. But this category is not confined to such services, and probably includes many commodities which are usually the subject of market-sale, their supply being controlled by individualistic demand: for example, fire-extinguishers which a householder buys to prevent fires in his own house and thereby saves neighbouring buildings from catching fire; silencers for motor-cars; houses the appearance of which may help to make or mar the neighbourhood for other citizens. Moreover, what applies to health or education services may well be held to apply to the supply of commodities such as primary necessities for the mass of the people or luxuries which have an educative influence or the reverse. Further examples which fall within this category are those things the supply of which is subject to decreasing cost as the supply of them is increased, owing either to the existence of large indivisible units of equipment which are not fully utilized or to economies of specialization to be

---

[1] This benefit may, of course, be negative as well as positive.

obtained from a large scale of production.[1] In these cases, which are common and numerous, an individual in increasing his purchases is conferring an incidental benefit on others in enabling them to be supplied more cheaply (*e.g.* in the use of transport facilities, or of electric light or power; or, conversely, in the use of roads or a health resort where each additional user may confer an additional cost of congestion on others).

When we consider such cases in detail, and add to them all those parallel cases where the individual desire for a thing is in large part conventional and depends on the fact that others desire and possess it, they would seem to be considerably more extensive than is customarily imagined, and possibly to cover the major part of consumers' expenditure. But there are two special examples of this general case which are of extensive importance, and which seem worthy of detailed mention if only because they are so frequently overlooked. These consist in the demand for variety and for variation, in both of which the individual interest, separately registered on a market, is apt to conflict with the collective interest of consumers. In the case of variable demand, the variation will tend to involve an additional cost to producers, owing to the uncertainty as to what level of demand to count upon and a consequent inability to adapt supply and productive equipment in the most economical way. Similarly, the taste for variety on the part of consumers

---

[1] Strictly speaking, the argument does not necessarily apply to *all* such cases, but only to those which are *most* subject to decreasing cost as output expands. If all lines of production were subject to decreasing cost and in equal and continuous degree, there would be no social advantage in any one expanding, since by doing so it would merely transfer labour and resources from some other line of production, and so raise costs in the latter as much as they were cheapened in the former.

may cause commodities, because they are produced in many instead of a few lines and types, to be produced at a higher cost than they could be if their production was more standardized. Each consumer, in registering his demand for some new type, will be influenced simply by the consideration as to whether his preference for one as against the other is equal to the *difference* in price between the new type and the old: he will not be influenced by the fact that his action, in preventing production from being as standardized as it might be, may raise the general cost of production of this and other types both for himself and for others. Similarly, he will change his demand from one type to another from time to time, if (provided the prices of varieties are the same) this variation seems to give him any advantage whatever: he will not balance this·advantage against the extra cost which his fickleness may involve for the whole industry, ultimately affecting both himself and others. For this reason it would seem that an individualistic consumers' market has a bias in favour of both greater variation and greater variety than the collective interest requires. This is not to say, of course, that collective interference would or should abolish either variation or variety: merely, that some collective overriding of the market's verdict would be necessary if these were to be limited to what the real interest of consumers demanded.

There seems to be little doubt that the utility-theory has considerably biassed the approach of economists to this whole problem, creating the presumption, as it has done, that demand is rooted in ultimate satisfactions, and that values on a free market interpret these satisfactions in an "optimum" way. The result has been to give this problem of "adjustment to demand" an importance in our minds much greater than it probably deserves. Actually the adjustment of supplies to the welfare-yielding qualities of different objects of consumption is of such a rough order of approximation, at best, in any form of market system, as to suggest that more may be gained by sacrificing niceties of adjustment to a more rapid *general* increase than by hampering general increase by devices designed to secure a nice adjustment of whatever is produced to demand as exhibited on a market. This is not to say that the latter has not some importance, and in extreme cases (like continuous bully-beef in the trenches) a great deal: it is merely to say that its quantitative importance has probably been exaggerated. It is certainly important for people to have variety from which to choose and for individuals to be able to choose differently according to taste; and there are certain broad classes of goods which it will be important for consumers to have in certain fairly definite proportions: for instance, meat compared to vegetables and cereals; house-room, furniture and recreation compared to food. If these proportions are seriously disturbed, people may suffer considerably. But it does not follow that if the different items or varieties inside these broad groups, most of which are close substitutes for one another, are not supplied precisely in quantities corresponding to initial preferences, consumers will suffer a hurt which is of a major order. Yet when economic writers speak about the complexities of the problem of adjustments to demand, it is usually of these finer adjustments within the main groups of consumption to which they refer. While I should certainly complain were meat in general to be scarce, or if I had no choice but to eat pork every day,

I hardly find it worthy of remark if my housekeeper supplies me with pork rather more frequently, and with beef and mutton less frequently, than I should myself have chosen if I ordered my own menu. It may be that I learn to respect her economical choosing above my own; at any rate, I should hardly dream of maintaining that my welfare was appreciably lessened by the divergence between her allocation and my ideal choice. In other words, in the case of demands which are inelastic in character, failure to meet them in the desired proportions is an important failure. But these are in fact demands for necessities or for broad types of goods, the need for which is most easily calculated, and is in general fairly constant as well as inelastic, so that supply can be soon adjusted on the basis of experience. On the other hand, luxuries and the multitudinous varieties within each of the broader types of consumption, where estimation of demand and its changes is admittedly a more baffling problem, are precisely the things which are characterized by an elastic demand, so that relatively little loss is caused by an adjustment of supply which gives consumers too much of one and too little of another. Where adjustment of supply to preferences is important, it is also relatively easy; where it is difficult, it would seem to be of a relatively minor order of importance.

Our conclusion, therefore, seems to be that the laws which will rule a socialist economy will be different in essential respects from those which rule a capitalist economy, for the reason that factors which are, *ex hypothesi*, unknown and unknowable to those who make the ruling decisions in the latter will be known in the former, and that part of what figured as dependent variables in the latter, and hence as actions and events determined by the given data, become subject to control and to conscious decision in the former, and hence are to be classed among the data of the problem. Is this to say, then, that no economic laws can be postulated of a socialist system; that events will there be arbitrary and that anything conceivable may occur? Does it mean that mere expectation will suffice to storm the heavens? Clearly this cannot be so. When Engels spoke of the historical transition from capitalism to socialism as a transition from "the realm of necessity to the realm of freedom", he clearly did not envisage a millennial realm of illimitable free choice. He presumably meant that in the former the individual will was blind, and human beings unconscious agents of the objective laws of the market; whereas in the latter man, collectively owning the instruments of his destiny, would become conscious of the laws which bound him and would consciously shape his actions to his purposes.

What then will such laws be which will limit economic events and the knowledge of which will at the same time enable a more perfect control of events? Clearly this cannot be answered *a priori* except in terms of analogies so general and abstract as to be of very limited use. What such laws in their full concreteness will be can only emerge from the actual problems of a planned economy and from classification and analysis of the experience which these afford. But one can tell something of the general shape which these laws will have, and from our knowledge of the essential elements of a socialist economy define some of the relations which will necessarily be included. In an individualist economy economic laws have the form of stating that, given certain conditions of nature and technique, and certain consumers' preferences, human beings as producers will behave in a certain way, the behaviour finding expression in certain value-relations. In a socialist economy they will have the form, rather, of stating that, given a certain purpose, a determinate course of action will achieve it, in view of the nature of the relationships which exist between material objects and between these objects and human organization. While the Political Economy that we know is concerned with postulating the determinate manner in which human beings behave (given certain data as to the situation), economic laws in a socialist economy will presumably be concerned with the manner in which the materials which man handles behave, since it will be these which will define his powers and (given his purposes) his actions. It is, in this sense, I think, that one can say that the determining relations which will control economic activity will be predominantly technical in character.

It might seem at first sight that this difference, as just expressed, is one of form but not of substance; and that to postulate the purpose first and then find the material situation which will produce it is a simple reversal of the process of studying situations and then deducing the results to which various types of material situation will give rise. In a limited sense this is true; and it is certainly important to remember that, when we speak here of "purpose", this cannot be conceived as something to be arbitrarily postulated, but that "purpose" will itself be conditioned and selected by the situation of which it is a part. But to go no further than this would be to deny that human action and the forms it takes are

316

part of the situation: to deny them any independent influence on events. Actually the order of the two statements of law, to which we have referred, is not a purely formal matter; and to say that the two are identical is to ignore the fact that the difference of order in their statement implies a real difference of fact: namely, that in a socialist economy certain new relations, and hence new possibilities, will emerge, in the shape of *a new type of social organization*. The very fact that the statement starts with purpose and proceeds to postulate the action appropriate to the situation implies that there is a new relationship between men which gives to collective purpose a new significance. The contrast can be likened, perhaps, to the problem of calculating the course of a derelict hulk adrift on the ocean and the problem of calculating the course of a sailing schooner manned by a captain and crew. In the former the course will be determinate given the necessary data concerning wind and currents. Any concept of will or purpose is irrelevant, even if there happen to be shipwrecked men aboard the hulk. In the latter case, data as to wind and currents will still be important. But purpose, and the instruments it uses, will no longer be irrelevant. Neither will it be omnipotent: many purposes will be impossible, given the data, and others will be rejected by their low possibility of achievement.[1] But the very fact that purpose enters as a relevant factor in this way is dependent on the existence of new relationships between man and the elements and the possibility of new types of event occurring (*e.g.* the possibility of "tacking" against a

---

[1] Of course, if purposes are defined precisely enough, *e.g.* to reach a certain port at a definite hour and day, no earlier and no later, at most one purpose will be attainable in any particular situation, and given the situation, both action and purpose will be determinate.

wind); and given the selected purpose, on the one hand, and the nature of wind and sea, on the other, and given too the type of ship and sails, a determinate line of action can be calculated which will achieve that purpose in the most effective way. There will then be a science of navigation, which will be something more than simply the laws of the winds and the tides. When one asks the question: is an economic plan a programme of intention or is it simply a scientific forecast? the answer can only be that it is both. What is commonly forgotten is that the sort of forecast on which a plan is based has to include among its data the fact that the plan itself will be one of the influences which determine the constellation of events.

Perhaps it will be said that laws of this kind would not properly be the field of economics but of technology. For this view there appears to be no very good reason. Clearly, there will exist a class of problem which is not identical with the problems of technology as customarily viewed: a class of problem to which the title of economic statistics could, perhaps, most suitably be given. Already to-day there are studies which seem to furnish a prototype of what such a fuller science will be. I refer to such inquiries as the nutrition and family budget, population, and productive-capacity studies which are assuming a growing importance, and which are already passing beyond the preliminary stage of pure description to the construction of elementary generalizations, competent to form the germs of a future science. A socialist economy would presumably both require and facilitate a great extension of such studies in the direction of assembling and generalizing the data of planning, of establishing the inter-relationships between the various elements of a given situation, and of constructing principles to determine what, in a given situation, could be and could not be done, and what mechanism of action, in a given situation, was competent to yield a given result. Economic laws, in the sense of generalizations about the behaviour of particular situations, would develop from concrete studies of particular situations themselves. Knowledge of how to plan would grow from the systematized experience of actual planning, and could grow in no other way. To guess what such laws would be, still more to seek to prescribe them dogmatically, on the basis of imperfectly understood analogies with the quite different situations of a capitalist world, is unlikely to be very productive and may be misleading.

If it be asked what part Political Economy as we know it as a theory of value would play, I would reply that its rôle would be small or non-existent, and at any rate a rapidly diminishing one. Here again it would be as unwise to be dogmatic in a negative as in a positive statement. But it has been a principal contention of certain earlier sections of this book that the traditional theory of value was an attempt to depict the behaviour of an individualist economy in a deterministic way, and that for this demonstration it relied on the postulation of certain data peculiar to an individualist system. It depicted the "necessary" relationships which emerge from a given situation—emerge "automatically" as the result of the interplay of numerous independent forces on the market, without this result being consciously designed. The theory of value originated as a theory of free competition; and while subsequent modifications have been introduced to allow for elements of monopoly, the deterministic statements which it makes still rely for their validity on the existence of substantial areas of competition (in the sense of diffused and independent decisions) within the economic system.[1] But the essence of a socialist economy is that the major decisions which govern investment and production are co-ordinated and unified and are no longer diffused among numerous autonomous individuals. True, there may still be areas of competition in a socialist economy: on the one hand, consumers purchasing in a free retail market, and on the other hand workers actuated in the choice of an occupation by wage-differences. But the significant contrast is that these areas of competition are external to the mechanism by which the major decisions, involving the most vital problems of the economic system, are made: the decisions which in a capitalist society figure as entrepreneur-decisions and in a socialist economy as the constituents of the economic plan. We sometimes forget that all the most important postulates of the law of value have been concerned with the way in which entrepreneurs behave—how their actions will be affected by given changes, such as taxation, or shifts in costs and shifts in demand. Their actions, as regulators of production, and in turn the effect of their actions on the shares of the various factors of production, have been the focus of interest. It is precisely this sphere about which no theory of value could tell one anything of major importance in a socialist economy; even if something remained for it to tell about the environment within which the planning mechanism

[1] Even in Mrs. Robinson's hypothetical "world of monopolies", there is still competition *between* monopolists in the various industries. (*Econs. of Imperfect Competition*, p. 309.) It was Edgeworth's opinion that the data would not suffice to yield a determinate result even in this case if the competing monopolists were few in number. (Cf. *Collected Papers*, Vol. I, pp. 136-8.)

worked. Suppose that in a capitalist economy one were to assume that all entrepreneur-decisions were fused, and all production was controlled by one monstrous monopolist (*a fortiori* if one were to assume him to be the owner of all capital and natural resources as well): would there be much of importance left for economic theory as it exists to-day to tell us except that this monster would extract as much product as possible from us all for the least return, and that he could best do this by making separate bargains with each of us according to the variations in our tastes and aversions, our incomes and physique? [1]

I do not speak here of a theory of value as a mere algebra of human choice or as the pattern of all rational action. What this has to say seems to be attenuated enough in any form of society; and any powers of prediction it may possess seem likely to be as small, and no smaller, in a socialist economy as they are to-day. Nor· is it to be denied that certain pieces of apparatus which economists use (*e.g.* elasticities and production-functions) would be used as part of the framework of generalization. Such apparatus is formal in character, borrowed from mathematics and by no means the peculiar creation of economic events; and it is not the framework but the real content which constitutes the law and determines the difference between one law and another. Nor again is it necessarily to be denied that any relationships can be postulated of a socialist economy by simple deduction and analogy. Certain relationships,

---

[1] Mrs. Robinson concludes that if, in her "world of monopolies", the various monopolists were to make common cause, "the powers of the monopolists would then be so great that they would only be restrained from exercis'ng them by the fear of provoking a revolution, and no precise analysis is possible of what would occur". (*Op. cit.*, p. 326.)

I think, it may be already possible to describe. I would assert merely that such postulates are no more than elementary, and can hardly be more than prolegomena to future studies. They can do little more than define conditions of consistency between the various categories in terms of which we define the problem. They do not suffice to forecast how the system as a whole will behave. To postulate them is merely to say that the parts of the system will be interdependent, and that this interdependence will include particular characteristics. Even so, statements of this kind must be regarded as tentative, since further knowledge may disclose that the categories by means of which we have defined the situation are unreal or incomplete.

First of such postulates is the simple axiom that the total money-value of finished consumers' goods must equal the total of wage-incomes over a given period (assuming that wages are the only form of personal money-income and that no part of personal income is voluntarily hoarded). If this equality does not hold, then the consumers' market must either, in the one case, accumulate stocks of unsold goods, or, in the other case, be limited by some form of rationing in such a way as to enforce an accumulation of an unspent margin of income. This can be expressed in the form:

$$x = I - G,$$

where G represents the value of consumers' goods, I total wage-income, while x, if it is positive, will represent the accumulated unspent margin of income, and if it is negative the accumulation of unsold stocks of goods. It follows that if, when $I = G$, individuals voluntarily decide to hoard a proportion of their income represented by $\frac{y}{I}$ (*e.g.* in additions to savings-bank deposits), then either a proportion of G will accumulate as unsold stocks or the prices of goods will necessarily be reduced by an average amount equal to $\frac{y}{G}\left(=\frac{y}{I}\right)$.

Retaining the assumption that wages paid out in the course of production (including transport, administration, distribution) are the only form of personal money-income, it will be seen that I will be a simple function of the size of the total labour-force (L), of the level of wages (*w*) (whether on a basis of piece-rates or time-rates) and the amount of work performed per unit of time by the average worker (which we will write as *k*). If a proportion ϕ of the labour-force is employed on *new* construction work, or in adding to the stocks of semi-finished commodities in process of production, then it will follow that industry in general will make a profit equal to ϕG, after counting as costs the wages paid out in current production and the wage-cost of current repair and maintenance of equipment. In other words, the ratio of costs to receipts for all finished goods produced in the period will depend upon the proportion of the labour-force which is transferred to new construction or is engaged in adding to the flow of goods-in-process which have not yet reached a finished form.[1] Where ϕ is zero (where no capital accumulation is taking place) industry can yield no surplus of receipts over costs; and the receipts of industry must exactly equal the wage-cost of goods sold during the period *plus* the depreciation of equip-

---

[1] Receipts will $= G = I$. Costs incurred for all finished goods will $= wkL - \phi wkL = I - \phi I$, if *k* and *w* are uniform over all industry. Receipts $-$ Costs $= \phi I$.

ment similarly estimated in terms of the wage-cost of repair and maintenance. This equality of receipts and costs will only hold, however, for industry as a whole: it would only hold uniformly for every separate industry if the technique of production in the case of every commodity was sufficiently uniform to permit a uniformity in the organic composition of capital (*i.e.* of capital : labour or of stored-up labour: current labour). To the extent that this technical constant is different in different industries, the industries which have an organic composition which is *above* the average will to that extent show a surplus of receipts over costs, while those industries which have an organic composition *below* the average will correspondingly show a deficit.[1]

This latter conclusion depends on a second postulate. This postulate is that an allocation of resources (whether machinery, constructional equipment or raw materials) in such a way as to achieve maximum productivity (measured in value) from their use will cause the prices of commodities which are produced under conditions

---

[1] This is, therefore, the element of truth in the statement of those, like Cassel, who assert that interest, as a sort of capital-rent, will exist as a category of cost in a socialist State. As a *differential* element between industries with divergent "technical coefficients" it will; but not as a net addition to price, and hence as a subtraction from wages. What will figure as a subtraction from wages will simply be the extent of capital accumulation, which will not bear any direct relation to "capital-rent" as a differential quantity between industries. A recent writer has said that if, in a planned economy, "purchasers of commodities embodying much capital are to bear an appropriate share of the cost of accumulating that capital, it is necessary to include in costs and prices an interest charge". (Raymond Burrows, *Problems and Practice of Economic Planning*, p. 51.) But the interest-rate never is an "appropriate" measure of "the cost of accumulating" the capital on which it is charged (whatever the latter may mean); and to add to the price of all goods an amount any higher than was necessary to finance *new* capital accumulation would merely result in goods remaining unsold.

of high organic composition of capital to be raised relatively to those produced under conditions of low organic composition; this effect on relative prices being proportional to the distance at which the economy is from the point which I have termed that of "capital saturation". "Distance" is here measured by the extent to which the physical productivity of additional labour devoted to capital-schemes as stored-up labour exceeds the physical productivity of additional labour used as current labour for purposes of immediate output. When the position of "capital saturation" has been attained (which alone can be spoken of as a position of "equilibrium" in a socialist economy), different technical conditions in different industries, and their resulting differences of "organic composition", will cease to exert any influence on relative prices. In other words, an economic plan which distributes capital resources in the most productive manner will necessarily, owing to the limited development of the productive forces at any one time, produce a system of prices analogous to Marx's "prices of production". But this will not be a position of equilibrium. In the degree that capital accumulation proceeds, and the productive equipment of society is extended, this dispersion of prices away from their labour-values will tend to disappear. In this final position prices will conform to labour-values, and all industries will attain equilibrium when their receipts cover their current wage-costs (as defined above).[1]

[1] The occurrence of new technical inventions, opening up new forms of "stored-up labour", would, of course, continually be jerking the economy away from this final position, so that it might never be actually attained, or never long maintained. All that is here being said is that the tendency towards this position would continue in the absence of technical invention or in the intervals between technical epochs.

The reason for this may be expressed by saying that, to the extent that labour is *under*-applied to certain of its uses, namely those where it is used as stored-up labour, the resulting scarcity (relatively speaking) of the products of those industries will raise their price; whence it follows that those products which embody proportionately more stored-up labour than others will show the strongest tendency to rise in price. But there is a more direct proof of the postulate which can be given in this form. To distribute resources of any kind in the most productive manner means that the product (measured in value) yielded by an addition of those resources to any use is everywhere equal. This is simply one way of defining what one means by "the most productive manner": if additional resources in one use yielded more than in another (*e.g.* if of a man's time spent on an allotment an extra hour on potatoes would yield more than an extra hour on cabbages), then a gain of productivity would result from transferring resources from the one use to the other (*e.g.* transferring labour-time from working cabbages to working potatoes), and the most productive allocation of resources would not yet have been attained. *Ex hypothesi*, this quantity (the product yielded by additional resources) is in every case greater in the case of stored-up labour than of labour currently used : a difference which will be uniform in all industries, since the two quantities themselves are uniform in all cases. Hence those industries which use a high ratio of stored-up to current labour will show an equivalently higher ratio of products to labour (both stored-up and current) involved in their production, when these products are valued at their current market-prices.[1] As, however, stored-up labour becomes increasingly plentiful relatively to current labour, this difference between the yield of additional stored-up labour and additional current labour will tend to grow smaller. When the difference has disappeared, any divergence of the proportions in which stored-up labour and current labour are combined between industries (provided that each is allocated in the most productive manner) will be irrelevant in this context; and the products of various industries, when valued at current market-prices, will be proportional to the labour (both stored-up and current) involved in their production.

A third group of postulates concerns the necessary "balance" between activity at different stages of production; stages being defined as parts of a process of producing a finished commodity which extends over a period of time. When such stages fall within one industrial plant or *congeries* of associated plants (such

---

[1] This follows, given a familiar assumption. If the increment of product yielded by stored-up labour be written as $\frac{dp}{dx}$ and that yielded by current labour $\frac{dp}{dy}$, and the amount of stored-up labour and of current labour used respectively as x and y; then on the assumption (given by Euler's theorem if we make abstraction of other factors of production) that the total product $= x \cdot \frac{dp}{dx} + y \cdot \frac{dp}{dy}$, it will follow that the larger the ratio of $x : y$, the larger will be the quantity $\dfrac{x \cdot \frac{dp}{dx} + y \cdot \frac{dp}{dy}}{x+y}$, if $\frac{dp}{dx} > \frac{dp}{dy}$. When $\frac{dp}{dx} = \frac{dp}{dy}$, the ratio of $x : y$ in any industry will not affect the magnitude of $\dfrac{x \cdot \frac{dp}{dx} + y \cdot \frac{dp}{dy}}{x+y}$, and this will be equal for all industries.

327

as blast-furnaces, steelworks and rolling mills), then the problem is simply the familiar technical one of achieving a "balanced process" so as to maintain a continuous flow of output without any waste from unused capacity at any stage. Where, however, different plants or even different industries are parts of a chain of successive stages in a process of production (as steelworks—engineering works making textile machinery—textile mills), the problem becomes one of a correct allocation of labour and resources between these plants and industries in proportions which enable a balance to be preserved between them. In an economy where production-processes are lengthy and capital accumulation is taking.place, certain rather complex relationships have to be observed, and particular importance attaches to the time-factor in connection with such a balance in a moving situation. The principles governing such relations involve the type of consideration discussed earlier in this chapter. Assuming a given economic policy with regard to investment and construction, it then follows that, given the data as to existing resources and technical conditions, there is a definite order in which development should proceed from construction schemes of one type to another, and labour be transferred from older technical methods to the construction of newer. Given the data, it will follow that there will be definite relations between stages of production, and a definite chronological order in which constructional development proceeds and new types of process are inaugurated, if there are to be no abrupt jerks or fluctuations in the flow of finished output, and no waste due to excess-capacity at certain stages or unduly rapid displacement of older technical methods. In other words, when labour is stored up in any concrete form it necessarily has reference to some point of time in the future when it will yield fruit in the production of finished goods. Conversely, the supply of finished goods to-day is dependent on the supply of equipment available to use in current production, and this in turn depends on decisions made in the past concerning the original construction of this equipment. To achieve a steady flow (or a steadily increasing flow) of goods, it is necessary for these preliminary investment decisions to conform to a certain pattern in time; otherwise there may be too much equipment of the type required, say, next year, and a consequent surplus of production, followed by a deficiency of the type of equipment required, say, the year after or five years hence, and consequent shortage of production at that period.

Some of these relations are examined in greater detail in a NOTE to this chapter. But the general character which such a theory of balances will have can perhaps be shown by a simple example. A community which was poor in resources might find it most consistent with a steady improvement in its living standards to start immediately building wooden structures of rapid construction and limited durability (as was done in the pioneering days of the American Middle West and is done to-day in some of the new Siberian towns), replacing these at a later date by brick structures, and still later by more complex and commodious buildings of steel and concrete when the productive powers of the community were more developed and resources more plentiful. Given the resources of this community and their rate of increase, and given the other needs of the community for food and clothing, etc., there would clearly be a "best" point of time for each stage of the transition, as well as a "best" volume and rate of construction at any one time. It would be uneconomic to construct so large and so many wooden buildings and to go on building them so long that many of them would become useless and abandoned before their physical life was complete, because superior brick buildings were suddenly constructed on a large scale to take their place. Moreover, as the constructional programme proceeded and changed its form, appropriate transfers of labour and resources would have to occur; probably (though not necessarily) [1] a larger proportion of the social labour-force being devoted to constructional work. To make this possible without any decline in the current output of consumption goods, such transfers would need to be timed to coincide with increased productivity in the latter trades as a result of the introduction of new technical equipment. Further, at some time prior to the transition from one building method to another, it would be necessary to achieve a similar ordered transition in the industries producing building materials. As soon as the period of brick-building started, the demand for timber would give way to the demand for brick, and later the demand for brick to the demand for cement and steel. Unless at some time prior to this transition investment in equipment in the timber industry, and, still earlier, investment in engineering firms making this equipment had been terminated and transferred to the

---

[1] If an invention of some new building method which, say, halved the period of construction occurred, then, of course, it would pay immediately to adopt it, and the result would tend to be that a *smaller* proportion of the social labour-force, *ceteris paribus*, would be employed on building than before (unless the demand for houses were very elastic).

making of equipment for brick-making, the transition when it came would inevitably involve, on the one hand, redundant plant and surplus capacity in the timber industry and in those industries which served it, and on the other hand a retardation of the construction of brick structures, due to limited productive power in the brick industry. It is to be noted that none of these decisions depend on the prior postulation of some relation termed a "rate of interest" before they can be made. They depend on a knowledge of certain data which would have also to be determined before any interest-rate could be calculated. Indeed, if the latter is defined simply as a relation between present and future income, then it can be no more than an abstract expression for the complex of such decisions: it depends on those decisions being made, not *vice versa*, and hence is logically consequent on them and not precedent to them.

Analysis has here been restricted in the main to what one may call the mechanics of the difference between a socialist and a capitalist economy, depending on one aspect of the difference between them: the contrast between a system of collective planning of production and the regulation of production through the agency of an atomistic market system. Of the other aspect, the difference of class relationships, little has explicitly been said. Yet it is this difference which is, in fact, the more fundamental, determining as it does the social relations between men, and hence the interests and the incentives, the conflicts and the policies which emerge. Actually, the two aspects cannot properly be separated; and much of what has already been said rests implicitly upon this more fundamental factor. The crucial data which shape the mechanics of either system are dependent on the social relations which prevail between men as producers. For instance, it is the class character of capitalist economy which determines that its *leit-motif* should be profit—the augmentation of surplus-value. From this it necessarily follows that policies or tendencies which serve this end are associated with prosperity to the system and tend to survive, while those which militate against this end are resisted as inconsistent and uneconomic, and give rise to conflict within the system. For this reason, as we have seen, foreign investment, a rise in wages, the "industrial reserve army", the existence of certain frictions in the market, have a unique significance in a capitalist economy and are associated with unique results. It has been suggested at various points in this and earlier chapters that capital accumulation, and the development dependent on it, is in a class society subject to special limits—limits which retard it in very considerable degree. The crucial limit seems to be the resistance which such a system imposes against the tendency of an approach to conditions of full employment in the labour market to raise wages to such an extent as to precipitate a sharp shrinkage of surplus-value, and consequently to change the value both of existing capital and of new investment. So abhorrent and unnatural does such a situation appear as to cause exceptional measures to be taken to clip the wings of labour—even, like the war-time "leaving certificates", to curtail the normal working of competitive forces—whenever labour scarcity shows signs of becoming an enduring condition of the labour market. It is an opinion which seems to have a growing currency to-day that, with the removal of such limits, not many decades of a somewhat enhanced rate of capital accumulation would suffice in advanced industrial countries with a stationary population so to saturate the known uses for capital as permanently to reduce the interest-rate to a very low figure and even to the neighbourhood of zero. The transformation of half a continent under the Soviet Five-Year Plans indicates how radically the economic face of a country may be changed within a decade by intensive constructional activity. Even John Stuart Mill, in the middle of last century, declared that, in the absence of foreign investment, of government loans for unproductive expenditure, and of wasteful employments of capital, "the mere continuance of the present annual increase of capital would suffice in a small number of years to reduce the rate of net profit to one per cent."[1] Yet can one seriously imagine this being allowed to occur, with the sharp rise of wages and the impoverishment of the propertied class which it would entail, in our class society as we know it? Can one not more readily imagine a campaign being launched to curb or break the overweening power of trade unions, or to start some new colonial venture as a profitable outlet for surplus funds? Such an outcome seems not only possible but extremely probable; since in a propertied system property is not only the greatest vested interest, but its possession confers the trump cards that are necessary to win the game. Reinforcing this resistance is the continual tendency of the present system, primarily motivated as it is by the desire to maintain the

---

[1] *Principles*, Ed. Ashley, p. 731. Cf. the remarks of Wicksell on the fact that "a collectivist society would afford a much better guarantee for the rapid accumulation of capital than does the existing individualistic society"; and that "capitalists as a class will gladly welcome all measures destructive of capital", whereas "the collectivist state will be quite unaffected by a lowering of the rate of interest as such". (*Lectures*, Vol. I, p. 212.)

333

earnings of capital, to restrict the utilization of plant and equipment as well as of labour, whenever this will permit a higher profit to be earned. Since such restriction may occur whenever output-policy is influenced by considerations of "overhead costs"—whenever the more intensive use of equipment is denied because price is designed to cover average and not marginal cost—the amount of chronic under-utilization of productive power which results from this cause alone is probably much more substantial than is generally realized. In such a society there seems every reason for interest to triumph over ideas, even over "the gradual encroachment of ideas", and abundant evidence that it does.

By contrast, in a socialist economy profit as an income-category ceases to possess any significance as an economic incentive or as an interest which shapes and limits policy, for the reason that it ceases to exist as a personal revenue. Moreover, since wages in one form or another are the only form of income, social incentives will be exclusively associated with work, and the sole aim of economic policy will presumably be to increase wages at the most rapid possible rate. Contrary to a common opinion, there seems little valid ground to doubt that the force of incentive to production would on balance be greatly increased by the change. The incomes of privilege and of property, which to-day account for nearly half the national income, are increasingly the fruit of, and hence incentive to, restrictive practices; while even work-incomes which are proportioned to productive effort lose much of their potency as incentives owing to the lack of social prestige attaching to labour compared with property, to the thwarting of ambition and the blunting effect of the rancour of envy and sense of injustice which unequal opportunity engenders. By contrast, a socialist economy rid of such negative factors is in a position to harness untapped sources of collective incentive, of which a society rooted in individualism and the subjection of servant to master can do no more than dream. If in such a society the rapid augmentation of wages is the dominant aim, it must follow that the attitude to all problems of capital accumulation and investment will necessarily be a different one. Given this as the ruling principle, the only limit to an increase of wage-income could be that which was set by existing productive powers and by considerations of future productive equipment. With the removal of the incentive to maintain reserves of unemployed resources, with a fuller utilization of capital equipment through time, and with an altered attitude towards present and future income, there is every reason to suppose that the rate of increase of productive power and of wage-income could be of a quite different order of magnitude to that to which we are accustomed in a capitalist economy. The words which J. B. Say once used of a slave economy in contrast to a free need little change to suit them to a modern context: "Labour can never be honourable, or even respectable, where it is executed by an inferior caste. The forced and unnatural superiority of the master over the slave is exhibited in the affectation of lordly indolence and inactivity: and the faculties of mind are debased in equal degree; the place of intelligence is usurped by violence and brutality. Slave and master are both degraded beings. . . . One of the productive classes benefits by the depression of the rest; and that would be all, were it not that the vicious system of production,

resulting from this derangement, opposes the introduction
of a better plan of industry." [1]

It is sometimes said that in a socialist society vested
interests of one kind or another would still remain to
thwart the social interest and to defy the dictates of
reason. Be this as it may, the power of interest would
be diminished, at least, by the removal of the interest
that is the most powerful in present society, the most
inimical to human welfare and the most predatory: the
vested interest of property. This contrast indeed between
a capitalist and a socialist economy is as crucial as it is
simple: that in the former it is the interest of property
which is dominant and the interest of human beings which
has minor weight or even no weight; while in the latter
the interest of human life would be paramount, and the
maintenance of the value of property of no account at all.
Of this subordination of human beings in capitalist society
the "shameful squandering of human labour-power for
the most despicable purposes" (owing to its cheapness),
to which Marx referred,[2] is merely one aspect. Two
consequences of this difference are eloquent enough;
but their significance is only too rarely appreciated. A
socialist economy, having no longer a place for profit as
an incentive to production and investment, would have
no interest in reducing wages as a solution for universal
unemployment and general excess-capacity, as is so
familiar a paradox of capitalism: in such circumstances
it would have always an interest in raising them. It also
follows that in the economic accounting of socialism the
"overhead costs" of capital would have no significance
and would be continually disregarded (once, at least,

---

[1] *Treatise on Pol. Econ.* (1821), Vol. I, pp. 319-20.
[2] *Capital*, Vol. I, p. 391.

the plant was in existence); and *a fortiori* the "overhead costs" of "goodwill" and of monopoly rights; but the maintenance of human beings, that most neglected investment of any hitherto, would become a prime charge. In the world as it is to-day we do not lack evidence, appalling evidence, that it is the maintenance of human beings and the blessings of human security which have no place in economic accounting, while it is the safeguarding of the value of capital which is the dominant concern: so dominant, according to the witness of contemporary events, as to be safeguarded by retarding invention and laying waste productive resources, by "Balkanizing" Europe and reviving the inspiration of the Middle Ages, by maintaining existing fields of exploitation and conquering new ones at the point of the sword.

The struggle of mankind to-day is as much—nay, more —a struggle to unseat a powerful interest whereby to banish the "mean and malignant" system which this interest upholds, as it was in the days when classical Political Economy launched its influential attacks, with unrestrained partisanship, upon the monopolistic system of its day. When interest obstructs reason, to preach reason is vain unless it preach to dethrone interest. Then it was a struggle of rising industrial capital against landed interests and trading monopolists. To-day the world is torn by the struggle of the unpropertied masses against the entrenched forces of monopolistic capital. If truth is to be gleaned from practice as well as inspire it, the economist can as little stand aloof *qua* economist as *qua* citizen of the world from such issues. To breathe life into the bones of abstract notions, he must, it would seem, not only descend from his cloister to walk in the market-places of the world, but must take part in their battles, since only then can he be of the world as well as in it. This is not to sell his birthright: it is to march in the best tradition of Political Economy. At any rate, if he does not, the world, and his cloister with it, may soon start tumbling about his ears.

NOTE TO CHAPTER VIII ON STORED-UP LABOUR AND INVESTMENT THROUGH TIME

THE significance of time has been variously estimated by economists; and discussions of its place in economic causation have been clouded by a good deal of mystification. The notion of time has even acquired what Marx termed a fetishistic character; attempts having been made to treat it as virtually a third ultimate factor of production (along with labour and nature) and to explain the phenomenon of surplus-value in terms of its productivity. As such, the notion is a more refined cousin to the older view which regarded capital as a unique entity which had a specific productivity and value, instead of as a particular form assumed by labour in the social division of labour. That this is so does not, however, prevent it from being true that time, properly regarded, must necessarily play an important part in the framework of a number of economic problems, particularly those of accumulation and investment. Into the wider question it is not the purpose of this NOTE to enter. The intention here is simply to analyse the considerations on which the *order* of investment in different types of construction-projects in a socialist economy would depend. In setting this as its intention, this NOTE does not claim to enunciate any final principle (which would require a much less abstract method) but merely to define the meaning of the problem in more explicit terms.

If we regard capital instruments as "stored-up labour" (*i.e.* as part of the social labour-force embodied in a certain form or use) we necessarily imply in this notion a time-dimension—the time for which the labour is stored, or the time separating the original expenditure of the labour (*e.g.* in building a power-station or a machine) and the emergence of the finished product. If all stored-up labour were of the simple type, which is represented

339

in the sowing of seed for a harvest or the planting of trees, the notion would have a simple quantitative significance: the time elapsing between the labour of sowing and the harvest or between the planting of trees and their fruit. This time could be represented as a definite quantity, and spoken of, not only as longer or shorter, but longer by a given amount. But in the greater complexity of durable instruments of production it is true that there are difficulties in giving to this notion any precise quantitative significance; and there are special problems connected with the fact of depreciation and maintenance of plant and equipment. Into these questions it is not necessary to enter here.[1] While a satisfactory solution of these problems is necessary if any high degree of precision is to be attached to the answers afforded to many questions, it is sufficient for our purpose that different types of stored-up labour should be capable of being broadly compared with respect to their time-dimensions, so as to be placed in an order and represented as being greater or less. It seems possible, at any rate, to make certain broad classifications of productive processes according to different types distinguishable as "longer" or "shorter"; and justifiable (indeed, essential) to use some such classification to enable general conclusions to be drawn with respect to *changes* in the use of different production-processes.

The crucial problem is this: if there is a series of n possible types of stored-up labour of different "lengths", what considerations determine the *order* in which these are adopted? In particular, what will determine whether labour will be devoted simultaneously to all the n types of stored-up labour, creating *some* of *all* of them in varying proportions, or whether labour will at first be devoted exclusively to constructing the first type in the series (the shortest or most quickly maturing) and then successively in future years passing through the series as longer and more complex types of stored-up labour are step by step created to take the place of the more primitive types when these latter fall into disuse?

[1] Some of these problems, especially those of maintenance, are handled by means of an original definition of "period of production" in Armstrong's *Saving and Investment*.

340

These various types of stored-up labour may stand in various relations to one another with regard to productivity. They may get more productive (absolutely) as they get "longer", and they may be more productive in greater or in less proportion to the increase in their length. Alternatively, some longer methods may be less productive than shorter ones. Presumably, however, the more productive application of labour will be preferred; and since the only obstacle in the way of investing immediately in the most productive known form of stored-up labour will be the length of time which must elapse ˋbefore the product appears, it will be increase of productivity with "length" which is alone significant.

Why, then, is not the most productive known form of stored-up labour immediately created, and created in sufficient quantity to maximize the productive power of social labour? The answer clearly is that, since this stored-up labour takes time to construct or to yield its product, the income of the community would be drastically curtailed in the intervening years. To satisfy the needs of these earlier years, "shorter" forms of stored-up labour are required. But it will be said: granted that *some* investment must take place in the "shorter" forms, to prevent the community from starving in the interim, why should not an immediate start be made in devoting at least *some* labour to the construction of the longer and more productive methods with an eye upon the income of the more distant future? In other words, suppose that stored-up labour took the form of fruit-trees which required an initial expenditure of labour to plant them, and after a certain period of growth yielded their fruit in a given year and then died; and suppose, further, that the period between planting and fruiting differed with various types of tree, the longer-fruiting trees yielding in general a larger fruit. Then two methods of planting would be possible. (A) It could be arranged that this year labour should be distributed between planting some one-year trees, some two-year trees, some three-year, some four-year, some five-year trees and so forth, so that each of the years into the future should have some fruit from this year's planting. When the near future had been adequately provided for by the earlier-maturing trees, labour would cease to be devoted to their planting and would be transferred instead directly to planting the most productive known type of tree. (B) Labour could be devoted at first *only* to planting one-year trees, to yield fruit next year and so make *next* year's income considerably larger than it could be, *ceteris paribus*, under (A); or at any rate restricted to planting one-year and two-year trees. Then next year, or the year after, the planting of one-year trees could be abandoned, and the more productive two-year trees concentrated upon instead; and so on successively up the scale. It is to be noted that under (B) the fruit of *earlier* years will tend to be *larger* than under (A); but, in so far as maximum productivity is reached more gradually, the fruit of *later* years will tend to be *smaller* under (B) than under (A).

On what considerations, then, will the choice between the two methods depend?

The crux of the matter seems to be that the more distant future always has a greater chance of being plentifully supplied, since there is the option of using part or all of the investments of intervening years in its interest; whereas the near future can only be enriched out of the labour of to-day and the immediate future, and will be benefited if this labour of to-day and of the immediate future is embodied in relatively short productive processes. In other words, concentration of labour on shorter methods will always benefit the *near* future at the expense of the more distant future. In certain circumstances it will benefit the near future *more* than it harms the distant future; and it is this fact which may cause method (B) to be preferred. As Mr. Armstrong has put it: "We can only produce for the future; we cannot produce in the future for the present. . . . We cannot make up in the future for the absence of income now by retrospective production; while the more distant the future the greater the number of ways in which we can provide income for that future by anticipatory production. Owing to this unidirectional nature of time, the principles which govern the distribution of resources through time are different from those which govern the distribution of resources through space." [1]

---

[1] *Op. cit.*, p. 21.

It is clear that the essential differences between the two methods is that method (*B*), by paying more attention to the income of the earlier years, will tend to attain to the higher productivity of the more advanced methods of production *more slowly* than will (*A*). Method (*A*), on the other hand, by investing earlier in production processes of a more advanced type, will attain to a given higher level of productivity much *sooner*, at the expense of providing a lower income for the earlier years. The more gradual method (*B*), in other words, represents the path by which a given higher level of productivity can be attained with the *smaller aggregate sacrifice*. (The method of *least* sacrifice would, of course, be one which raised income so gradually as to attain maximum productivity at infinity.) But it does not by any means follow that the method involving the smaller aggregate sacrifice is the most economic: it may well be advantageous for the community to incur additional sacrifice to purchase the benefit of attaining the higher level of productivity sooner and enjoying this higher level of income for a greater number of years.

The method which attained to maximum productivity (or to a given higher level of productivity) most speedily would unquestionably be the one to be adopted if a given addition to a small income were of no greater importance than a similar addition to a larger income; since in this case the loss of income in the earlier years would invariably be more than repaid by the earlier attainment of maximum productivity and the consequent gain of income in subsequent years. It is the fact that this condition does not hold—that to give a family one room to dwell in is usually more important than to provide a second, and to have shoes on one's feet at all is more important than to possess a change of footwear—which may render the more gradual method the appropriate course of action. What is clearly decisive is whether or not the rate at which productivity increases as the time for which labour is stored up increases is greater than the rate at which the importance of increments to income declines as the level of income rises. If the former is slower than the latter, a method which yields a tardier attainment of the higher level of productivity, but involves a smaller

343

sacrifice of income in the earlier years, will be preferable. If the former is faster than the latter, the method which attains to the higher level of productivity at the most rapid possible rate will be preferable, since the large absolute addition to the income of distant years will then outweigh the (smaller) loss of income in the nearer years. It has been maintained that the importance of increments to income declines in greater proportion than increase of income: a statement which seems clearly to be true of increases of income near the starvation level and again of increases at high levels of income. But it seems not unreasonable to suppose that, even if this be true of intermediate levels of income per head, the importance of increments to income does not decline *much* more rapidly than the increase of income within the range of *per capita* income-levels appropriate to advanced industrial countries. In this case there is a presumption that method (*A*) will be the most economic in technical situations which are such that the productivity of different forms of stored-up labour increases in an appreciably greater proportion than the time for which labour is stored up. In general, we may say that periods which are technical epochs, in the sense that there are very large possibilities of increased productivity of labour from the adoption of new (and "longer") processes of stored-up labour, will be periods in which method (*A*) is most likely to be adopted. Part of the labour directed to constructional work in those years will need to be directed to relatively primitive, but more quickly maturing, forms of construction to supply the needs of the nearer future. But at the same time part of the labour will be directed to commencing the construction immediately of more advanced, but more slowly maturing, processes; since the earlier attainment of the increased productivity resulting from the latter will outweigh the loss resulting from a smaller investment in the former (with the consequent lower levels of production in the earlier years).

It must be noted that the difference between our two methods is one of degree. Method (*B*), if its transition through the various types is accelerated sufficiently, will approximate to method (*A*) and may be indistinguishable from it; particularly

344

if the latter is interpreted in the sense of requiring a certain minimum income (and, *a fortiori*, if a gradually rising minimum) to be secured to the earlier years. When the two methods are so qualified as to approximate to one another in this way, there is a feature of method (*B*) which will give it a superiority over method (*A*). In other words, if the only condition attaching to the two methods is that a certain minimum income is to be provided for the earlier years, method (*B*) will actually be the speedier method of attaining to maximum productivity. The reason for this is that method (*B*) gives priority to the satisfaction of the needs of the earlier years. The paradoxical result that maximum productivity is soonest reached by a method which refrains from immediately constructing the most advanced methods depends on the fact that, since the needs of earlier years can only be satisfied by means of the less productive and shorter processes, the more labour that can be concentrated at the outset on providing for the needs of these earlier years, the greater the speed with which labour can be released to be invested in the more productive methods.[1] It is like a party of rope-climbers ascending a mountain: the top may be reached the sooner if the guide at the head of the party spends more of his energies helping up the slower members of the party than in accelerating the speed of his own ascent. When other considerations are equal, therefore, this fact will weigh in favour of method (*B*). But it remains true that, since method (*A*) is essentially the method by which, as a rule, the income of the earlier years is stinted in the interests of a more rapid attainment of higher levels of productivity, it is likely to be the appropriate path of development in situations where relatively large increases of productivity are to be anticipated by lengthening the time for which labour is stored up, or at periods in which political and social reasons may give an unusual importance to speed of development.

[1] Of course, a certain preliminary increase of productivity is *bound* to come earlier under (*A*), since the construction of the more productive methods is commenced earlier. But in the later stages the increase of productivity will be greater, *ceteris paribus*, under (*B*), since the labour previously devoted to supplying the minimum needs of the earlier years will be more rapidly released.

But the adoption of this method (A) will only be possible in an economy which has sufficient foresight to be able, with some approximation to certainty, to calculate the movement of investment and productivity over future years. Such a degree of foresight is clearly impossible in an individualist economy; so that anything approximating to method (A) is rarely adopted, and even then only over a relatively short span of time. For this type of economy method (B) is the only practicable method available; the step-by-step transition to new methods taking place under the prompting of changes in interest-rates as investment and income change. Any other method would require a grading of interest-rates for investments of different periods of maturity, such as is hardly conceivable in an economy so much the prey to uncertainty and to the vagaries of business expectations, which in face of such uncertainty can have little objective basis. Moreover, it is to be noted that this transition to the new method would require to come *in advance* of the year in which the income had actually increased to the point which made an addition to it less important than an increase of productive power for the more distant future—namely, in the year in which investment for the benefit of that richer future year was actually being undertaken. Since in an individualist economy such a transition will tend to take place only when that change of income has *already become apparent*—namely, in the future year itself—it follows that an individualist system will have an additional reason for pursuing a tardier course of development of its productive forces than will a socialist economy; having a recurrent tendency to over-invest in shorter and obsolete processes and myopically to inflate the income of the *near* future at the expense of under-development of the productive power of the more distant future. This retardation will, on the one hand, tend to maintain interest-rates and, on the other hand, tend to provoke fluctuations; and this quite apart from any monetary influences. As productive processes become longer, the results of this retarding tendency are likely to become progressively greater.

Labour, however, will be required to work machines as well as to make them. The proportions (capable of limited variation)

346

in which the labour-force of society requires to be divided between this current labour and stored-up labour will be determined by what has been termed the "technical coefficients" of industry, which will be relative to the state of technique in various industries at any one time and to the relative sizes of different industries of varying technical coefficients. It is clear that the social labour-force is only being employed in the most productive possible way if no gain in productivity would result from transferring labour from current uses to stored-up uses. This implies that the product (valued in terms of current income) resulting from an additional application of labour as current labour (operating existing machines) equals the product resulting from an additional application of labour as stored-up labour (valued in terms of anticipated future income).[1] Let us assume that there is a gradual progression through various types of production-process according to method (B) as the usual path of development (broken by fluctuations) in an individualist economy. As long as new investment is taking place, the income of future years will be rising; and as more of the social labour-force is devoted to stored-up labour, the product (valued in future income) resulting from each addition in this direction will fall, while the labour available as current labour to work the existing machines will grow relatively more scarce and indispensable. If only one type of stored-up labour were known and available, this transfer of labour to stored-up labour would continue until the product resulting from additional applications of labour in each of the two directions was equal. This is what may be called a point of *capital saturation*, at which the *average productivity of the social labour-force is at its maximum*.[2] But this maximum would represent a low or a high level of productivity according to whether this one and only known form of stored-

---

[1] *I.e.* $\frac{dP_1}{dL_1}k = \frac{dP_2}{dL_2}$, where k represents a relation between future income and current income.

[2] This point seems to be synonymous with what Mr. Meade has termed "the optimum supply of labour relatively to capital". (*Introduction to Economic Analysis and Policy*, p. 259 *seq.*) This point is *not*, however, necessarily the same as Mr. Meade's "optimum supply of capital", for the reasons set out below.

up labour was of a technically primitive or advanced type. If other and more advanced types were known, their existence would preclude this point from being reached. Before the product resulting from additional labour devoted to the existing type of stored-up labour had fallen beyond a certain point, it would pay to transfer this labour instead to more productive and "longer" types of stored-up labour. Such successive transfers to more productive methods would proceed until there was no known more productive type of stored-up labour; and equilibrium would be reached when sufficient labour had been devoted to this type of stored-up labour to make any gain from further transfer zero (*i.e.* $\frac{dP}{dL}$ was the same in both directions). Existing stored-up labour would continue to be replaced each year as it wore out; but it would not be added to, and the existing proportions between stored-up and current labour would, *ceteris paribus*, be maintained. Here, again, the average productivity of the social labour-force would be at its maximum. But it would be (relative to existing knowledge) a *maximum maximorum*.

Traditional classifications of technical inventions as "labour-saving" or "capital-saving" are generally made to turn on the effect of these changes on the relative prices of labour-power and of capital. For purposes of analysing capital-development through time it would seem that a classification in terms of the effect of technical change on the ratio in which stored-up labour and current labour require to be combined is more useful and less ambiguous—namely, in terms of labour-units and not of prices.[1] Technical changes which have the effect of increasing the proportion of current-labour to stored-up labour will tend

[1] These ratios will not, of course, necessarily be rigid, but will have the form of a given "production-function" defining the changes of productivity as the proportions in which stored-up labour and current labour are combined. For simplicity we have spoken above only of the proportion between current labour and stored-up labour at the *end* stage of production. Corresponding to it will be the (possibly different) proportions in which at all earlier and intermediate stages of production fresh labour has to be used to work up or to work with stored-up labour, which is product of a still earlier stage.

to retard (temporarily at least) development towards the point of maximum productivity by leaving less of the social labour-force available for new construction-work; and conversely technical changes which diminish the proportion of current labour to stored-up labour will tend to accelerate this development. They will not, however, affect the point of capital saturation itself; in the sense that this will still consist in the most productive known type of stored-up labour. Technical change will only shift this point if it creates a new type of construction which is absolutely more productive than any previously known and available—if it discloses a new mountain-summit to be mastered, higher than any which was visible before.

It is to be noted that as progress towards this point of capital saturation occurs, the intensive utilization of existing plant and machinery by current labour will grow less; until at the point of capital saturation it will not be economic to carry intensive utilization by labour of existing plant beyond the point where diminishing returns to this utilization sets in. The types of stored-up labour which are in use will be so productive that it will pay to employ the major part of the social labour-force on maintaining or replacing society's large stock of machines and equipment, and relatively little of it in the operation and utilization of machines. Labour, in other words, will have become predominantly a process of machine-controlling, with actual manual operations reduced to a minimum. What Mr. Meade has defined [1] as the points of "optimum supply of labour relatively to capital" and of "optimum supply of capital relatively to labour" will, at this point (but only at this point), have become identical (apart from possible unexhausted economies of division of labour in the finishing industries).

[1] *Op. cit.*, p. 259 *seq.* and p. 273 *seq.* If one is speaking in terms of a flexible "production-function", it is to say that on any indifference-curve expressing such a function that point will be chosen which represents the greatest economy of labour (both in using and in making machines) to yield a given output. This would only represent the *smallest* possible use of labour in operating machines if capital goods, once made, needed neither repair nor replacement. Only then would it be the case that such goods would have to become "free goods" before the point of "capital saturation" was reached.

349

INDEX